TURN IT
UP

TURN IT
UP

A GUIDED TOUR THROUGH THE WORLDS
OF POP, ROCK, RAP AND MORE

GREG KOT

Chicago Tribune

MIDWAY

AN AGATE IMPRINT

CHICAGO

Turn It Up
ISBN 13: 978-1-57284-253-3
ISBN 10: 1-57284-253-9
eISBN 13: 978-1-57284-471-1
eISBN 10: 1-57284-471-X

Printed in the United States of America

Chicago Tribune: R. Bruce Dold, Publisher & Editor-in-Chief; Peter Kendall, Managing Editor; Colin McMahon, Associate Editor; Amy Carr, Associate Managing Editor/Features; Joe Knowles, Associate Managing Editor/Sports.

10 9 8 7 6 5 4 3 2 1

Midway Books is an imprint of Agate Publishing. Agate books are available in bulk at discount prices. For more information, visit agatepublishing.com.

CONTENTS

ABOUT THIS BOOK

The columns in this book appeared in the Chicago Tribune between 2000 and 2013. The material has been carefully selected and edited to present information in book format about the essential musical acts and issues of the early 21st century.

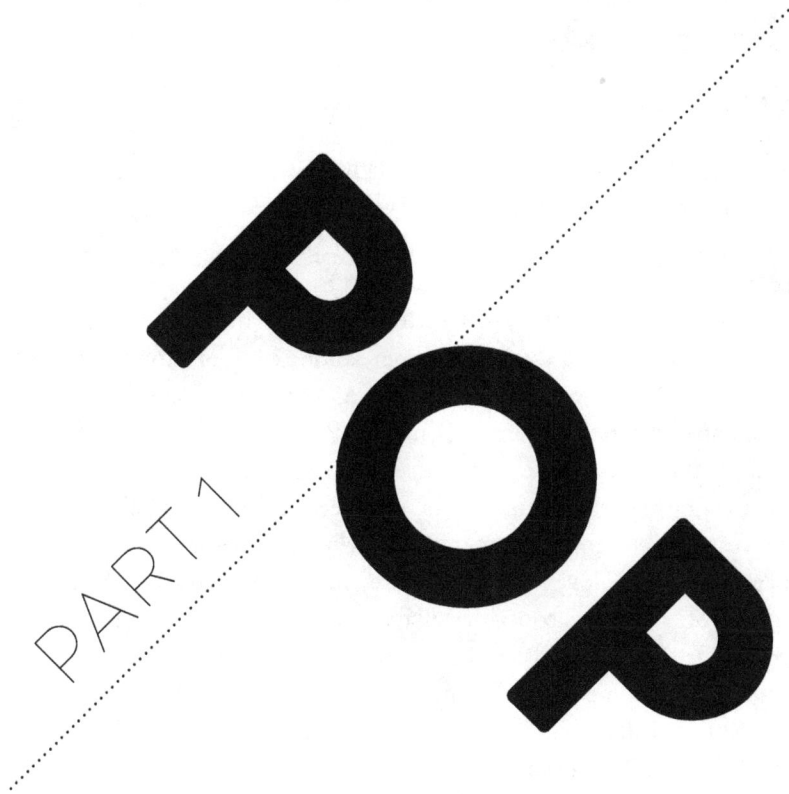

PART 1

POP

....

Nelly Furtado boldly blends a host of different styles

MARCH 2, 2001

N elly Furtado's "Whoa, Nelly!" (Dreamworks) is a rare achieve-ment: a joyous, catchy-as-all-get-out pop record that neither insults the intelligence of listeners past puberty nor bogs down in so-hip-it-hurts cool.

Like Beck's "Odelay" or Cornershop's "Woman's Gotta Have It," Furtado treats world music like a big sandbox full of exotic toys, and why not? A first-generation Canadian, her parents are Portuguese, she sings in three languages (English, Portuguese, Hindi) and stud-ied trombone, ukulele and guitar even as she was immersing herself in hip-hop's world of turntables, samplers and drum machines. The 22-year-old's performing aspirations kicked in a decade ago when she began warbling along to Mariah Carey records and copying the dance moves off Janet Jackson videos; she went from playing in an experi-mental trip-hop duo at age 16 to strumming a guitar and sharing the stage with Sarah McLachlan and Beth Orton at the 1999 Lilith Fair.

Now, her debut album has cracked the top-100 on the strength of the hit single "I'm Like a Bird" despite the album's experimental flair: trip-hopper Tricky meets the trancy violins of the Kronos Quartet on "Hey, Man!," and TLC communes with the spirit of the late Pakistani singer Nusrat Fateh Ali Khan on "Turn Off the Light." Furtado, who brings her band to the Park West, explained in an interview how such mix-and-match audacity comes second nature to her.

Q: On the record, you combine elements that shouldn't go together, but somehow do: Big Britney Spears-type melodies with surreal production. It's like you wanted to liberate pop music from the low-est common denominator.

A: That's part of the love of it, the challenge of making pop music. To be original and musical in that format is extremely challenging.

Everything I did before was like boot camp for this record: trip-hop, electronic music, drums 'n' bass, hip-hop. I'm lucky because I have two sides to me. One side is the formally trained musician, and the other side just loves expression. I have a lot of ammunition, more than the average 22-year-old because I started so young. I grew up listening to [Brazilian Tropicalia artists such as] Caetano Veloso, because of my parents' Portuguese heritage. I was inspired by singers like Nusrat Fateh Ali Khan and Jeff Buckley. Those elements aren't all immediately apparent on a 12-song pop album, but that's the research that goes into it. It's like when you're doing a term paper in college, and you take these books out of a library. Those were the books I took out of the library, and I studied them.

Q: Yet all that diversity must have made it hard to fit in with any kind of musical scene.

A: I never fit into the underground because of that: The hooks always stood out too much [laughs]. It was never one thing or the other with me. My favorite music has a solid footing in the underground world and solid footing in the commercial world at the same time. I think it's great when you can be two things at the same time.

Q: So do you approach the songs like a traditional singer-songwriter, strumming your guitar into a tape recorder? Or is it more of a hip-hop, freestyling approach?

A: Both. That's the theme of my life—paradox, duality. There's the Neil Young, sit-down-with-the-guitar-and-craft-a-song side. Once I tackled that discipline, I felt comfortable in my urbanness, the girl who from age 12 just wrote melodies in her head. My album isn't a hip-hop album, but it represents my generation, which has grown up around this hip-hop energy. It's become a code for my generation, and I don't think we've yet seen the full repercussion of hip-hop. For a while I was hiding behind trip-hop and electronic music, because I was afraid to be myself musically. Meeting my producers [Gerald Eaton and Brian West of the trip-hop group the Philosopher Kings] was great, because they made me less afraid of my pop side, the girl who loved Mariah Carey when she was 12. Then touring with Lilith Fair and Sarah

McLaughlin, it was uplifting, it showed me that I didn't have to be a tortured artist my whole life.

Q: I can't believe you were flirting with the "tortured artist" cliche.

A: Can you believe that? I was hiding from myself. I'm impressed with people who can tour behind those kinds of songs, like Radiohead, or PJ Harvey. Plus, it's hard to make uplifting music that doesn't seem slight. But seeing Cornershop three years ago, I said, "This is it!" This is what I feel when I listen to East Indian or Brazilian music. That's what I want. I realized I was capable of it. I had the background. I could do musical pop music. Who are the artists who real inspire people? Stevie Wonder, Bob Marley, Finley Quaye, Beck, Cornershop—great artists with integrity, but they're joyful, uplifting. That's what I wanted to be, especially when I'm young and want to be smiling.

....

No Doubt about this band's impact

APRIL 8, 2002

As rock and hip-hop get heavier and harder, the pop side of the commercial spectrum has been dominated by bellybutton-baring teen acts (Britney Spears), moonlighting actresses (Jennifer Lopez) and aging boy bands ('N Sync) proffering romantic fantasies for adolescents. Some of it is catchy, but too much of it sounds like the by-product of a marketing meeting.

All is not lost for connoisseurs of musical whip-cream, however. Nelly Furtado, Garbage and Craig David are crafting pop that is both frothy and ambitious, often rewarding multiple listens with its giddy inventiveness. Also back in the hunt for guilty pleasure-seekers is No Doubt, who headlined the sold-out Aragon [*April 6, 2002*].

After a decade of scuffling in the Southern California ska-punk scene, the quartet broke through in 1995 with an 11-million-selling album, "Tragic Kingdom." They fell victim to self-seriousness on the follow-up, the ballad-heavy, we're-not-a-kiddie-act-anymore, "Return of Saturn." But No Doubt's latest, "Rock Steady," is loaded with the

Gwen Stefani with No Doubt at the Aragon Ballroom April 6, 2002.
PETER THOMPSON

kind of feisty, fizzy pop that breaks down barriers: smart, witty, dance-able and fun. It takes the band's '80s influences and massages them with 21st Century production touches.

Like the most ambitious pop acts, No Doubt employs a bevy of producers to concoct an album that is more a collection of potential singles rather than a cohesive statement. It's a formula that has re-stored the band's standing as hit-makers, and the 4,500 tickets to its Aragon show were sold weeks in advance. Despite a pointless set of stage props—eight Darth Vader-style villains cluttered up the pro-ceedings at the start and finish of the concert—No Doubt otherwise relied on putting across its songs with frill-free, fire-drill urgency. The opening "Hella Good" set the tempo, a loose remake of the Bangles' "Walk Like An Egyptian" with a techno face lift that had everybody pogoing on stage, including drummer Adrian Young.

Singer Gwen Stefani has a bellybutton, too, and she's not afraid to use it. But, if anything her Lydia Lunch-meets-Betty Boop warble has toughened up, and her voice sounded strong despite leading what seemed to evoke an aerobics class; Stefani even pumped out 10 push-ups before delivering her feminist anthem "Just a Girl." Without the choreography and fireworks that reduce most big pop shows to the equivalent of a tightly scripted long-form video shoot, No Doubt re-lied on combustible performance, emphasizing the best songs appear-ing on its last three albums.

Unfortunately, the nuances that make "Rock Steady" such a de-light were lost in the Aragon's brutal acoustics. Stefani's voice and Tony Kanal's reggae-deep bass lines were consistently in the foreground of the mix, at the expense of Tom DuMont's guitar and the keyboards that give the new album its electro-rock dazzle.

The quartet, abetted by two animated multi-instrumentalists, com-pensated with manic energy that drew on their background in '80s new wave ("Don't Let Me Down"), the frenetic Los Angeles punk of Fishbone ("Sunday Morning") and the Twin-Tone ska of the English Beat ("Spiderwebs"). There were moments of introspection, with the big ballad "Don't Speak" and the melancholy folk-rock strum of "Sim-ple Kind of Life." And the stripped-down percussion of "In My Head" emphasized Kanal's snaking, almost subliminal bass.

Such nuances weren't the first order of the evening, however. This was all about pop with an exclamation point, almost cartoonish in its zeal. "Hey Baby" was aggressively nonsensical, with two rappers joining Stefani. The song served its purpose: The hit single got No Doubt back on the charts, compelled the 'N Sync-Britney crowd to pay attention to the band, and pleased the audience at the Aragon. A few years from now, will anyone care? And will it matter? The questions are irrelevant. Pop is music for the moment, and once again the moment belongs to No Doubt.

Artistic leap puts Pink on right track

JUNE 14, 2002

Pink, the thinking teen's pop diva, paused between songs at the Rosemont Theatre [*June 12, 2002*] to reveal the key to her recent success: "I did everything everyone told me I should not do."

The pronouncement was cheered by a house packed with teen girls who relate to the 22-year-old singer less as a star and more as a peer coping with many of the same issues they are: squabbling family members, disrespectful boyfriends, clueless authority figures. Pink backed up her assertion that "music is freedom" by relying on exactly that.

Unlike concert tours by pop singers from Madonna to Britney Spears, this was not a show about dance steps or production razzle-dazzle, but about introspective songs performed with a muscular co-ed, biracial five-piece band.

The concert affirmed a rapid transformation from pop tart to credible rock artist. Only two years ago, Pink appeared to be just another pop diva-in-training on her debut album, "Can't Take Me Home," with its processed beats and overly derivative arrangements positioning her as Britney Spears' tomboyish sister.

Last year *[2001]*, she made it even easier to write her off by cavorting with Christina Aguilera, Lil' Kim, Mya and Missy Elliott on an uninspired remake of La Belle's "Lady Marmalade."

Pink at the Rosemont Theatre June 12, 2002.
JOHN BARTLEY

But the singer—born Alecia Moore in Doylestown, Pa.—broke the pre-fabricated mold on the recent follow-up, "Missundaztood," which demands a complete rethink about who Pink is and what she represents. The disc is more daring and personal than the collected works of Spears, Aguilera, the Backstreet Boys and 'N Sync, and it came out over the objections of Pink's employer, Arista Records mogul L.A. Reid, who fretted that it was too great a departure from the debut and would derail her career.

Sales of 2 million albums later, Pink is prancing all the way to the bank, as she sang on "Don't Let Me Get Me": "L.A. told me/You'll be a pop star/All you have to change/Is everything you are/Tired of being compared/To damn Britney Spears/She's so pretty/That just ain't me."

The song provided an ebullient finale to a show in which the singer solidified her credentials as the latest bad girl to seduce the mainstream. She's a cross between Joan Jett's rock moxie and Fiona Apple's singer-songwriter introspection, with a dash of Salt and a pinch of Pepa's attitude. While not yet as credible as those predecessors, the artistic leap made by Pink suggests she's on the right track.

Her audience was a sea of pink shirts, glow sticks and hair, but the contrarian singer arrived with a working girl's 'do and auto mechanic's overalls. Newsflash: She sang, rather than lip-synced. Her voice veered from a bluesy growl to a world-weary-beyond-her-years trill.

She paid tribute to her songwriting partner, Linda Perry, with a gutsy cover of "What's Up," a 1993 hit by Perry's old group, 4 Non Blondes. And she took a valiant run at the Janis Joplin trifecta, with a medley of "Summertime," "Me and Bobby McGee" and "Piece of My Heart."

At times, as on "My Vietnam," which equates her personal turmoil with a national tragedy, her callowness as a songwriter becomes apparent. But what's encouraging about "Missundaztood" is that it has a personal point of view, complete with growing pains. It's the type of coming-of-age party that Britney and her ilk want desperately, but so far haven't been able to pull off. Pink blows off the image-by-committee approach employed on so many pop albums to focus on autobiographical tunes that balance vulnerability ("Dear Diary" quotes Apple—"I've been a bad, bad girl"—in a ballad set over a shuffling, trip-hop beat) with toughness ("You can run me over with a . . . truck, and I won't give up," she sang on the anthemic "18 Wheeler").

She's got a feel for pop tunefulness, but she and her band rock as hard as any teen act since Jett's Runaways. Pink next comes to town as the opening act for Lenny Kravitz, and judging by this performance, Kravitz had better be at the top of his game or risk being upstaged.

....

Shania Twain marks her success by what sells

JULY 25, 2003

Shania Twain and Duke Ellington have at least one thing in common: They're not much for categorizing music. For Ellington, there were only two types of music: good and bad. For Twain, there's the stuff that sells, and the stuff that doesn't.

"I never was comfortable being typecast as one thing," Twain said in an interview before launching a two-year world tour that brings her to Grant Park for a free concert [July 27, 2002]. "My biggest problem when I went to get my record deal is I couldn't decide what genre to go do. I had to fit into something, which was very awkward for me. That I became a country singer had a lot to do with the timing, the fact that labels were taking on new country artists. But the type of country I was doing by that time wasn't what country people call 'country.'"

Though she was one of Nashville's core artists through most of the '90s—her 1997 album, "Come On Over," is the sixth-biggest seller of all time—Twain looked more like a cross between Cat Woman and Pat Benatar when she performed at the Super Bowl halftime last January.

What's more, Twain liked her latest album so much she made it thrice, and only one of those versions had even the slightest hint of a twang.

The cross-format chemistry experiment that was "Up!" (Mercury)—which offers separate 19-song mixes for pop (the "red" album), country ("green") and world-beat ("blue")—is state-of-the-art marketing, if not music-making, and it's produced 3.9 million sales in eight months.

For a singer who has always measured herself by mass appeal rather than hipness, chart staying power rather than artistry, "Up!" represents the latest and most calculated step in a career that's all about creating a franchise, even as it keeps her fans at arm's distance with songs that don't present a distinct personality so much as a factory assembled utility. Twain's completely shaken off the country tag that got hung on her when the Canadian singer signed to the Nashville branch of Mercury Records in the early '90s, and taking dead aim at the kind of beyond-genre appeal that has turned the likes of Celine Dion, Cher and Madonna into juggernauts.

In collaboration with her husband, producer-co-writer Robert John "Mutt" Lange, Twain first bent Nashville to her will by crafting songs loaded with country signifiers such as pedal steel guitars and fiddles, then piling on the pop hooks and bombastic arena-rock orchestrations. "Up!" cuts out the pretense—compared to the countrified "green" mix, even Garth Brooks sounds like an Appalachian hillbilly—and steers straight for the lucrative suburban market, which finds country too rustic, hip-hop too ghetto and rock too harsh. It makes Lange's work for past clients such as AC/DC, Def Leppard and Bryan Adams sound like just a warm-up: Here's a pop album that's all about surface pleasure, the guiltier the better. It warms over artistically bankrupt but commercially success-ful styles such as hair-metal power ballads and Euro-pop novelties into a collection of marginally clever anthems that dispense a little self-help advice while portraying Twain as frisky, independent and in control.

It wasn't always so.

"As a teenager my music was much more introspective," she says of her days as a struggling singer on the Canadian bar circuit. "I didn't care so much if the songs made sense to anybody else. I used them as more of an escape than anything. I was into artists like Kate Bush, and though I didn't necessarily understand her songs, I wanted to write like her."

But Twain couldn't afford to be strictly in it for the self-expression; she raised her three younger siblings after her parents died in a car accident. "If it was rock they wanted in the bars, I played rock," she says. "If it was dance, I did dance music. If it was country, I did country. I did whatever was paying."

Now, Twain says, "being hip doesn't matter to me." Her biggest in-fluences, she says, come from the top-40 music she grew up with: the Bee Gees, Supertramp, Loverboy, Nazareth.

"I steered away from writing introspective songs because of live per-formance," she says. "You're on stage for two hours a night, and I want people to be able to relate to what I'm singing. I try to make the lyrics conversational and realistic, but not heavy. It's supposed to be a party. It's just not the place I want to get lost in myself."

She and Lange get lost in other ways; they live in Switzerland, far removed from the record industry, with their young son. She wants to dominate the music world, but not impose her inner secrets on it, revealing little about herself in interviews, and even less in her songs.

"I was never really comfortable as a child in the environment of sing-ing in a bar," she says. "So I learned to hide behind the music. That's how I keep it fun."

....

Britney Spears is the poster child for a crippled music industry that sells celebrity first

NOV. 16, 2003

Hmmm, let's see, what's Britney Spears selling this week? Oh, yes, she's got a new album, "In the Zone" (Jive), out [*Nov. 18, 2003*]. As for the music it contains —does it really matter?

No wonder the music industry, crippled by years of declining revenue, is getting out of the business of strictly selling music. Its future lies in pushing one-woman self-marketing machines like Spears for whom music is just another product line.

With CD sales plunging and consumers by the tens of millions turning to the Internet for a free music fix, the multinational corporations who dominate the $12 billion business know they need to embrace a new entertainment model to lead them back to profitability. The new question becomes: how to sell music-related product in an age when recorded music has lost substantial commercial value?

Enter Spears as the poster child for the new music business, a role model for a wave of telegenic performers who sell . . . everything. It's easy to overlook the idea that Spears is a singer amid all the other stuff she's been pushing in recent years: the risque video shoots, the derriere-baring and topless magazine covers, the soft-drink commercials, the step-into-my-shower concert finales, the breathless interviews about when she did what with whom (insert name of tattooed and pierced pop celebrity here). In the end what sticks isn't the music but the titillation: the ex-Mouseketeer traipsing down the hall in her schoolgirl outfit, the did-she-or-didn't-she sexual escapades of her teen-pop romantic summit with Justin Timberlake, the French kiss with Madonna.

Once these activities might have been perceived as distractions. Now they're necessities, and the music is the afterthought. The erstwhile teen-princess, now a 21-year-old multimillionaire, has a career that's only getting bigger. Those who predicted that her Lolita-esque

Britney Spears at the Allstate Arena in April 2004.
JOHN LEE

boy-toy routine had run past its allotted 15 minutes were focused too much on the meaninglessness of the music, and not enough on the whip cream, the froth that turns lowercase personalities into uppercase

Celebrities whose every activity generates "news" and marketing opportunities. It's a world in which she is now first among pop stars, both old (Madonna, Cher, Michael and Janet Jackson) and new (Timberlake, Jennifer Lopez, Christina Aguilera), performers who can be bought and sold in a variety of formats: television, movies, DVDs, video games, T-shirts, lunch boxes, soft drinks.

Though the music industry has always wanted to produce multimedia stars, in the past these cross-marketing strategies hinged on music as the one indispensable ingredient. Bing Crosby, Frank Sinatra, Elvis Presley, The Beatles and even Bob Dylan went Hollywood. Johnny Cash hosted a prime-time television show, and Ricky Nelson and the Monkees were created as performers to star on the tube. Yet music remained essential to how those performers were perceived and marketed. Even Nelson and the Monkees were able to build long careers—if not by becoming credible artists, at least by performing credible songs.

A cosmetic quality

But for Spears, the music has always been cosmetic. Yes, there is a new Spears album, but more important, "In the Zone" is accompanied by a relentless and pricey marketing campaign. [J]ournalists around the nation received a cardboard box, shipped for a $1.50 mailing fee, that contained nothing more than a poster with pink and white lettering on a blue background announcing "her brand new album . . . featuring Madonna." It was a gesture designed to prove that Spears' label will spare no expense in promoting its most valuable product. Factor in at least four or five videos, and there's little doubt that the marketing expenses for Spears' new album will eventually hit eight digits.

Spears has become the ultimate commodity in a rapidly consolidating and increasingly panicky music industry not because of her music, but almost in spite of it. Time Warner Inc., EMI Group, BMG Entertainment, Sony Music Entertainment Inc. and Universal Music Group—the multinationals that dominate the $12 billion a year music business—are in a tailspin, bedeviled by their inability to keep up with the rapidly expanding world of Internet file-sharing. Sales have plummeted for three straight years, and the downward spiral shows no signs of abating; album sales are down an additional 6.4 percent so far this year *[2003]*, to 461 million. Even Spears was caught in the downturn: after selling 22 million copies of her first two albums, her 2001 release, "Britney," was a relative flop, with 4 million sales.

In its desperation to reverse the slide, the industry has shifted its goals away from its former strengths: developing artists and letting them grow over an extended career. The big labels are now transforming themselves into mega-marketing companies with an eye on celebrities and potential cross-format stars rather than artists. The industry has already begun to proffer restructured contracts that turn artists and labels into business partners across a broad spectrum of potential revenue streams, rather than just albums. Labels realize that to survive, they must become increasingly diversified entertainment companies. And they'll likely get even bigger: Sony and Bertelsmann are talking merger, as are Time Warner and EMI. That would leave three major labels running the show, which will mean more bands and jobs will be cut. Only the biggest, most easily marketable entertainers will be retained (at the same time opening up unprecedented opportunities for smaller artists on indie labels and through the Internet).

Some legitimate artists will still get a major-label shot, but they won't be indulged the way musicians from previous generations were; they'll be expected to turn into big sellers quickly, or be dropped before they turn into a financial liability.

In the future, expect to hear and see more carefully groomed entertainers across a broad spectrum of media, from photo books to Internet pop-up ads. The middle tier of the mainstream music industry, the one capable of sustaining artists who sold 300,000 or fewer albums, will disappear. It will leave an upper crust dominated by multimillion-selling entertainers, and a huge lower tier of artists, bands and independent record labels for whom 100,000 sales is a huge hit.

Image is everything

The shift has already begun. Movie stars-turned-singers such as Hilary Duff and Jennifer Lopez are priority acts at their record labels. The "American Idol" television series has turned nobodies such as Kelly Clarkson and Clay Aiken into icons. In each of these instances, a relationship with the consumer has been established in which music is not nearly as critical or compelling as the story and the image. Whereas in the past, the music urged us to know the performer, now the music is merely a byproduct of celebrity, a convenient way of buying into it. The American public is being fed a steady diet of media melodrama, and its hunger remains unsated: the cameras in Ozzy Osbourne's bathroom, "Joe Millionaire," Kobe and Shaq, J. Lo and Ben, Kid Rock and Pamela, Martha Stewart's decline, Rosie O'Donnell's dueling lawsuits, Elizabeth Smart's abduction-turned-made-for-TV movie, Gov.-elect Arnold Schwarzenegger.

In a culture where the celebrity feeding frenzy shows no sign of abating, performers such as Spears are the music industry's new meal tickets. She'll be everywhere in coming weeks as she promotes "In the Zone," though her musical talents remain safely buried beneath layers of top-shelf production. Abetted by the finest producers that a bottomless corporate budget can buy, including R. Kelly, Moby and the Matrix, the album reeks of Madonna envy, circa the Material Girl's trancy "Erotica" phase, ornamented with Caribbean and South Asian "Bollywood" accents. Spears' heavily processed voice ranges from a pinched nasal whine on "Me Against Music" to a faux Jamaican patois on "The Hookup." Like the latest albums by Lopez and Duff, "In the Zone" is so expertly constructed that it doesn't require a real personality or heavy-duty voice to make it fun. The clever arrangements are entertainments in themselves: the way a hip-hop back-beat morphs into a banjo lick on "(I Got That) Boom Boom," the way fluttering flutes and sexy-siren violins conspired to create a woozy hangover feeling on "Early Mornin'," the giddy juxtaposition of spaghetti western guitars and swooping ELO-like strings in "Toxic."

Those looking for insights into Spears' personality will have to settle for a few lines in the closing song. The billowy ballad "Everytime" could be interpreted as an apology to her ex-boyfriend, Timberlake: "My weakness caused you pain." Otherwise, the new "adult" Spears sounds like a lap-dancer seducing a client: "After the screaming's at an end, why don't we do it again"; "I find myself flirting with the verge of obscene"; "don't stop, because I'm halfway there." On Kelly's "Outrageous," she equates sex with a shopping spree. "Touch of My Hand" is about pleasuring herself.

In the Britney-approved bio accompanying the album sent to the media, Spears defends the song and, presumably, her more sexually active "In the Zone" persona: "It's not freaky freaky, it's just a little freaky."

Also a little freaky is how, after announcing last year [2002] she was taking a "hiatus" from the music biz, she's only gotten bigger. What's her secret? Call it the Madonna Factor: an ability to exploit the media as much as it exploits her. There was the full-on lip-lock with her role model, Madonna, at the MTV Video Music Awards, which caused such a scandal that the Atlanta Journal-Constitution was compelled to apologize to outraged readers who objected to a Page 1 photo of the smooch. Her relationship and subsequent breakup with Timberlake has been keeping tabloids in business for months, and Limp Bizkit's Fred Durst regaled Howard Stern's listeners with graphic tales of his relationship with Spears, which inspired a new round of he-said, she-said "reportage." Then there were her recent appearances—topless and bottomless—on the covers of glossy general-interest magazines such as Rolling Stone and Esquire.

None of it had anything to do with the music, but it all had everything to do with a business losing its dependence on music. CDs may not be worth as much as they used to be, but the price of celebrity—and Britney Spears—is at an all-time high.

....

Avril Lavigne seeks maturity with 'Skin'

MAY 27, 2004

With one multimillion-selling album, Avril Lavigne turned teen-pop's agenda away from its Lolita-grows-up fantasies toward tomboyish petulance.

Suddenly, Britney and Christina and the Backstreet Boys were so over, and Lavigne and spiky haired popsters Good Charlotte represented the Everyteen fantasy: sincere but not smarmy, self-confident but not cocky, attractive but not aggressively so. Plus they could play their own instruments and write their own songs, at least some of the time.

Now Lavigne's back with "Under My Skin" (RCA), the follow-up to her 2002 debut, "Let Go." Despite the first album's success, she's got something to prove. Though she was portrayed as a punky alternative to the teen princesses, it turned out she was no more punk than any high schooler with a Green Day record in her collection. And though, in interviews, she described herself as the primary songwriter on "Let Go," she got plenty of help from her producers, particularly the hit-making troika known as the Matrix, who helped craft her biggest hits, including the breakthrough singles

"Complicated" and "Sk8er Boi." The sound, bristling with melodic hooks and fine-tuned pop exuberance, even won over Liz Phair, who hired the Matrix to work on her 2003 self-titled album and hailed "Complicated" as the inspiration.

On "Under My Skin," Lavigne is eager to prove she's matured. She's not only 19, she's not working with the Matrix anymore, instead collaborating with fellow Canadian singer-songwriter Chantal Kreviazuk on half the album, and writing several songs herself. The sound isn't markedly different from "Let Go," however: Precisely sung tunes with soaring choruses and lyrics that can be charmingly blunt or simply clumsy. Lavigne will keep her young legion of acolytes because she comes across as a guileless peer who won't be pushed around, even as her music embraces glossy formula and her lyrics brim with cliches.

In an interview, she veers between rehearsed calculation and blunt honesty. She's still in the netherworld between adolescence and adulthood, and "Under My Skin" will speak to youngsters who find themselves in the same place.

Q: Liz Phair says "Let Go" influenced her last album.

A: Are you kidding me? That is so funny.

Q: Do you know who Liz Phair is?

A: Not really. I guess she used the producers I used, right? She seems cool. I should go get her album, because I haven't heard it. I've never heard her music, actually. But it was nice of her to say that.

Q: The perception is you killed teen-pop with "Let Go." Are you buying that?

A: It was different than what was out there, which was great, because I don't ever want to be like anybody else, or follow any trends. I just want to do my own thing. That's always worked for me. I don't think of anybody else as competition. I don't get hung up on that stuff.

Q: Did selling that many records give you more or less freedom to make the music you want to make?

A: It gave me more. I told the record company I wanted to work on this record, and don't ask to hear any songs until I'm ready. What happened on the last record and what tends to happen is we write and record our songs and immediately FedEx them to the label, and they hear it and judge it. This time I wanted to have a clear mind away from all that. I wanted to focus on making the record without other people's opinions getting in the way. I feel if I had done it that way there would have been more pressure. So I went into the studio and said go away until I'm ready to give you the songs. And they were cool with that, which was important, because that makes me, as an artist, more comfortable. Especially because I write extremely personal songs. I feel like I'm handing out pages of my diary about me.

Q: Did you enjoy working with the Matrix on "Let Go," and why didn't you work with them again?

A: I enjoyed it at the time, but I didn't need to work with them again. I had written songs on tour, and I wrote some more songs with my friend. So I had the music. I want to work with new people, and different people, and the record company was cool with that.

Q: These songs sound therapeutic, like you're getting a few things off your chest about old boyfriends.

A: Totally. It's how I deal with my emotions. I sing them away, and strum them away. I usually just do music first, and then come up with lyrics and melody at the same time. I write pretty quickly. I have a song on my record called "Together" that took me 10 minutes to write. When I start lyrics, they come straight from my heart, and what is going on in my life at the time. If there's something on my mind, the songs come.

Q: Do you hope your ex-boyfriends are going to hear these songs?

A: [laughs] I think they might.

Q: Do you ever hear from them after you write a song about them?

A: No. Not yet. But I'm waiting.

Q: Did you feel you had something to prove because of people questioning your songwriting on the last album?

A: People who said I wasn't a writer, you can't listen to this record without totally knowing that the songs came from me. There are emotions in my lyrics and in the way that I sing these songs. I'm not going to sit here and lie. I'm a writer, and those songs came from me. People who have a problem believing that, then that's their problem. I don't really care. That's in the past. I know there have been people questioning whether I'm a writer or not. Whatever. People are going to question things. People are going to say mean things. People are going to love you; people are going to hate you. I'll get over it.

Q: It sounds a lot like high school.

A: Yeah. High school is a rough place, isn't it?

Q: I barely remember high school. I think I've tried to blot it out of my memory.

A: Uh-huh. I feel like everyone has masks on in the hallways. Yeccch. Not good. Everyone has an agenda, and it's all about the crowd you're hanging out with. You're involved in this crowd, so you can't hang out with that crowd. That's where I came up with a lot of the lyrics for "Sk8er Boi." This preppy girl had a crush on this dude who was in the skater group, and she didn't want her friends to make fun of her. I saw a lot of that when I went to school. In the end, the song is about following your heart, and do what you want, and don't try to please other people. The No. 1 thing is don't worry what other people think.

....

Neil Diamond
Still cool after all these years

JULY 31, 2005

I f there was a dictionary of hipness, Neil Diamond would be MIA. In the 474-page Rolling Stone History of Rock & Roll, he barely exists, dismissed as a singer who "sold millions of records to a market hungry for maudlin middle-of-the-road pop rock." He appeared in the Band's legendary 1976 farewell concert, "The Last Waltz," but few people seem to know why. Even Diamond himself says, "I don't fit in."

At 63, Diamond remains something of a musical vagabond, a singer and song-writer who has visited many camps, yet calls none of them home. Yet, as he head-lines two concerts [*Aug. 1 and 2, 2005*] at the United Center, he stands as one of the most successful—and surprisingly influential—performers of the last 40 years.

On his previous tour, in 2001–02, Diamond played to more than 1.5 million fans in the United States, Canada and Europe and hauled in revenue of $88 million as he sold out 98 of 117 shows. In the '90s, he earned $182 million from 461 shows, the decade's most successful touring act, according to Billboard. In addition, he has sold more than 120 million albums worldwide.

Beyond the numbers, Diamond's songs have endured. While everyone from the Monkees ("I'm a Believer," a No. 1 hit that helped launch their career in 1966) to Frank Sinatra ("Sweet Caroline") has covered his songs, he has also made an impression on several generations of musicians who might not necessarily be typecast as Diamond buffs. His "Kentucky Woman" was covered by British hard rockers Deep Purple in 1968 and hit the top 40, UB40 had a hit with a reggae version of his "Red Red Wine" in 1984, Urge Overkill provided a defining moment in Quentin Tarantino's 1994 movie "Pulp Fiction" with its version of "Girl, You'll Be a Woman Soon," and Johnny Cash titled his 2000 album "American III: Solitary Man" after a Diamond song that he recorded with producer Rick Rubin.

Neil Diamond at the United Center Aug. 1, 2005.
NUCCIO DINUZZO

And this year *[2005]*, the singer recorded an album with Rubin, who has also previously worked with Slayer, the Beastie Boys and Rage Against the Machine—none of whom, you can bet, would ever be in regular rotation on Neil Diamond's iPod. The November 2005 collaboration is built on Diamond's songs, voice and guitar-playing. It was designed by the producer as a throwback to the singer's earliest days as one of the '60s' most distinctive singer-songwriters.

"The whole album is guitar-based and I was scared at the beginning," Diamond says in an interview from his adopted hometown of Los Angeles. "I was basically forced [by Rubin] to play guitar on every one of those songs I had written. I had been away from it since I wrote 'Kentucky Woman' and 'Cherry, Cherry' in the '60s, only because I felt there were better guitar players out there. We had an argument pretty much every day or any time we faced a new song. I tried to figure out a way where one of the other guitar players could cover my parts, so I could just worry about singing it. And Rick was pretty insistent that I play the part, and as it turned out he was absolutely right. The vocal performances he got out of me are better than I've heard in a long time, because Rick was trying to involve the artist and the instrument as one, and it became real intimate."

Collaboration

Rubin, in an interview in his Los Angeles mansion before the recording sessions began, says he had been aiming to make a record with Diamond for years. The singer was finally persuaded to meet with Rubin, and was impressed by the bearded producer's approach: "It's all about great songs, and creating an environment for great songs to emerge," Rubin says.

"Neil Diamond is one of my all-time favorite artists," the producer says. "The live show is simply amazing. [Diamond's 1972 double-album] 'Hot August Night' is probably my favorite live album. He's got better songs on it than [The Who's] 'Live at Leeds.'"

Diamond, born to a working-class family in Brooklyn, New York, in 1941, dropped out of New York University in 1962 to concentrate on songwriting. He scuffled around the famed Brill Building, where songwriters such as Ellie Greenwich, Jeff Barry, Gerry Goffin and Carole King cranked out hits for the Ronettes, Righteous Brothers and countless other acts. "I was an abject failure," Diamond says. "I spent eight years trying to get a break."

Finding his voice

It wasn't until he was encouraged to sing and perform his own songs by Greenwich that he broke through. "Solitary Man," his debut for the Bang Records label, established him as a distinctive voice in the hurly-burly world made by The Beatles, Bob Dylan and the Rolling Stones in 1966: dark, brooding, introspective. He followed it with a string of now-classic hits: "Cherry, Cherry," "You Got to Me," "Girl, You'll Be a Woman Soon," "Kentucky Woman," "Sweet Caroline," "Holly Holy," "Shilo."

The music touched on everything from rock and country to folk and gospel. Later on, he would flirt with symphonic orchestration and jazz harmonics.

"I felt it was important for me to change the musical presentation for the singles," he says. "The Beatles led the way with that. They would come up with a hard-rock track, and then a softer ballad, and then an artier thing, a show thing. It kept the public interested, and they were very good at it. By the time I started making records, two or three years after The Beatles hit, it was something I consciously tried to do."

Today, such willful stylistic hop-scotching would be frowned upon by a music industry that insists on slotting artists into particular formats and demographics. But in the '60s, Diamond says, such distinctions were blurred.

"This was before genres and radio formats," he says. In the early '60s, "all you needed was a big pompadour and a half-decent song, and they'd let it fly. Then The Beatles hit and opened it up even more."

In 1976, he recorded one of his best albums, "Beautiful Noise," with the Band's Robbie Robertson as producer. Later that year, Robertson invited Diamond to perform with the Band at its farewell show in San Francisco. The performance was filmed by Martin Scorsese, and "The Last Waltz" became one of rock's most revered documentaries. Diamond's appearance alongside counterculture figures such as Dylan, Van Morrison, Muddy Waters and Neil Young puzzled many observers. By then, Diamond had written songs that were more redolent of Broadway show tunes than the early folk-rock hits that first established him as an artist.

But upon the release of a boxed set documenting the concert in 2002, Robertson said Diamond was a crucial piece of the Band's history.

"The Tin Pan Alley songwriters in New York crafted brilliant songs for people to record, but they weren't performers," Robertson said. "Neil Diamond bridged that world. When I worked with him on his record, people said, 'Is this a put-on?' No, it wasn't. This guy is really good at what he does and comes from this tradition of songwriting. He wanted to be one of those people: [Jerry] Leiber and [Mike] Stoller, Carole King, Gerry Goffin. I thought what he does is as good as anybody who played 'The Last Waltz.' He was filling more arenas than any of us, that's for sure. And he's still doing it. He's a phenomenon in his own kind of way. And he has written a lot of songs, a lot of great songs. But they were just a little bit on the other side of the tracks from most of the people on 'The Last Waltz.' He was never the critic's darling because he didn't fit in with what was deemed 'cool.'"

An audience-grabber

The hits dried up for Diamond in the '80s, but his tours continued to play to capacity audiences in arenas around the world.

"It's amazing when any band can rock the last person in the third tier in the back row," says Urge Overkill's Nash Kato. "But for one person to do it—it's a dying art form. All the way back to the enormo-dome, he grabs the audience."

Some of Diamond's more maudlin songs through the '70s and '80s cost him credibility with tastemakers. But Diamond's passion for performing, Kato insists, crushes all quibbles.

"He believes more than anyone in these songs," Kato says. "And he believes he is Neil Diamond. If there was one iota of doubt in his mind, I think the whole thing would collapse. You either buy it or you don't, but what's not up for debate is his conviction. Critics had a field day with him. But he would say, 'The dogs may bark, but the caravan rolls on.'"

The Chicago trio was citing Diamond as an influence when the band was carving out its identity on the indie-rock circuit in the late '80s. "It's like Neil Diamond appearing on 'Star Trek,'" Kato once said of the band's early shows, a mix of Rat Pack-era Vegas swagger and guitar rock. The band recorded a gritty version of "Girl, You'll Be a Woman Soon" to fill out a 1992 EP, "Stull," and Tarantino later used it in "Pulp Fiction." But first he sought Diamond's permission to use the song in a key scene when a date between the characters played by John Travolta and Uma Thurman takes a sickening turn.

"I got sent the script and I read some of it, and I thought this is some kind of exploitation movie," Diamond says. "The drugs, the shooting— I didn't want any part of it, so I turned it down. Soon after, my music publisher called and said that Tarantino is a great filmmaker, and he doesn't make exploitation movies, and would I reconsider? So I read it again. And from the eyes of a filmmaker, it started to make some sense. So I gave the OK. If you bought the movie to begin with, everything was part of the package and it seemed to work on that level. I thought

Urge Overkill's version was fine. They communicated what the director wanted in that scene."

Kato still isn't thrilled with the band's interpretation, though it became the biggest hit of Urge's career.

"When we recorded it, pitch, meter and tuning went right out the window," he says. "It's a squishy demo version of a great tune. But Tarantino is a genius of putting sound with vision: It was the wrong tune in the wrong scene that he made perfectly right. He gave it this creepy, haunting twist. It made sense, because the Neil of the Bang era was a dark guy. Dylan was the prophet, Cash was the man in black, but Neil was the solitary man. He bucked the trend. He was one of the first guys who not only wrote songs but sang them. He was this big-nosed Jewish kid from Brooklyn who defied all odds."

The singer and his songs

In an interview, Neil Diamond discusses his songs and songwriting:

His favorite cover: "Frank Sinatra's version of `Sweet Caroline' is my all-time favorite version of one of my songs. He did it like big-band swing. It's one of my favorite records ever."

His take on Johnny Cash's version of "Solitary Man": "I was saddened by that album. It was a very difficult album to listen to. I agree that it was a song that suited him, but I never got past the fact that this man was seriously ill and yet he was in the recording studio working on his music. That's a tough thing for me to hear."

His biggest influences: "The Everly Brothers sang like an angelic choir. I still adore them. I hear an Everly Brothers record now and still smile at the beauty of their sound. And the Weavers . . . knew all these songs, Woody Guthrie songs, that you could sing around the campfire. Those were the first songs I learned . . . to play on the guitar."

On songwriting: "I still do think of myself as a songwriter. That's what I started out to be, and it's what I continue to do. Songwriting is a lot harder than giving a live performance. It's something that has always attracted me, but it's always a struggle. You're always forced to create music and lyrics that cover new ground, and it's always been the hardest thing that I do because there is no magic formula."

....

Kelly Clarkson aims to survive clash with record company

JUNE 24, 2007

There are few sure things in pop music, but bet on this: Natalie Maines and the rest of the Dixie Chicks know exactly what Kelly Clarkson is going through right now, and not just because they all are from Texas.

With a career-at-the-crossroads album, "My December" (RCA), coming out [*June 26, 2007*], Clarkson is shaping up as this year's version of the Dixie Chicks.

The Chicks tried to reinvent themselves on their 2006 album, "Taking the Long Way," while ticking off radio programmers and the White House, alienating fans and canceling under-selling tour dates with their increasing outspokenness. A few days ago, Clarkson canceled her summer arena tour because of poor ticket sales and fired her manager. She's also been feuding with the chairman of her record label, Clive Davis, over the direction of her new album.

Sound familiar?

Here's the kicker: "Taking the Long Way" wasn't nearly the radical departure from the Chicks' country-pop sound that last year's *[2006]* uproar suggested, and neither is "My December" the radio-phobic dud Davis apparently believes it is. On the contrary, it's fascinating that pop albums so well-crafted, so thoroughly middle-of-the-road, so undeniably catchy in spite of their more personal lyrical tone, could stir up such outrage.

For the Chicks' fall from grace, politics certainly played a major role in how the music was perceived. They had the temerity to criticize President Bush for invading Iraq, and their fan base protested by refusing to buy their albums and concert tickets. For Clarkson, it's politics of a different sort that threatens her career. Without the enthusiastic support of Davis—a powerbroker who launched the careers of Janis Joplin, Carlos Santana, Bruce Springsteen, Barry Manilow and Whitney

Kelly Clarkson at the Chicago Theatre Nov. 1, 2007.
MILBERT O. BROWN

Houston, among others—Clarkson could find herself short of the kind of marketing muscle required to prop up a major hit.

The Clarkson-Davis spat says a lot about how our entertainment gurus like to package things for consumers in neat little boxes. And when an entertainer tries to push out of that box, the gurus get nervous. They fear that change and growth can't be good, because those variables make it more difficult to predict public acceptance and massive sales. To follow that logic, Kelly Clarkson and the Dixie Chicks would've been better off by staying exactly as they once were, rather than jeopardizing their record companies' profit margins by thinking for themselves.

Art vs. commerce

The Clarkson controversy offers the latest twist on the old art vs. commerce debate, and the stakes are unusually high: Clarkson not only won the first "American Idol" competition in 2002, which instantly elevated the Texas waitress to celebrity status, she made something of it. After a mild-mannered debut album, she racked up 10 million sales and two Grammy Awards with her 2004 release, "Breakaway." The record was more aggressive in tone, and recast Clarkson as an Avril Lavigne-style pop-rocker, with production from John Shanks (who has worked with Ashlee Simpson) and Max Martin (the songwriter-producer behind Britney Spears). Not exactly groundbreaking, but it showed there was more to Clarkson than originally imagined.

Buoyed by that success, RCA is counting on "My December" to lift the label out of the sales doldrums. In the past, the big labels counted on their biggest hitters, whether U2, Madonna or Mariah Carey, to rack up huge numbers to make up for the rest of the underperforming albums on the roster. With sales down 16 percent industry-wide this year, the pressure is on Clarkson to deliver a blockbuster.

It's a sick business model, but it's the world that Clive Davis helped create and that "American Idol" has plugged into. As the most successful of the "Idol" singers, Clarkson was groomed to play by the rules, and on her first two albums, she pretty much did as she was told.

But "My December" finds Clarkson trying to develop a personality. Bad idea, in the eyes of King Clive. Davis' criticism of the disc stems in part from his time-tested belief that an artist's success hinges on catchy pop singles, and he was distressed that Clarkson stopped working with the producers who helped her craft "Breakaway." He didn't feel the songwriting was up to snuff, and he told Clarkson as much a few weeks ago.

As the title would suggest, "My December" isn't exactly the feel-good album of the year. A nasty breakup underlines many of the lyrics and betrayal and despair shade many of the songs. The kickoff track, "Never Again," echoes the spiteful tone of Alanis Morissette's 1995 breakthrough hit, "You Oughta Know."

"I hope the ring you gave to her/Turns her finger green/I hope when you're in bed with her/You think of me," Clarkson hisses.

On "Sober," she compares her recovery from a soured relationship to an alcoholic addiction she can't shake. "Irvine" concludes the album with a last-ditch prayer, a sparse tour de force built on voice, acoustic guitar and a wordless backing choir. It makes an impact in part because it's so totally unexpected: No listener coming to this track cold would guess that the singer ever had anything to do with "American Idol" and its florid displays of ballad-belting.

No pity party

Yet, despite its sometimes wrenching lyrics, "My December" doesn't come off as a pity party. The radio-friendly hooks—and the potential hits—are still very much in evidence. Producer David Kahne (who produced hit albums by Sugar Ray and Sublime) knows how to massage songs into shiny objects designed for mass consumption as well as the singer's previous producers did. "Haunted" pushes the singer into the goth-pop terrain of Evanescence. And the petulant guitar pop of "Don't Waste Your Time" sounds as if it would've fit nicely on Lavigne's latest album, which has been in the Billboard Top 10 for weeks.

Kahne also deftly replicates some moves from his old new-wave days with Romeo Void and the Bangles, and the punchy guitar riffs in "Hole" and "How I Feel," the jabbing keyboards of "One Minute" and "Judas" and the faux-soul horns of "Yeah" suit Clarkson well.

Even when she professes to feel numb, as on "Hole," Clarkson doesn't wallow in histrionics. Though she occasionally flirts with the showboating vocal tics that "Idol" has turned into a national pastime, for the most part her performances are lean and combative. The songs are all pretty conventionally structured, and build to the type of choruses her fans—including those from the "Idol" days—will expect and recognize.

It's a smartly accomplished pop album, nothing more, nothing less, and it shows Clarkson is going to be around a bit longer than the 15 minutes allotted to even the most celebrated "Idols" contestants.

Like the Dixie Chicks, she's probably going to take a hit at the box office. But like her fellow Texans, she's starting to earn something she once lacked: credibility.

The key question then becomes: If sales dive, will Clarkson still insist on taking the high road?

Or will she even have that choice?

....

Michael Jackson's masterpiece
Innovative artist couldn't maintain success

JULY 5, 2009

The record will show that Michael Jackson died June 25, 2009, but in many ways he was dead creatively long before that. The beginning of the end can be traced to Nov. 30, 1982—the day "Thriller" was released.

What George Lucas and Steven Spielberg did for the Hollywood movie, Jackson did for the pop album. These icons of spectacle ushered in the blockbuster era for film and music, and the mega-billion-dollar industries that grew around them. Celebrity careers were created and lots of money was made, but in the end the art took a beating. And in Jackson's case, the need to top himself became all-consuming, until he literally stopped making music, unable to live up to his outsize expectations.

It all started innocently enough. Lucas' "Star Wars," Spielberg's "E.T." and Jackson's "Thriller" were popular masterpieces, the kind of mass entertainment on which your grandmother and 8-year-old nephew could agree.

"Thriller," of course, ended up selling more than 100 million copies worldwide and helped shape what would become a $15 billion a year music industry by the end of 1999. That industry was built on "Thriller"-like blockbusters from bands and artists such as U2, Metallica, Shania Twain and Mariah Carey.

Jackson showed them all how to do it. He didn't teach the world to sing, but he may have taught it how to dance. He created a pastiche of funk, soul, disco, rock, B-movie shlock and ballads embodied by his long-limbed power and grace in white socks and loafers. He was a multimedia star, and everyone wanted a piece of him. When he co-wrote the charity single "We Are the World," the superstars lined up around the block to be a part of the 1985 recording session.

His timing was perfect: Jackson was the first major artist to break big at the dawn of the compact disc era, the video pioneer who broke down racial barriers at the still relatively young MTV, and the self-conscious marketing maven who tailored his songs for a series of commercial-radio formats. There was the song for rockers ("Beat It" with Eddie Van Halen's guitar), the scary cartoonish movie for kids ("Thriller," with a Vincent Price cameo), the duet with an aging classic-rock icon ("The Girl Is Mine" with Paul McCartney), the bedroom ballad ("The Lady in My Life"), the world-music nod (the Swahili chant in "Wanna Be Startin' Somethin'"), hard funk ("Billie Jean") and straight-up disco ("P.Y.T.").

The calculation was masked by the artistry. In collaboration with producer Quincy Jones, Jackson created enduring art that also happened to be extremely popular. But Jackson would in many ways destroy his own career by attempting—with increasing futility—to emulate that formula in subsequent years. Jones described the malady as "paralysis by analysis" and soon after stopped working with the singer, who turned his every public gesture into a grandiose—and eventually grotesque—spectacle. There were videos that cost more than an entire album to make, the monstrous statues depicting Jackson in military garb, the long lead times between albums requiring years to make and promote. As the music slowed to a trickle, Jackson's private life became a series of scandals and outrages, reducing a once-gifted entertainer to a punch line.

The music industry, in the midst of a huge, two-decade growth spurt, was happy to ride the wave started by "Thriller." Artist development had been the cornerstone of the music industry—the idea that talent should be nurtured over a number of albums in order for artists to find their voice and establish their sound. But after "Thriller," the industry became addicted to blockbusters. One mega-selling album could make up for a lot of mistakes, and the industry thrived in the '90s on the back of 10 million-sellers by Garth Brooks, Alanis Morissette and the Backstreet Boys, among dozens of others.

But as the albums got bigger, did the music actually get better? "Thriller" was a once-in-a-generation success and it led to years of music powered by marketing demands. Idiosyncrasy and personality were subsumed by the need to sell as much product to as many consumers as possible, a trend exacerbated by the increasing consolidation of the industry into multinational corporations in the '90s that were beholden to stockholders and quarterly profit statements.

Similarly, the pipeline to MTV and commercial radio narrowed until it was open only to the best-financed performers. By the end of the '90s, the big labels were spending tens of millions on marketing, publicity and promotion to break acts such as Jennifer Lopez and Alicia Keys. Whereas Jackson had worked with one producer, Jones, to create his multifaceted music, artists began hiring studio specialists to produce individual tracks on each album, ratcheting up recording costs to multimillion-dollar levels and putting a premium on breaking these expensive tracks on radio and MTV.

Blockbuster albums came and went: MC Hammer, Vanilla Ice, Michael Bolton, Creed, Britney Spears and dozens more. The industry's thirst for superstars caused it to ignore almost everything else that didn't sell in massive quantities, and a lot of worthy artists who simply didn't sell in big enough quantities were kicked to the curb.

As for Jackson, he was barely heard from in the last two decades of his life. His records came fewer and farther between, and each sounded more strained and formulaic. In the last 18 years, he managed to release only one album of entirely original music, "Invincible," in 2001. He left his label soon after, upset by a perceived lack of promotion. In an era of mega-marketing budgets, the self-proclaimed King of Pop went out like a pauper.

....

Out of her hurt, anger, Rihanna creates art

NOV. 23, 2009

"To those of you who think you can take it, we say welcome to the Mad House."

The opening monologue, intoned by a sinister-sounding voice, sounds a little ridiculous, the introduction to a low-rent slasher movie.

But the trauma Rihanna addresses on her fourth studio album, "Rated R" (Def Jam), is a good deal more jarring than that cheesy prelude.

Rihanna at the Rihanna benefit concert for the Believe Foundation at Vision Night Club March 26, 2008.

YVETTE MARIE DOSTATNI

The Barbados native, born Robyn Rihanna Fenty 21 years ago, has graduated from the light dance-pop of "SOS" and "Umbrella" that helped her sell 12 million records to a sound a good deal darker and harder.

How could she not? Her romance with R&B singer Chris Brown ended in a violent argument in February [2009] that left Rihanna bloodied and bruised. Brown pleaded guilty to felony assault in July [2009] and received probation. He's on a brief club tour trying to restore his gravely tainted image, with a stop on Thanksgiving in Chicago at the House of Blues. Rihanna, meanwhile, went to work on her album, and it's impossible not to hear the anger and hurt in her voice.

She poses on the cover like a 21st century version of the dance-club maverick Grace Jones, a feral, not-to-be-messed-with dominatrix. In the same way, the music has lost much of its ingratiating-if-innocuous airiness. She always has favored Caribbean accents in her music, but she adds more pronounced rock guitar, and the beats and orchestrations reference Goth rock and new wave as much as dance music and electro-pop.

The album was written and produced by top-tier collaborators such as Ne-Yo, Justin Timberlake, The Dream, Tricky Stewart, will.i.am and Stargate. A few moments in "Rated R" feel detached: the gimmicky "Rock Star 101" with a cameo appearance by Slash, the overblown "The Last Song." But Rihanna personalizes most of these songs in a way that suggests she had a much greater voice in this album than any of her previous efforts.

"Russian Roulette" was a gutsy choice as a first single; it compares a relationship to a potentially fatal game of chance. Rihanna's voice is a delicate instrument, often the least interesting element in her productions. But on this track, she's squarely in the center of the action. A sparse piano-and-synth backdrop plays out over a heartbeat bass line, framing her story. She gives it a dramatic reading worthy of its jarring conclusion: an audible shiver followed by the sound of a gunshot.

Nothing else on the album can top that song, but they certainly complement it and make its startling conclusion feel sadly inevitable.

She turns the tables on "G4L." Over a stark, eerie backing track that sounds like whips cracking against cold pavement, she purrs, "I lick the gun when I'm done because I know revenge is sweet." It's not a threat so much as a way of protecting herself, the sound of a violent-crime victim venturing out again into the streets, fighting off fear with bravado. "Can't hurt us again when you come around here," she sings.

The narrator in these songs refuses to play the victim. She's wary of men even when she's flirting with them in "Wait Your Turn": "I'm such a (expletive) lady," she growls. She lashes out in "Hard," with help from an even harder-edged MC, Young Jeezy.

But the album is most haunting when she allows vulnerability to peer through the tougher exterior. She looks back at the wreckage in "Photographs" and "Cold Case Love," over appropriately desolate musical settings.

Even more devastating is "Stupid in Love," as rueful as a pop song can get. Over finger snaps and an undulating piano line, the narrator berates herself for being duped by a suitor. Even smart people make decisions they later come to regret.

In Rihanna's case, she turned that regret into powerful and moving art.

....

Mariah Carey concert shows the diva can laugh at herself

FEB. 15, 2010

Mariah Carey was doing that diva thing in the first of two shows [*Feb. 13, 2010*] at the Chicago Theatre: Poured into a gleaming, silver gown; eyes closed; self-absorbed in the moment of singing how her lover had done "The Impossible." All the while, a male dancer a few feet off her left shoulder was bumping, grinding and eventually popping his pectorals like a circus act.

Carey didn't break stride, but then as the song wound down, she cracked up. "Did you enjoy that?" she asked the audience with a laugh, as if to let everyone know she was in on the joke all along.

The singer, who has sold more than 62 million albums in the U.S. in a career that spans two decades, has always had a prodigious voice. But now she's developing a personality to go with it, and that made all the

Mariah Carey at the Chicago Theatre Feb. 13, 2010.
WILLIAM DESHAZER

difference in a concert in which the singer both played up her cartoon image and undercut it.

As the concert opened, Carey descended from the rafters on a swing, like a fairy-tale princess. Throughout the night her collection of gowns and miniskirts were so tight-fitting, her heels so high, that she could barely move, a Jessica Rabbit with hair cascading down her back and curves on top of curves. Unlike many of her peers, for whom gyrating like an aerobics instructor is all but required, Carey didn't so much move as mince a bit, though at one point she was painstakingly hoisted to shoulder level by two of her dancers—a creaky and slightly ridiculous bit of choreography.

"If you're gonna call me a diva then, damn it, I'm gonna act like a diva," she cracked as two assistants applied makeup midshow.

She sipped from a glass of champagne and fretted about starting yet another product line. "If I did a shoe line, would you guys buy them?" she asked.

It all made Carey seem a bit eccentric and slightly daft, in the same way that Patti LaBelle deflates her larger-than-life status by making fun of it even as she exaggerates it.

Of course none of it would work if Carey didn't have the voice to back it up. Her latest album, "Memoirs of an Imperfect Angel," is her best work yet, a warmer and more subtle album that makes her more relatable to those of us who aren't Mariah die-hards—or "lambs," as she refers to them. The thaw-out carried over into the show, and gave new perspective to older songs that once were defined strictly by technique.

> ### Mariah Carey set list at Chicago Theatre
> 1. Butterfly Intro/ Daydream Interlude
> 2. Shake It Off
> 3. Touch My Body
> 4. Fly Like a Bird
> 5. Make It Happen
> 6. Angels Cry
> 7. Always Be My Baby
> 8. It's Like That
> 9. The Impossible
> 10. Love Hangover/ Heartbreaker
> 11. Honey
> 12. My All
> 13. Emotions
> 14. Obsessed
> 15. We Belong Together
> *Encore:*
> 16. Hero

For many, her defining moment was the 1993 hit "Hero," her encore. It's a template for the generation of singers featured on "American Idol," a singing style that dictates emotions instead of evoking them. In concert, she trotted out a few of those dog-whistle trills that she popularized in the early '90s, turning Minnie Ripperton's soul into a vocal tic. In the late '90s she flirted with hip-hop, a rhythmic flexibility that carried over into her performances of "Honey" and "Heartbreaker."

But it has always been the ballads that kept her swimming in bling, and so it was here. Whether ramping up some gospel-style fervor on "Fly Like a Bird" or dialing it down to a near whisper on "Angels Cry," Carey has slightly less vocal range but is a much better singer now than when she was enjoying her biggest sellers.

Part of it may have to do with her career nosedive circa 2001–2002. Things got so bad her record company paid her to leave. The bumps and bruises haven't changed her assembly-line pop all that much. But as a personality and a performer, the brief tumble from her pedestal has worked wonders. Before that, she was a somewhat bland presence on stage. Now she knows how to have a laugh, sometimes at her own expense.

....

Lady Gaga

Anything goes for the pop singer, but there's substance to the circus

MARCH 2, 2011

"It's raining unicorns and gay teddy bears," Lady Gaga said [*Feb. 28, 2011*] at the sold-out United Center as the audience hurled gifts at her. Then she bit the heads off several dolls, but allowed a mini-Paul Stanley to live another day and watch the show from the lip of the stage. Kiss, and Kiss-style spectacle, still rules in the Land of Gaga.

The singer appreciates the circus of performing, and has turned herself into the pop world's most incisive commentator on its seductions and pitfalls. Every eye-catching moment had a few more layers to it that made this 100-minute performance something more than just a collection of stunts.

Last time through town, headlining the Lollapalooza festival in August 2010, the singer born, Stefani Joanne Angelina Germanotta 24 years ago, wore a chip on her shoulder the size of one of her oversized stage props. She was ranting, raving and doing a lot of preaching while her concert proceeded in fits and starts.

But she was a more relaxed, down-to-earth Lady Gaga, her show the equivalent of a repressed kid joy-riding through the streets toppling taboos like so many trash cans. There were intimations of cannibalism, sparkler-spewing bras, a celebrity-eating monster and Lady Gaga in costumes that disturbed as often as they provoked. Many outfits accented jutting limbs, mutant hands.

Lady Gaga at Rosemont Theatre on Jan. 8, 2010.
CHRIS SWEDA

"Do you think I'm sexy?" she purred as she smeared herself with fake blood.

Self-empowerment messages were the big theme, and Lady Gaga strived for solidarity of the you-can-do-it-too variety. While the message was beaten into the ground by the end, she gave it a provocative twist as she advocated forcefully for gay rights and virtually limitless self-expression. Her closing song, "Born This Way," was far more persuasive on the stage than it is as a recording, where it comes across as a knockoff of Madonna ("Express Yourself") by way of the Staple Singers ("Respect Yourself"). It came alive as an anthem in performance, with Lady Gaga and her backing singers amping up the song's gospel underpinning to ecstatic heights.

The singer affirmed that she has a strong, pliant voice, and, without naming names, pointedly dripped disdain for performers who lip sync. She went out of her way to showcase that she was not only singing and playing live, but also backed by a six-piece band that delivered gothic drama and glam-rock strut.

The show's centerpiece was an epic reading of a new ballad, "You and I," scheduled to be part of her second album, due in May 2011. It began with Lady Gaga singing a bluesy lament at the piano and evolved into a big hand-waving crowd-pleaser, complete with a bombastic guitar solo straight out of Guns N' Roses' "November Rain" video. But then she let dissonance consume the song, pounding her boot heel into the piano while the guitar sputtered feedback. She settled back in and began singing the praises of her favorite Chicago burger stand (Kuma's Corner) and baseball team (Cubs—much to the chagrin of some very vocal White Sox loyalists), as if holding court at a piano bar after hours with 20,000 of her closest friends.

Lady Gaga set list at the United Center

1. Intro
2. Dance in the Dark
3. Glitter and Grease
4. Just Dance
5. Beautiful, Dirty, Rich
6. The Fame
7. LoveGame
8. Boys Boys Boys
9. Money Honey
10. Telephone
11. You and I
12. Monster
13. Teeth
14. Alejandro
15. Poker Face
16. Paparazzi
Encore:
17. Bad Romance
18. Born This Way

It could be argued that Lady Gaga is the sum of her predecessors, and some parts of the show certainly were: "Alejandro" was a mashup of an ABBA song ("Fernando") and the blasphemy-tweaking imagery in a Madonna video ("Like a Prayer"). Would she exist without superstar chameleons such as David Bowie or cult figures such as Klaus Nomi as inspiration?

But her ideas run more than skin-deep, a visual mix of striking movie references, from Alfred Hitchcock's "The Birds" to Martin Scorsese's "After Hours," and a sound that spans flamenco and goth to disco and heavy metal. In that sense she is the best of what pop can be: expansive, pushy, humorous, inclusive. Even gay teddy bears and unicorns are welcome.

....

Emeli Sande delivers poetry, therapy

MAY 18, 2012

Before emerging as one of the most acclaimed young songwriters and artists in the U.K., Emeli Sande took a little medical detour.

Who is Sande? Her inaugural North American tour brings her to Lincoln Hall [*May 30, 2012*], but she's already a star overseas. Her resume includes credits on a string of songs by major U.K. artists, collaborations with Alicia Keys, an opening slot on Coldplay's upcoming U.S. arena tour, a Brit Critics Choice Award (previously won by Adele and Florence & the Machine) and a debut album, "Our Version of Events" (Capitol), that ties together soul, electronic music, pop and rock with sharp, literate songwriting.

Yet before plunging into music full time, the 24-year-old singer studied neuroscience for more than three years at the University of Glasgow in her native Scotland. Reminded that the neuroscientist-musician career combo is fairly rare, Sande laughs. Music was always a driving force in her life, she says. But growing up in a biracial family with a Zambian father who was a respected educator meant that a premium was put on schooling and making sound career choices. Her passion for music was never discouraged, but college was never not an option.

"All the way through my childhood, I loved school, and my dad underlined the importance of education," Sande says. "I wanted to be a musician, but I also wanted a degree to give me more stability and power in my life."

Couldn't she have picked something a little less complicated than neuroscience, though? "I just find the whole human body so fascinating, and the brain in particular, the mystery of it. I thought that it would be fun to study."

As it turned out, spending six hours a day studying the brain under a microscope was a chore, she says. But working in hospitals and treating patients proved inspiring.

"I would love someday to pursue a career where I can merge music with medicine, and its therapeutic effects on people," she says.

Music worked its own therapy on the young Emeli. At age 7, her parents overheard her singing. "Their validation motivated me more than anything to give music a try."

By the time she was 11, she was writing songs on piano and drawing inspiration from her father's record collection, which included Nina Simone, Joni Mitchell, and lots of African music and jazz. Her father took 16-year-old Emeli and her younger sister to an Alicia Keys concert in Glasgow, and Sande came away with a lasting image of what she wanted to be.

"We sat way back in the arena, but the whole vibe of it, the way she presented herself, the way the crowd was reacting to her was exciting," she says. "The moment I heard her songs, I felt I was hearing an intelligent woman doing exactly what she wanted to do without compromise, and yet all these people were coming to see her. She was making a connection through her music without losing her integrity. She showed me that you could have both."

While on a weekend break from college, Sande played a solo set at a London club with producer Naughty Boy (aka Shahid Khan) in the audience. Afterward, he introduced himself and suggested they collaborate on some songs. The success of "Diamond Rings" in 2009 and her signing to Virgin Records a year later prompted Sande to hang up her lab coat to focus on music.

Demand for her work increased, and she wrote songs for a parade of singers and rappers, including Leona Lewis, Susan Boyle, Tinie Tempah and Cheryl Cole. Meanwhile, she and Naughty Boy worked on her debut album, with an array of genre-busting styles: from the propulsive, Massive Attack-like electro-soul of "Heaven" to the raw, acoustic "Breaking the Law."

"I want to put the poetry back into pop music," Sande says. "Melody is a way to get people to listen, and maybe to encourage them to sing along. But the words have to say something. I try to look at an ordinary event and take a different angle on it."

"Heaven" is a typical example. It grew out of a late-night discussion in the studio with Naughty Boy about religion, and what it means to be a "good" person in a world full of distractions and temptations. "At one point, he said, 'I guess you just have to keep your heart clean,' and that line triggered something in my head," she says. "After that, it was a flow of consciousness. We had a piano loop going around with the chords, and once I had the concept for the lyric, the song came easily."

Another key track on the debut, "Hope," she co-wrote with Keys. Sande met her idol after Keys invited her to open a show in London.

"She reached out asking if I wanted to write with her," Sande says. "We've been working a lot since then, and we have a great relationship. She's taught me a lot."

The biggest lessons she's gleaned from Keys? "She reminded me to enjoy the moment, to take time to celebrate the successes, because everything moves so fast. We're always trying to get to the next thing, so it's important to embrace the things we've gained."

Keys also reinforced a notion that Sande has tried to live up to since she first saw the singer-pianist as a 16-year-old: "With music, she told me to strive to be different, don't try to fit in. Make the music that I feel, that I want to hear, and don't worry about what anyone else thinks."

Superstar Madonna flashes pop-art fetish

SEPT. 21, 2012

It was a concert that opened with an act of contrition and closed with a robed church choir paving the road to a celebration. In between there was fake blood, pretend guns, the return of the infamous conical bra, whiffs of sadomasochism and poison-tipped political commentary, as well as allusions to the pop art of Roy Lichtenstein, movies by Oliver Stone and Stanley Kubrick, Brecht-Weil cabaret, Asian mysticism, Cirque du Soleil-style tightrope acrobatics and Basque folk music.

Madonna was in town, and though she's one of the most famous celebrities in the world—and also one of the priciest, as evidenced by those $355 seats —[*the Sept. 19, 2012*] show, the first of two shows at the United Center, had all the hallmarks of a cult artist indulging a serious art-pop fetish.

Madonna at the United Center Sept. 19, 2012.
NUCCIO DINUZZO

The easy route would've been a greatest hits tour, but even at 54, something of a godmother to two eras of pop singers from Britney Spears to Lady Gaga, Madonna appears to get bored much too easily to do something that rote. She's almost perverse in the way she tries to upend and reconfigure her songs to fit a theme, and this was no exception, a self-described two-hour, four-part "journey of a soul from darkness to light."

Got that? Sometimes it wasn't always easy to follow Madonna's lead. Where's this going, exactly? And how much of this was gratuitous shock theater rather than soul-baring personal statement? But there was no denying the blend of art, artifice and sheer sensory overload. Besides the 16 dancers, four musicians and two backing singers, a stage that stretched into the middle of the arena and the sumptuous visuals made for something grandly watchable. It made every other recent arena tour that traffics in spectacle look rather puny in comparison. And, somehow, a few emotional payoffs sneaked through the dazzle too.

Once regarded as a chirpy ingenue destined to burn up her 15 minutes and fade, Madonna has turned reinvention into 300 million worldwide record sales and nearly 30 years of stardom. She has taken a few knocks *[in 2012]* as her latest album, "MDNA," tumbled down the charts soon after a muddled halftime performance at the Super Bowl.

Though the album was panned as a late, unsuccessful attempt to ride the coattails of the burgeoning electronic dance music movement, it was sold short. It was that rare recent Madonna album with an emotional center, with several songs zeroing in on the toll of her broken marriage, and that filtered into her performance.

Her concert tours use music as just one of many elements in a multimedia scramble of dance, performance art, theater and video, and "MDNA" was no exception. The visually spectacular first segment was set in a Gothic cathedral with shafts of light piercing through the "windows" and hooded monks ringing a bell and burning incense, suggesting some strange hybrid of Kubrick's ritualistic sex scenes in "Eyes Wide Shut" and a foreboding medieval ceremony. The set morphed into a tawdry hotel straight out of Stone's "Natural Born Killers," with Madonna gunning down masked assailants with disturbing glee, smearing the joint with blood and curse-splattered bravado. The music rumbled with menace, Madonna's voice auto-tuned almost beyond recognition, the once-bouncy "Papa Don't Preach" and the exuberant "Hung Up" slowed and twisted to a crawl.

Segment two was more organic and exuded a highly unusual quality for a Madonna tour: something like warmth. She still uses her guitar, which was often barely audible, as more of a prop than an instrument, and her voice remains thin. But her dancing was energetic and at times astonishingly athletic. "Open Your Heart" inspired an ensemble performance that suggested a mating of gypsy kicks and hip-hop break dancing.

The next segment was all ice-queen Berlin cabaret, topped by an oddly moving, slowed-nearly-beyond-recognition "Like a Virgin." Here was Madonna's signature song (or at least one of them) sung from the perspective of a much older woman looking back on her life, trying to conjure up a feeling she could barely remember, let alone ever experience again. It concluded with a tortured, erotic ballet involving Madonna, another dancer and a corset. A vulnerable Madonna? You saw it here first.

After that, the singer sent her fans home dancing with the sound of sitars on "I'm a Sinner," a choir on "Like a Prayer" and an aerobics class sponsored by Kraftwerk on "Celebration." Amid a fleet of fluorescent modules, she was briefly the dance-pop icon of the '80s and '90s again. Some of her fans would surely be glad if she stayed there for an entire concert. But for Madonna that would mean turning into a nostalgia act, and she's not having it.

Live or taped, Beyonce captivates

FEB. 4, 2013

Beyonce looked like she stepped off from the recent air-brushed perfection of her GQ magazine cover, danced like a junior Tina Turner and generally owned her 12 minutes on a worldwide stage [*Feb. 3, 2013*] like few Super Bowl performers ever have.

But there were a few nagging questions: Was she live or was she canned? Or perhaps more to the point: Did it matter?

Beyonce's performance had the lip-sync police out in force. The pop star fessed up to singing with a backing tape at the presidential inauguration a few weeks ago, but that should come as no surprise. Canned performances have been business as usual at Super Bowl-size events for decades. For most performers, the question isn't whether to use a backing tape, but whether to sing into an open microphone while the tape serves as a kind of aural safety net.

Sound engineers note that the entire performance has to be set up in 6 minutes at halftime, with no guarantee that the singer will be able to hear herself or that there won't be technical glitches that compromise the performance.

Most artists are in it strictly to look and sound good anyway. They don't view it as a "performance" so much as a way to promote product to

Beyonce at President Barack Obama's inauguration ceremonies in Washington, Jan. 21, 2013.
BRIAN CASSELLA

more than 100 million TV viewers; in Beyonce's case, it was a free ad for her recent reunion and greatest hits album with Destiny's Child.

And, wow, guess what? There she was with her Destiny's Child companions Kelly Rowland and Michelle Williams! Williams coyly said there was nothing to the reunion rumors a few years ago, citing her commitment to appear in a touring version of the Broadway play "Fela!," but miraculously she found a way to clear her schedule just in time.

The leather-clad trio looked like a walking, strutting advertisement for a dominatrix-boutique franchise. But Rowland and Williams came off as Beyonce's backing band, dutifully singing harmonies on one of the singer's biggest solo singles, "Single Ladies (Put a Ring on It)." Her Destiny's Child accomplices were part of a huge ensemble of dancers and musicians that appeared to consist entirely of women.

Otherwise, it was the high-heeled Beyonce stomping her imprint on libidos everywhere: the silhouetted opening count-off into "Crazy in Love," topped with a firecracker-spewing guitar solo; the Jamaican dance hall flavor of "Baby Boy"; the closing, signature ballad "Halo." On the last of those, the close-up TV images suggested that the singer was indeed belting it out, at least semi-"live." But by then the verdict was already in: Beyonce affirmed that she's the reigning all-purpose multimedia celebrity of our era, and she knows how to entertain.

The musical prelude to the game was relatively low-key by comparison. Marvin Gaye gave one of the longest and most celebrated versions of the national anthem at a sporting event, in 1983 at the NBA All-Star Game. But at 2 minutes, 40 seconds, Alicia Keys went 6 seconds longer than Gaye in her interpretation before kickoff.

Seated at a white grand piano, Keys offered a blues and jazz-tinged version of the technically demanding song. Like Gaye, she made the song seem fragile, even poignant, the intimacy undercutting any threat of the showboating that sank Christina Aguilera's interpretation two years ago. There are many ways to perform the anthem—Kelly Clarkson belted out a concise, fat-free version in 1 minute, 34 seconds at last year's [2012] Super Bowl. But Keys certainly delivered one of the best of recent vintage.

Its tone was appropriate, given what preceded it: Jennifer Hudson's "America the Beautiful." The singer gave a dignified reading, but the focus was deservedly on her smiling choir: 26 white-shirted, beribboned students from Sandy Hook Elementary School in Connecticut, the scene of a mass murder last year that, including the shooter, claimed 27 lives. Hudson herself has been a victim of gun violence; her performance of the national anthem at the 2009 Super Bowl came only months after her mother, brother and nephew were killed in their Englewood home in Chicago.

ROCK

PART 2

Beck strays within blurry lines for quite a show

FEB. 2, 2000

n a way, Beck's entire frazzled, frayed, funhouse of a career has been building to what transpired during the final improbable moments of his concert at the Aragon [*Jan. 31, 2000*].

Entrance music was provided by DJ Swamp, who whirled like a short-order cook, flipping 12-inch pancakes of vinyl on the turntables and scratching out sounds that faithfully mimicked the guitar riffs from "Louie Louie" and "Smoke on the Water." As Swamp smashed the last platter against the decks with a triumphant flourish, Beck took the stage for his final encore, a caped superhero leading what looked like a kabuki hair-metal band—part Kiss, part "Seven Sumarai."

"Got a devil's haircut in my mind," Beck brayed, flapping his elbows in a chicken strut while the horn section rolled around in slow-motion at his feet. A trombonist ambled past in a daze, and Beck began loading up on baggage—a microphone stand, a guitar, another guitar, wires, keyboards—before hitting the road. He wandered off, the eternal busker from his imaginary planet of static, the short-wave radio in his brain tuned to some funky frequency channeling Dr. Seuss, Parliament-Funkadelic's George Clinton, Frank Zappa and Salvador Dali.

This was no attempt at a grand summation of Beck's night at the rock opera. If anything, it was a mock opera, fun for its own sake, grand theater that took nothing—especially itself— seriously. Beck's music is sly and witty, but rarely is it profound—nor was it meant to be. But it is captivating pop that blurs the lines separating rock and rap, R&B and country, blues and the avant-garde, lounge music and psychedelia.

There was Beck hijacking a roadie's cell phone and placing an impromptu call while demanding the abolition of all "Sexx Laws," or singing about "going back to Houston to get me some pants" as if it were his sole mission in life. He rhymed "She looks so Israeli" with—

Beck at the Aragon Jan. 31, 2000.
CHARLES CHERNEY

what else?—"nicotine and gravy," imitated the Stones imitating Gram Parsons on "Lord Only Knows," and ambled from the sexy strut of horn-swathed R&B to the dreamy incantations of "Jack-Ass."

He dropped to one knee and yowled like a lust-crazed Prince on "Debra," skated like James Brown's valet, cranked out some clunky robot moves from a Devo video and played the tambourine-shaking sex symbol with the invisible hips and the ill-fitting suits as the mood swayed him. With a nine-piece band and two back-up singers, Beck picked through rock history utterly uninterested in the stuff that obsesses most connoisseurs, but with the practiced eye of a junk man examining a lot of shattered cars, finding revelations in the rust.

Those looking for Beck to make some kind of sense might as well have consulted the Mad Hatter for insight—his art is in the artifice. He's a poser, but an entertaining one, revving up the rate of change in David Bowie's chameleon act for a new, more restless generation; whereas Bowie changed personas every year, Beck dials into a new set of clothes with every song.

For those who like their artists to ante up a piece of their heart with each performance, they were in the wrong place. But that doesn't make Beck's shtick meaningless. Rather than diminishing the styles he dabbles in, he celebrates their equality—mixing them until he overloads the senses. He understands that rock is filled with plenty of would-be kings and prefab queens, but not enough jesters—and nobody wears that boogaloo hat better than Beck.

Patti Smith's renewed Declaration of Independence

APRIL 9, 2000

"You are all important! You all mean something! Your collective voice can make a difference!"

Patti Smith isn't running for president, though on this cold St. Patrick's Day evening [*in 2000*] she is agitating like a rock 'n' roll politician. She raises a fist to the stars with a guitar strapped around her neck and a crowd of thousands sprawled out before her, at a concert just a few hundred yards from the Texas state Capitol building.

Smith is the mother of two children, a widow and a poet. She is also the first riot grrrl, a rocker who streaked her punk iconoclasm with hippie idealism and post-feminist politics. She has always viewed rock as the ideal forum to uplift, enlighten and agitate, yet

Patti Smith performs a free outdoor concert at Waterloo Park in Austin, Texas, on March 17, 2000, as part of the South by Southwest Music Conference.
JACK PLUNKETT

she's never climbed into the machine that creates and cannibalizes rock stars. Over eight albums spanning 25 years, she's preferred to work the margins of an industry perpetually in love with less complicated personalities.

For a brief time, in 1978, she was at the center of the pre-MTV swirl, presenting a bold new vision of rock femininity and finding herself swept onto the pop charts for the only time by "Because the Night," co-written with Bruce Springsteen. Within two years, Smith disappeared from the music-making mill to start a family in Detroit with former MC5 guitarist Fred "Sonic" Smith—a stunning anti-career move by a then-32-year-old performer at the top of her game.

"All I knew how to say at that point in my life had been said," Smith now says simply.

Two decades later, Smith finds herself on the outside again, knocking on the door of a culture much too preoccupied with 'N Sync and the latest doings of Puffy, Britney and the Backstreet Boys to bother

with a 53-year-old woman whose sexuality was always more feral than
cosmetic and whose last hit was more than 20 years ago. But after
the deaths of her husband and brother, as well as close friend Robert
Mapplethorpe, the time was right. She spent two albums pulling herself out of mourning, with "Gone Again" (1996) and "Peace and Noise"
(1997). Now, with "Gung Ho" (Arista), Smith has regained her swagger. Her great theme is self-empowerment, and in a pop landscape
bereft of big ideas and righteous voices, she stands taller and more
necessary than ever.

Greeting a visitor at her hotel suite door, she still dresses the part
of the boho rabblerouser who seized the New York underground by
its throat in the early '70s: jeans drooping out of scuffed black boots,
graying hair falling around her shoulders, flushed cheeks and blue-
gray eyes unaccented by makeup, a black jacket bearing a ribbon that
was a gift from presidential candidate Bill Bradley. She raves about
Chicago, the place of her birth and the site of one of her greatest
performances, in 1998 at the Riviera. "That," she says, "was an unbe-
lievable night."

**Q: That show is certainly the only time I've ever seen the Declaration
of Independence read with guitar feedback. What prompted that?**

A: Ever since I was a little kid I was fascinated with the Declaration
of Independence, this beautiful document on parchment paper. But I
don't think I fully comprehended what rights it gives me as an American. So I finally picked up a book devoted to it in San Francisco and
read it on the 18-hour flight to Australia. A few days later, I was watching a documentary on Ho Chi Minh's early years, and his involvement
in the fight for Vietnamese independence. Ho Chi Minh had done a
serious amount of study of the American Revolution, Thomas Paine,
Thomas Jefferson, the Declaration of Independence, and he used this
knowledge when he structured the Vietnamese Declaration of Independence. I thought it was time for me as an American citizen to know
as much about our Declaration of Independence and how we developed our freedom and constitution as Ho Chi Minh did. The song
"Gung Ho" came out of that experience.

Q: You're saying "Awake, people, arise" and "Lift up your voice" on this album. You're not hearing too many rock artists say that these days.

A: We're not hearing these kinds of things talked about much at all except occasionally by a politician like Bill Bradley or Jesse Jackson. We're pretty complacent right now as a people. The economy is going good, we're not at war, people are not being drafted. Even things like the AIDS epidemic don't seem as scary as they did a decade ago. But our children are murdering each other. The gun situation in America is way out of control. We're polarizing racially. The moral fabric of the country is unraveling. But everyone thinks we're doing fine because we've got credit cards and computers. People see what I'm talking about as "'60s stuff." But I look at it as a continual necessity. We have to constantly remind ourselves of the value of the individual, and the strength of our collective voice. Those views should never be looked upon as old-fashioned.

Q: But so many layers of irony and distance have come between art and politics since the '60s. When music and art address political issues, what kind of change can they effect?

A: We're in this era of the golden calf, and the golden calf is pop music. We have a form like rap music that has the potential to become a forum for speaking out on things, creating change in a community and uniting people. But the people in these forms are self-involved, calculating, materialistic. I feel that no one is really using these forms to unite, educate. A lot of it is just offensive for no apparent reason. A forum to vent and make a lot of money.

Q: Is it getting worse?

A: I haven't seen enough positive changes coming from the music that has been created in the last decade and I see more and more young people, instead of being inspired or incited, being targeted demographically. I have a 12-year-old daughter who is just a target for new products and it's heartbreaking to me. Young people are made to feel more and more peer pressure in terms of what they look like, how they're dressed, how they feel sexually, in every way. They're just being conditioned to consume. It reminds me of Hansel and Gretel and the witch who kept giving them candy and goodies to fatten them up for the kill.

Q: So maybe if you'd kept making records in the '80s and early '90s, you could have helped counter some of that. Why did you go away for so long?

A: I ended up being involved in the arena of rock 'n' roll out of necessity, because I felt that there were things that needed to be said, and there was space to be created for future generations to work in. But by 1979, it was mission accomplished and unless I evolved as a human being, learned more things, or did more study, I should just go away. I wasn't in that arena to get rich and famous. If I had stayed, perhaps that's what would have happened, but that wasn't interesting enough to me to stick around. I liked the public service aspect of rock 'n' roll, but I also seek illumination. And I wasn't getting any more illumination. I felt stagnant as an artist and as a human being. That's why I had to leave.

Q: In 1976, you told writer Nick Tosches that "when I'm 40 I don't want to try and do a rock 'n' roll record like Gene Vincent tried to do right before he popped off. It would have been much better if he'd written a book." You're 53, and you just made a rock 'n' roll record. Any second thoughts about rock 'n' roll at 40 and beyond?

A: I still believe that rock 'n' roll is a young people's forum. But I believe that within that forum I still have things to say and the authority to say them. I was really concerned about rock 'n' roll in the '70s because I began to see what I perceived as a withering away of a strong, unique and immediate form that had been developed as a cultural, political and artistic force by people from Elvis Presley and Bob Dylan to Jim Morrison and Jimi Hendrix. To appreciate a painting like (Picasso's) "Guernica" you had to go see it, but with a rock 'n' roll record you could affect thousands of people all over the world simultaneously. I started getting involved in 1973 because I thought people were losing sight of that power and using rock 'n' roll to get famous and indulge in drugs and sexual fantasies. It was losing cultural importance, and I didn't want that to happen. I think there are kids out there, the bands of the future, who don't want that to happen now either.

Q: You're three albums deep into the second phase of your career. What's different about it now?

A: In the past, I always felt I was like one of the people, a fan who crossed the line and who had some things to say. I don't feel like I'm in the same place anymore. I don't feel so much like a fan at this point. In a way, I feel more like an outsider than ever.

Q: You're still playing the Paul Revere role.

A: When I used that analogy in the '70s, people might have thought it was conceited of me. But Paul Revere was a very modest guy, an engraver, a silver maker, and he got on his horse and yelled, "The British are coming!" because someone needed to do it. I don't have the intellect of a Thomas Jefferson or a Thomas Paine. But I can relate to someone like Paul Revere who looked around and saw what needed to be done, and he just did it. I always viewed my role that way. We're all given a voice, but hardly any American uses his voice, his rights. People died, lost their homes and families to ensure that we have these rights, and we seldom use them. I feel like it's not only my privilege but my duty to exercise these rights we've been given.

....

George Harrison
Beatle's influence anything but quiet

DEC. 1, 2001

George Harrison, the former Beatles guitarist who helped revolutionize popular music and culture while playing in the most revered rock band of all time and then went on to a successful solo career in music and movie production, died [*Nov. 29, 2001*] in Los Angeles after a long bout of cancer. He was 58.

Harrison's longtime friend and noted celebrity security expert Gavin De Becker said Harrison's wife, Olivia Harrison, and son Dhani, 23, were with him.

"He left this world as he lived in it, conscious of God, fearless of

Avoiding their screaming fans, George, John, Ringo and Paul prepare to take a limousine into Chicago from an outlying O'Hare hangar on Aug. 11, 1966. The Beatles were on their third and final U.S. tour. While in Chicago, John Lennon apologized for saying the group was "bigger than Jesus."
TRIBUNE ARCHIVE

death, and at peace, surrounded by family and friends," the Harrison family said in a statement. "He often said, 'Everything else can wait but the search for God cannot wait, and love one another.'"

With Harrison's death, there are two surviving Beatles, Paul Mc-Cartney and Ringo Starr. John Lennon was shot to death by a deranged fan in 1980. Harrison died at De Becker's house.

"I am devastated and very, very sad," McCartney told reporters outside his home near London. "He was a lovely guy and a very brave man and had a wonderful sense of humor. He is really just my baby brother."

In a statement, Starr said: "George was a best friend of mine. I loved him very much and I will miss him greatly."

It was not immediately known whether there would be a public funeral for Harrison. A private ceremony already had taken place, De Becker said.

As word of Harrison's death spread in Henley-on-Thames in England, where he lived for almost three decades, a stream of people stopped to leave bouquets and tributes at the gate of his 19th Century Gothic mansion.

"My guitar will gently weep forever," said a note pinned to some yellow roses, alluding to one of Harrison's Beatles compositions.

In New York's Central Park, fans began gathering before dawn in Strawberry Fields, named for a Lennon-McCartney song. In Los Angeles, fans placed flowers on the Beatle's star on Hollywood Boulevard. Meanwhile, Harrison's 1970 album "All Things Must Pass" jumped to No. 1 on the Amazon.com sales chart.

Harrison underwent radiation treatment for an inoperable brain tumor *[in November 2001]* at Staten Island University Hospital in New York, where fellow Beatles McCartney and Starr reportedly held a tearful reunion. Over the summer he received radiotherapy in Switzerland for the brain tumor, and *[in the]* spring he was a lung cancer patient at the Mayo Clinic in Rochester, Minn. In 1997, he underwent surgery to remove a cancerous lump from his throat, a condition he blamed on his years of smoking.

Harrison was the quietest of pop superstars, with a reputation as an inscrutable mystic who valued his privacy.

"I'm really quite simple," he declared in his 1979 memoir, "I Me Mine." "I don't want to be in the business full time because I'm a gardener; I plant flowers and watch them grow. I stay at home and watch the river flow."

Those self-effacing comments belied a career in which The Beatles, with Harrison as their primary guitarist, reinvigorated rock 'n' roll. Through the 1960s, they transformed the once-primitive brand of youth entertainment into an art form with increasingly sophisticated songcraft that has endured into the new century. As recently as 2000, a collection of Beatles songs, "1," sold millions of copies and debuted at No. 1 on the pop album chart, ahead of such contemporary competition as the Backstreet Boys. The collection included Harrison's most famous Beatles composition, "Something," which the late Frank Sinatra declared "the greatest love song of the past 50 years."

The Beatle years

Born in Liverpool, England, on Feb. 25, 1943, George Harrison grew up in a public housing project as the youngest of three sons. When he was 13, his mother bought him his first guitar and he formed a band called the Rebels. At age 15, he joined the Quarrymen with John Lennon and Paul McCartney. The three young men—along with a fellow named Ringo—would eventually change the course of musical history as The Beatles.

1960: The Quarrymen become The Beatles and begin working at the Indra Club in Hamburg, Germany. When they perform at a rival club, the Indra owner tells police George is only 17, too young to work in a club, and the group returns to England.

January 1961: The Beatles make their debut at the Cavern Club in Liverpool.

May 9, 1962: The Beatles are signed by producer George Martin of Parlophone, a subsidiary of EMI. After one session, Pete Best is replaced by local drummer Ringo Starr.

October 1962: "Love Me Do" becomes The Beatles' first Top 20 hit, allegedly because manager Brian Epstein purchases 10,000 copies to ensure that the song would reach the charts.

February 1963: The Beatles record 10 songs in one day for their first album, "Please Please Me."

1963: Capitol Records, the American partner of EMI, refuses to release the early Beatles singles. Instead, Chicago independent label Vee Jay Records releases them as "Introducing The Beatles," technically the band's first U.S. album.

1964: After a court awards EMI/Capitol rights to all Beatles material, Capitol releases "Meet The Beatles!" which contains songs from earlier British records.

Feb. 9 and 16, 1964: The Beatles perform to a live TV audience on "The Ed Sullivan Show."

March 1964: Shooting begins on The Beatles' first feature film, "A Hard Day's Night." Harrison meets future wife Patti Boyd during the filming.

Sept. 5, 1964: Beatles play first Chicago concert at the International Amphitheatre.

1965: Harrison studies under Indian sitar player Ravi Shankar. Harrison becomes interested in Eastern religion and starts associating with spiritual leader Maharishi Mahesh Yogi.

The Beatle years, cont.

Aug. 20, 1965: The Beatles play at Comiskey Park, part of a 10-city North American tour. On the same tour, they meet Elvis Presley for the first time. Not knowing their names, Presley simply addresses each of them as "Beatle."

Jan. 21, 1966: Harrison marries Pattie Boyd.

Aug. 12, 1966: The Beatles' final tour opens in Chicago at the Amphitheatre. They perform their final concert on Aug. 30 at Candlestick Park in San Francisco.

June 1967: Landmark LP "Sgt. Pepper's Lonely Hearts Club Band" released.

1968: In the first solo outing for a Beatle, Harrison travels to Bombay and contributes sitar-based songs to the movie "Wonderwall Music."

Jan. 30 1969: Harrison performs for the last time with The Beatles on the rooftop of Abbey Road studios.

April 10, 1970: McCartney announces that he is leaving The Beatles—leading to the breakup of the band.

Looking 'good again'

"Rock isn't just teenybopper music anymore," Harrison told the Tribune in a 1992 interview in explaining The Beatles' continuing prestige, influence and commercial power with typically self-deprecating insight. "You've got audiences now from three generations. And as the music has gotten worse and worse over the years, it's made us start to look good again."

The youngest of The Beatles, Harrison was born Feb. 25, 1943, in Liverpool, England, and, unlike his bandmates, lived in a stable family with his parents, two brothers and a sister. He and McCartney became friends in their teens and practiced guitar together.

Eventually Harrison joined the rock band that McCartney had formed with John Lennon, which changed its name from the Quarrymen to Johnny and the Moondogs to the Silver Beatles to The Beatles. The band's first extended gig at a Hamburg, Germany, club in 1960 was cut short when the 17-year-old Harrison was expelled for being underage.

Harrison, McCartney, Starr and Lennon went on to influence fashion, humor, counterculture politics and even hairstyles during their heyday. Their blend of wit, style and charisma transcended music and invaded daily life through movies, news conferences, television appearances, concerts and other media—even lunch boxes and a Saturday morning Beatles cartoon. Initially derided as a mop-topped fad, The Beatles gained acceptance from establishment tastemakers as their music evolved, inevitably shifting the cultural landscape with each new phase in their rapid development.

"We modeled ourselves after The Beatles in that with every album we tried to take a step forward," said drummer Bun E. Carlos of Cheap Trick, which has covered numerous Beatles songs in its 25-year career and once collaborated with Lennon. "Our only problem was we're not Lennon, McCartney, Harrison and Starr. They encouraged rock musicians to be musicians, and it was about four separate personalities becoming one band."

The Beatles' first two appearances on "The Ed Sullivan Show" in February 1964, heralding their arrival in the United States, were each viewed by more than 70 million people. That year, The Beatles had six records that reached No. 1 or No. 2 on the American pop charts, and Harrison's terse, melodic precision on his instrument inspired legions of would-be guitarists.

Countless bands were formed as a result of the Beatles-led "British Invasion," and the band pushed rock 'n' roll out of its infancy by introducing Eastern instruments and classical arrangement ideas while pioneering the use of recording technology to create albums that were richer, denser and more complex than pop music ever had been.

Harrison earned the nickname "the quiet Beatle" as he was overshadowed by Lennon and McCartney's outsize talents and Starr's cuddly goofball persona, but it was an inaccurate stereotype.

Did more with less

He was an essential and innovative component of the band's sound as his guitar playing advanced from twangy rockabilly licks influenced by '50s rock 'n' rollers Chuck Berry, Carl Perkins and Scotty Moore to incorporate a broad palette of avant-garde textures that enhanced The

Beatles' increasingly diverse songs. Never a flashy soloist, few guitarists did more with less: Harrison could make a short introductory statement such as the one that opens his Beatles classic "Here Comes the Sun" seem like a song in itself.

Harrison also proved hugely influential with his pioneering use of the 12-string Rickenbacker guitar, its chiming sound adopted by the Byrds, Tom Petty and countless others. He also introduced Eastern instruments to the rock lexicon, first with the sitar on the Lennon-McCartney tune "Norwegian Wood" and then with a full complement of exotic orchestrations on his own Beatles compositions "Love You Too" and "Within You Without You." By the time of his first solo album, in 1970, he had also developed a signature tone as a slide guitarist, a sweet sighing sound that was his unique interpretation of the Southern blues idiom.

Just as Harrison's fuss-free guitar playing belied his inventiveness, so did Harrison's reserved demeanor mask his wry humor. At the group's first recording session with George Martin, the producer asked whether there was anything they didn't like, and Harrison replied, "Well, I don't like your tie for a start." He also fired off some of the best zingers in the groundbreaking feature films "A Hard Day's Night" and "Help!"—movies that broadened the group's following by emphasizing their madcap humor and unthreatening sex appeal.

His sense of humor remained until the end. Harrison recorded a new song, "Horse to the Water," and credited it to "RIP Ltd. 2001" that was released this month on a record by British musician Jools Holland.

"To me, George was, always will be, above all, a real gentleman, in the full meaning of the word," said Rolling Stones guitarist Keith Richards. "We both felt we held similar positions in our respective bands, which formed a special knowing bond between us. Let's hope he's jamming with John."

The most introspective of The Beatles also set the band's social agenda during the late '60s, when the quartet's every move was scrutinized by fans around the world. He instigated The Beatles' visit to India and helped introduce a new generation in the West to Eastern religion. Unlike his bandmates, Harrison adopted many of the principles of Eastern religion and used them as inspiration for his music. He began to

Beyond The Beatles

While a member of The Beatles, Harrison often was overshadowed by Lennon and McCartney. But it was Harrison who had the first No. 1 single—"My Sweet Lord"—and the first No. 1 album—"All Things Must Pass"—as a solo artist.

1970: Harrison records his first true solo album, "All Things Must Pass," a critically acclaimed triple LP that reaches No. 1 on the U.S. charts. It includes the hit "My Sweet Lord" as well as "Isn't It a Pity," "What Is Life," "Beware of Darkness" and "Wah-Wah." Ringo Starr plays drums on a few tracks.

1971: Produces an album for the group Badfinger and contributes work to Lennon's "Imagine" record.

Aug. 1, 1971: Organizes and performs in the Concert for Bangladesh to raise money for the poverty-stricken country.

1973: Records the album "Living in the Material World," featuring the hit "Give Me Love (Give Me Peace On Earth)."

1974: Hastily records the album "Dark Horse" and then embarks on his first solo North American tour.

1975: Releases the record "Extra Texture." It flops, ending his relationship with EMI, The Beatles' production company. Harrison creates his own Dark Horse record label and releases "Thirty Three & 1/3" the next year.

1976: A court rules that Harrison "subconsciously" borrowed the melody from the 1962 Chiffons hit "He's So Fine" for the song "My Sweet Lord." Harrison is ordered to pay $1.6 million in damages. The case is not completely settled until the 1990s.

1977: Pattie Boyd leaves Harrison for another guitarist, Eric Clapton.

1978: Harrison decides to shift his artistic focus toward movies and establishes HandMade Film, which later produces titles such as "Time Bandits" and "Monty Python's Life of Brian."

Aug. 1, 1978: Son Dhani is born to Harrison and Olivia Arias, who worked as a secretary for Dark Horse Records.

1981: Harrison's LP "Somewhere in England" includes a tribute to the late John Lennon, "All Those Years Ago," which also features McCartney and Starr.

1987: Releases "Cloud 9," the biggest-selling LP of his solo career. It includes a cover of Rudy Clark's "I Got My Mind Set On You," which becomes a No. 1 hit. It remains the most recent No. 1 song by any of The Beatles.

Beyond The Beatles, cont.

1988: Along with Bob Dylan, Roy Orbison, Tom Petty and Electric Light Orchestra frontman Jeff Lynne, Harrison forms the Traveling Wilburys. The group records two platinum-selling albums before disbanding in 1990.

1991: Harrison tours with Clapton and releases a live album from the tour the following year.

1994: With profits sliding, Harrison sells HandMade Film.

1995–96: The three-volume Beatles "Anthology" CD sets are released, featuring two songs—"Free as a Bird" and "Real Love"—created by mixing new music performed by Harrison, McCartney and Starr with vocal tracks sung by Lennon in the late 1970s.

1997: Harrison has treatment for throat cancer.

1999: Harrison is stabbed several times by an intruder in his London-area mansion . He suffers a punctured lung and his wife, Olivia, suffers minor injuries. The intruder, a 33-year-old former heroin addict Michael Abram, was later found not guilty by reason of insanity.

Nov. 29, 2001: Harrison dies at age 58 of cancer in Los Angeles.

express his beliefs in openly spiritual songs that longed for redemption in a corrupt material world. Many of those songs would emerge after The Beatles broke up in 1970, a cultural watershed in part brought about by Harrison's increasing frustration as a songwriter whose contributions were not always taken seriously by McCartney and Lennon.

He quickly made up for lost time, launching his solo career with the landmark 1970 triple album "All Things Must Pass," stockpiled with songs The Beatles had dismissed. Harrison went on to record eight more studio albums, including the 1987 hit "Cloud Nine." Though he lost a lawsuit over the No. 1 single "My Sweet Lord," which the authors of the Chiffons' 1961 hit "He's So Fine" claim he plagiarized, Harrison's songwriting remains an influence on contemporary artists ranging from Elliott Smith to the Dandy Warhols.

"He was pushed out of the picture in The Beatles, so all his best writing was on those solo albums," Cheap Trick's Carlos said. "But he was as big an influence on us as Lennon was. That he could contribute so much to his band even though he wasn't the main songwriter is something we appreciate."

Though Harrison's deferential personality hindered his progress in The Beatles, it proved helpful in building long-lasting relationships outside his famous band. He was befriended by legendary talents Bob Dylan and Eric Clapton, and collaborated several times with both. He later formed the Traveling Wilburys with Dylan, Petty, Roy Orbison and Jeff Lynne, and co-produced two successful albums with the supergroup in 1988 and '90. "All Things Must Pass" featured contributions from Dylan and Clapton, as did Harrison's 1971 concert for Bangladesh hunger relief, which presaged all-star charity events such as Live Aid and the Concert for New York.

Harrison's relationship with Clapton was particularly fascinating, one of rock's most complex and tumultuous collaborations. Harrison co-wrote the song "Badge" for Clapton's group Cream, and Clapton played the guitar solo on Harrison's Beatles classic "While My Guitar Gently Weeps." Meanwhile, Clapton was falling in love with Harrison's then-wife, model Pattie Boyd, and wrote the 1970 rock masterpiece "Layla" as a testament to his unrequited passion.

Boyd eventually divorced Harrison in 1977 and married Clapton in '79, yet the two guitarists remained friends. It was Clapton who coaxed Harrison out on tour for the final time, a 1991 jaunt across Japan that yielded the former Beatle's final solo album, "Live in Japan."

"I finished with the wife and he married her, then he finished with her," Harrison once told the Tribune with nonchalance typical of his feelings toward Clapton. "I mean, we've been through a lot of similar things, similar wives. It's just the way it is."

Fatherhood, focus on film

Harrison remarried in 1978, to Olivia Arias, who had been working at his record label, Dark Horse, and they had a son, Dhani. In the late '70s and early '80s, as his recording career slowed down, Harrison devoted most of his attention to his HandMade Film production company, which financed "Monty Python's Life of Brian," Terry Gilliam's "Time Bandits," Neil Jordan's "Mona Lisa" and Bruce Robinson's "Withnail and I," among other movies.

He spent most of his recent years as a relative recluse, living on his country estate outside London or spending time in his secluded Maui digs.

He re-emerged to participate in the "Beatles Anthology" multihour documentary project in 1995, and he, McCartney and Starr added vocals and instruments to the unfinished Lennon tracks "Free as a Bird" and "Real Love," the first new Beatles recordings since 1969. All three retrospective double-CDs in the "Anthology" campaign entered the pop charts at No. 1 and sparked a new generation's interest in the band.

But Harrison never gave the OK for an onstage reunion of the surviving Beatles.

"Personally, I'd stay as far away as possible from that," he told the Tribune. "It wouldn't be what people expect. They'd show up, and it would just be three old men on stage."

Although he preferred a peaceful life—"the adulation or the superstardom is something I could leave out quite happily," he told the Tribune—his last years were filled with turmoil. On top of the cancer, he suffered multiple stab wounds when a deranged fan attacked him in his English home on Dec. 30, 1999. He and wife Olivia fought off and subdued the 33-year-old attacker, who a court later determined was insane.

"I had a little throat cancer. I had a piece of my lung removed in 1997. And then I was almost murdered," Harrison told the AP *[in 2001]*. "But I seem to feel stronger."

Throughout his life, Harrison maintained his reputation as The Beatles' least flamboyant and most humble personality. He tended to credit his following of Eastern religion—an amalgam of faiths—for his staying grounded.

"Practicing it is what counts," he told the Tribune. "I believe that we're a mirror, and so much dust accumulates that we can't see in or out. We have to clean off the dust and reveal to ourselves what we are. And the key to doing that is not to become too attached to this world."

....

Peter Gabriel talks death, birth, music making

SEPT. 22, 2002

Where have you gone, Peter Gabriel? A founding member of Genesis who became a rock superstar in the '80s with hits such as "Biko," "Shock the Monkey" and "Sledgehammer," Gabriel last released a studio album of pop-oriented songs in what seems like a different world:

Bill Clinton was running for the presidency against the father of the current president, George W. Bush.

Fledgling Mouseketeer Britney Spears hadn't even filmed her first episode of "The New Mickey Mouse Club."

Guns N' Roses was the planet's biggest rock band.

Now, as the Gunners' Axl Rose could tell him, times have changed. Like Rose, Gabriel has been hunkered down in a studio on and off for the last decade, tinkering with songs and plotting his next move. "Up" (Geffen), will finally be released, a 10-song concept album about "death and birth and things that are above and beneath life," Gabriel says in an interview, "the stuff outside the main view of the windshield."

Would that be a literary conceit or something he says just to satisfy nosy journalists? Even Gabriel, who treads cautiously through interviews with a blend of monkish calm and an undertaker's dourness, has to laugh.

"It's really the sort of B.S. I start coming up with when I start doing interviews," he says. "The theme of the album usually doesn't emerge until I talk to a few journalists, and one of them comes up with a good theory, and I think, 'Yeah, that's it!'"

Lacking levity

One wishes a bit of that humor had found its way into "Up," which comes off as an unusually sober and sobering listening experience, even by Gabriel's exacting standards. Long noted for breaking ground rhythmically, and for his breathtaking blends of exotica, rock groove

Peter Gabriel at the United Center June 20, 2011.
NUCCIO DINUZZO

and psychodramatic introspection, the artist sounds unusually inert on the new album.

A sense of stasis and self-seriousness shrouds the entire enterprise, and Gabriel sounds like yesterday's news when he slings darts at exploitive talk-show hosts on "The Barry Williams Show," an unfortunate choice for the first single.

There are a handful of glorious moments, notably the celebratory soul groove that puts an unexpectedly uplifting spin on the elegiac "I Grieve." But mostly, the album feels labored, the product of too much time in the studio instead of not enough.

The advent of home-recording technology and studios has given artists more freedom than ever to produce music at their own pace, rather than a record company's. Without having to worry about mounting studio costs, musicians are free to explore myriad options at a pace that makes the rockers of the past appear even more dizzyingly prolific than they actually were. Whereas in the '60s and '70s major acts such as The Beatles and Elton John were recording and releasing as many as three albums a year, the pace has slowed dramatically in the last decade. Now big-name performers are expected to take their time between studio releases, turning each into media events: witness the protracted media campaigns for Bruce Springsteen's recent release, "The Rising," and U2's 2000 opus, "All That You Can't Leave Behind."

But the more deliberate pace demanded by these promotion schedules also promotes creative hand-wringing. Rose has been working on "Chinese Democracy," the 11-years-in-the-making sequel to Guns 'N Roses' "Use Your Illusion" albums, so long that he has become a punch line for rock-star excess. Springsteen similarly has recorded and scrapped countless tracks and at least one finished album over the years; "The Rising" is his first studio album since 1995 and only his fifth in 17 years. Nine Inch Nails'Trent Reznor took five years to create "The Fragile," the follow-up to his 1994 breakthrough "The Downward Spiral," and found himself struggling to reclaim his audience.

The slow track

Gabriel has also been working at an increasingly deliberate basis. Whereas his first four groundbreaking solo albums came out in five years, his next three required 20, with increasingly diminishing artistic results. It's not that he's been dithering. His Real World Studios, near Bath, England, has become a workshop, sanctuary and meeting place for musicians from around the world. While developing the songs for "Up," Gabriel completed two other projects: Ovo, the multiethnic score for the Millennium Dome Show, and "Long Walk Home," the soundtrack for the Australian movie "Rabbit-Proof Fence."

"There were 130 songs in various stages of completion the last 10 years," Gabriel says. "I guess I just enjoy the business of making music better than selling it. I didn't have a producer on board whipping me into shape, and so deadlines become things you pass through on the way to finishing."

Gabriel brushes aside the notion that isolation breeds a kind of insularity, a lack of outside input that hampers his ability to make decisions quickly.

"Real World isn't an isolated lighthouse, it's a bit more like a train station with people coming from all over the world, so there is always a lot of stuff to inspire me, and a few musicians to try and kidnap."

A few of them appear on "Up," including the late Pakistani sacred singer Nusrat Fateh Ali Khan and the gospel group the Blind Boys of Alabama. They bring a richness to the recording that is undeniable. But Gabriel's songwriting lacks the sense of surprise and subversiveness that marks his finest work.

A natural fit

If Gabriel feels daunted by that legacy, he doesn't let on.

"Music has never been a problem for me," he says. "If I had to produce a song a day, as the songwriters were required to do in the old days of the Brill Building, I think I could do that. The problem comes when I try to strap some words on top. And then to get something that I am satisfied with, or even half-satisfied with, will take a week or two weeks. I have to go away. I can't do it at home or in the studio, because I'm a master of distractions. I could make a career out of distractions, and I wouldn't get anything done."

Gabriel says he does not work with collaborators because he is after something specific, if elusive, when he writes songs. "I think of the songs like journeys, a train journey," he says. "You've got to decide what place you want to go, and then try to make it interesting and real for you. It's not something that necessarily lends itself to sharing with others."

Ultimately, it's a lonely process, and as the incubation time lengthens between albums, the audience an artist has taken a career to cultivate may no longer be there.

"I have no idea what sort of audience there will be for me anymore," he says. "It's been a long time since I've had a radio song out. On this album, at the last minute I pulled a track ['Burn You Up, Burn You Down'] for a future project because it didn't seem, on reflection, to come from the same family as the rest of the songs on the album. I got a few protests about that from the European label, because they think it's a radio-friendly song. But I have a history of doing that sort of thing. If this album dies a horrible death, the record company will be at my door."

At his pace

Gabriel doesn't sound particularly concerned. Because of his stature, the weight of his previous accomplishments, he is an artist who has earned the luxury of making his own decisions, in his own good time.

There is a nobility even in the singer's failures, because they are untainted by compromise or outside meddling. But as the time between albums expands, one has to wonder if Gabriel has fallen victim to a work schedule that allows almost too much creative freedom.

....

Wilco
A band famous for reinventing itself continues to flourish

JUNE 6, 2004

Wilco's forthcoming album, "A Ghost Is Born" (Nonesuch), ends not with a bang but with a wink. The final song, "Late Greats," takes a wry look at anonymity:

> *The best songs will never get sung*
> *The best life never leaves your lungs*
> *So good you won't ever know*
> *You can't hear it on the radio*

A listener familiar with Wilco's recent past will be tempted to hear those lines as at least partially autobiographical. Three years ago this month, the Chicago band was being shown the door by its old record company. Wilco's fourth record, "Yankee Hotel Foxtrot," wasn't deemed hit-worthy enough for Reprise Records to even bother releasing it.

Then a funny thing happened on the way to record-industry oblivion. Wilco took back its album, released it on the Internet, and then sold it to another label, Nonesuch Records. More than 400,000 sales later, Wilco had become a commercial force and a cause celebre with its own

Wilco band members (L-R) Glenn Kotche, Mike Jorgensen, John Stirratt and
Jeff Tweedy, in their Chicago studio in 2004.
ALEX GARCIA

made-for-TV-worthy script (little band trumps big corporation). "Yankee Hotel Foxtrot" was named album of the year in the annual Village
Voice critics poll, and the band concluded its 2002–03 world tour by
selling out two shows at the Auditorium Theatre—a $200,000 weekend
that by itself would've paid for the recording costs of "Foxtrot."

This non-commercial band was suddenly doing very well commercially, and "A Ghost Is Born" became one of the most anticipated
releases of 2004. Then the floor began to give way, again. Keyboardist Leroy Bach quit the band a few months ago, the fifth defection
or firing in the band's 10-year history. His amicable departure was
closely followed by the hiring of two new musicians—guitarist Nels
Cline and keyboardist Pat Sansone—on the eve of a world tour.
Then band leader Jeff Tweedy checked himself into a rehab clinic
to try to break an addiction to painkillers brought on by persistent
migraine headaches.

"With the new band members and the new album, there was a lot
of [expletive] at stake," drummer Glenn Kotche says. "We were going

to be on the road the next two years. Jeff had to do this to get healthy, otherwise it could've turned out bad for everyone."

Tweedy emerged from rehab a few weeks ago with the migraines under control, saying that he felt better than he has in years. And after a handful of canceled tour dates, the new six-piece lineup was preparing for the June 22 release of "A Ghost Is Born" and a sold-out concert at the Vic. They warmed up with two shows at Otto's, a DeKalb club that had become a favored haunt in recent years.

The band sounded formidable even at this early stage, with Cline's guitar adding muscle and nuance to the attack, and Sansone's keyboards coupling with Mikael Jorgenson's to bring orchestral richness to the more ornate songs. "This could be the most exciting live lineup we've had," bassist John Stirratt says.

But even Stirratt realizes it could all end in a flash. "Jeff's situation makes you realize how precarious it all is, especially when you're depending on one person," he says. "If it all ended, I think we've had a pretty good run. It's been a long run, longer than most bands. We're living on borrowed time in a way."

That what-have-we-got-to-lose? attitude has served the band well. Rather than progressing in baby steps or simply refining its best moves, Wilco has turned each album into a new opportunity to reinvent itself. The sole exception was "A.M." (1995), which blended twang with punk, a tentative extension of Tweedy's work with Stirratt in Uncle Tupelo. "Being There" (1996) was the great leap forward, as it touched on everything from country-soul to noise rock. "Summerteeth" (1999) explored lush orchestral pop, and "Yankee Hotel Foxtrot" (2002) tucked meditative folk-rock songs inside meticulously layered soundscapes. Sprinkled in between were a pair of "Mermaid Avenue" albums with British folkie Billy Bragg that offered a fresh take on the lyrics of Dust Bowl balladeer Woody Guthrie.

No easy routes

"A Ghost Is Born" is yet one more left turn down a dark alley of new possibilities. It finds Tweedy becoming an even more adventurous singer: the intimacy he conveys in the opening seconds of "At Least That's What You Said," the falsetto he unveils in "Hummingbird," the treacherous seductiveness he conveys in "Hell Is Chrome." The album also showcases a group of complementary musicians who know how to shape a song: Stirratt's melodic bass playing in "Handshake Drugs," the luxurious keyboard orchestration of "Company in My Back," the gospel-tinged accents and shuffling soul moves of "Theologians."

Then there's Tweedy's emergence as a lead guitarist, a job he had previously assigned to other, more technically accomplished musicians in the band. Now he's out front taking solos that shriek and shudder like the poltergeist referenced in the album title. When he tears loose over Kotche's boisterous drumming in the final bars of "At Least That's What You Said," it's exhilarating. Two songs later, on "Spiders (Kidsmoke)," his guitar darts in and out over a relentless trance-rock groove. Like many of the songs on "Ghost," the song had been performed in concert by the band for more than a year, but in a vastly different arrangement.

It was "a bombastic track that reminded us a little too much of Coldplay or U2," Stirratt says. In the studio, Kotche and Stirratt locked into a rhythm pattern that wouldn't have sounded out of place on an early album by German art-rockers Neu! The band cut two epic versions of the song, and called it a day.

"We were just jamming on it—I thought we'd go back to it and edit it together later," Kotche recalls. "But no, sure enough, it was two full, complete takes, and one of them ended up on the album."

The spontaneity of "Spiders" epitomized the spirit of the entire album, which was less about the studio-as-instrument experiments that characterized "Summerteeth" and "Yankee Hotel Foxtrot" and more about the musicians playing together in a room with a minimum of overdubs. Whereas Kotche applied a variety of drums and percussion instruments on "Foxtrot," he used a single trap kit for most of "Ghost." The arrangements are more spacious, the interaction of the band as crucial as the words. For Tweedy, celebrated for his forthright lyricism, this marks a bold departure.

"I was having a tougher time getting all the emotion I wanted to get out of the words," Tweedy says. "I started to trust my guitar-playing more, just by working at it, and I felt a lot of things come out that I wasn't able to get to lyrically. I'm not as fast or proficient as 90 percent of the guitarists out there making a living. But I can sound like me."

Not thin-skinned

Darin Gray, an old musician friend of Tweedy's from pre-Uncle Tupelo days, says the guitarist's willingness "to just put it out there, no
matter what anyone says," has enabled him to take risks other artists
avoid. "I don't think he's saying, 'Look at me, I'm a great guitarist,' but
he's confident in his ability to express himself. Before he might default
to other, more accomplished musicians, like Jay Farrar in Uncle Tupelo or Jay Bennett in Wilco, but now there are no crutches left. He's
just more confident in his own skin, but he's also of the mind-set that
'What have I got to lose?' It's not worth it to him if there's not a sense
that he's turning a corner and trying something new."

That approach doesn't always sit well with the fans, who are already
upbraiding the band on various Internet message boards for turning
the concert favorite "Spiders (Kidsmoke)" into an 11-minute guitar
"wankfest," and for appending a 12-minute instrumental drone to one
of Tweedy's most intimate songs, "Less Than You Think."

Tweedy understands the fans' consternation, though he makes no
concessions to it. "I know that 99 percent of our fans won't like 'Less
Than You Think,' that they will think the record is flawed because of
that, or that it was a ridiculous indulgence. But I wouldn't have put it
on the record if I didn't think it was valuable, that it wouldn't reward
someone's attention if they decided to sit down and just listen."

The song sits near the end of a record that Tweedy feels is about identity, or the lack of one. In song after song, the question of "What do you
want me to be?" recurs. In "Less Than You Think," identity is subsumed
completely by music. Each Wilco member set up a sound installation in
the studio, running their instruments through a series of effects boxes.
The noise was recorded, then sculpted into a slow-moving sonic parabola
that ascends, peaks, then fades. The sound of a ghost being born?

'Higher power'

"Nobody plays anything—there is so much less to this than you think,"
Tweedy says. "It's identity again. Why is this here? Because anybody
could do it. Anything can happen. It's not up to us. It's that big idea of
a higher power."

"Less Than You Think" melts into album finale "The Late Greats," which serves as something of a subtle punch line. Tweedy pokes fun at his self-indulgence, and those who might've fast-forwarded through the previous track. "The greatest lost track of all time," he sings. "Can't hear it anywhere you go."

At that moment, another theme threading its way through "A Ghost Is Born" becomes apparent. When Tweedy insists that "the best songs will never get sung, the best life never leaves your lungs," he posits that all we need to "be" is ourselves. But as the monthslong Internet discussions about the merits of "Spiders" and "Less Than You Think" illustrate, Tweedy and Wilco make music that also demands something more. It's not enough simply to be. "A Ghost Is Born" is also an attack on complacency. It is the sound of a band challenging itself to work outside its prescribed boundaries and challenging its audience to respond, even if it means walking across the room to push the fast-forward button on the stereo.

"Hearing the songs is just as important as singing them," Tweedy says. "And what the listeners bring to them, and what they pour into it, and how they see themselves is everything about how this album, and that song in particular, will work. It's something that's come up before in our albums, only now I'm making the point in much more aggravating fashion: That it's your album too."

....

Bono: 'We need to talk'

MAY 22, 2005

Bono is steamed.

It's not every day that I answer my cell phone and hear the lead singer of U2 expressing serious disagreement with something I've written, but that day has arrived.

"You've offended us," he says as I weave up Lake Shore Drive during evening rush hour, trying not to crash into a concrete barrier while I reach for my notebook. "There's a dark cloud over us and we need to talk."

I've covered the band for 15 years, interviewed Bono a half-dozen times and attended virtually every one of U2's Chicago concerts since the Irish quartet first played at Park West in 1981. Along with R.E.M., U2 is the most important mainstream rock band of my generation, a band that set a new standard for how an arena rock concert could feel and what it could communicate. In the '90s, Bono, guitarist The Edge, drummer Larry Mullen Jr. and bassist Adam Clayton gave their well-honed approach a twist on such adventurous albums as "Achtung Baby" (1991), "Zooropa" (1993), the "Passengers: Original Soundtracks I" side project (1995) and "Pop" (1997).

But "Pop" bombed commercially by U2 standards, and the band seemed to lose its nerve. It made two consecutive albums, "All That You Can't Leave Behind" (2000) and "How to Dismantle an Atomic Bomb" (2004), that retreated from the innovations of the '90s and settled for a retro '80s sound. In February [*2005*], the Tribune published an article in which I chastised the band for a series of dubious artistic and business decisions. It was prompted by a flood of irate e-mails from fans who had paid $40 to join U2's fan club in order to gain access to pre-sale tickets for the band's North American tour. The sale was a public-relations disaster. Some fan-club members reported they couldn't even get tickets, or paid nearly $200 for third-balcony seats, while scalpers were selling tickets on eBay for more than $600. It was the latest in a series of missteps that prompted me to question whether this once-vital band was turning into the Rolling Stones, more of a corporation focused on perpetuating itself than a creative force.

There was the ubiquitous television ad (for which they were not paid) in which "Vertigo," the first single from "Atomic Bomb," was turned into a commercial for Apple's portable music device, the iPod. There were the unusually conservative albums, evidence that the band had run out of ideas or the will to challenge itself and its audience. There was the live appearance at the Super Bowl halftime in February 2002, the type of marketing opportunity that presented even the most idealistic brand of rock as just another product.

It was these criticisms that prompted Bono's Lake Shore Drive call. A day after that conversation, I attended the first concert in U2's four-night sold-out run at the United Center. My review focused on the tired set list. U2 played some new songs early in the two-hour performance, but instead of building a case for the new album and possibly redeeming it, the quartet reserved all the big-bang moments for its greatest hits, songs that had been in the set list for a decade or more. They sounded more than ever like the bands they once arose to replace, the dinosaur acts of the '60s.

All of this is part of what should be the relationship among the artist, the critic and even the audience, which at the United Center was wildly cheering (as they always do) every note. Critics, on the other hand, are not cheerleaders. They are paid to honestly and passionately react to what the artist does—for better or worse. When it's the latter, audiences are often more vocal in their defense than the artists. But Bono was different.

After the review appeared in the Tribune, Bono invited me to attend another show. Later, he would acknowledge that my review of the first concert wasn't off base. "We weren't at our best," he said. When I attended the final show of the four-night stand, the song deck had been shuffled, and the band grew more daring. A new song that wasn't in the first night's set, "Original of the Species," was a highlight. It's a soul ballad with a melody so suggestive that it compelled me to go back and hear what I had missed the first time on the "Atomic Bomb" album. If not a return to the old boldness, the performance certainly made me aware of something that I had missed about the album several months before: the classic beauty of some of the less-immediate songs.

The next morning, Bono and I met at a corner table in a swanky restaurant overlooking Michigan Avenue. "Stick 'em up," he rasped as he approached from behind, finger on an imaginary trigger pressing into my left kidney. It was 9 a.m., and the previous night's concert had left the unshaven singer a touch hoarse. But he was in a spry mood and claimed to do all his best work before noon. "I sometimes wish we could play our concerts right after I wake up," he said, peering out from behind his tinted wraparound glasses after ordering a breakfast of poached eggs and toast. The ire in his voice of the previous week had softened to a contentious but melodious brogue.

"Larry [Mullen, the band's drummer] is going to kill me for doing this," Bono said. "But I want this on the record. Some of what is going around as a result of your article is not just unhelpful to our group and our relationship to our audience, but just really problematic for what in the broad sense you might call rock music. The things you think are wrong with it, and the things that I think are wrong with rock music, are polar opposite. Your vision of rock and mine are 180 degrees apart. And that's why I need to talk to you."

A portion of that 90-minute conversation, edited for length, clarity and language, follows.

Q: You're an important band for my generation. A band that led by example: This is how to do it, how to be a successful band without compromising your principles. But when the ticket sale went wrong this year *[2005]*, I got hundreds of e-mails from fans who felt you had let them down, that their loyalty was betrayed.

A: Everybody in this band knows about that debacle, and regrets it, and we've taken steps to prevent it from happening again. I think most fans understand what happened. Our eyes were not on that ball the way they normally would be. Our eyes were on trying to determine whether we would be going on tour at all. There are things that we can't discuss in the interview that were going on within the band that just took precedence. Most U2 fans knew what that was [serious health problems in the family of a band member]. I thought it was really disingenuous of them and you not to recognize that this is not normal behavior from this band. Complain, yeah. Something did go wrong. That was a mistake, and we tried to put it right.

Q: The first I heard about the internal problems in the band was when Larry apologized about it at the Grammys. Before the article was published, I tried for three weeks to get information from the band, to interview you. Yes, this was not normal behavior from U2. Instead, you steer me to the record company president and the tour promoter. You let these business guys answer for you.

A: I'm really sorry about that. It's our fault that didn't happen. But it's done, and we've taken care of it.

Q: The ticket sale to me was just the tip of a larger issue, which is: Is the band losing sight of what it once was? The iPod ad, the Super Bowl halftime appearance, the Grammy Awards appearances—I didn't think U2 was about that sort of promotion.

A: That's a really important point that I want to get across to you. There's this poverty of ambition, in terms of what rock people will do to promote their work. That's a critical issue to me. The excitement of punk rock, in the Irish and UK scene when we were coming up, was seeing our favorite band on "Top of the Pops," right next to the "enemy." That would be exciting. We did talk shows, TV shows, back then. The great moments of rock 'n' roll were never off in some corner of the music world, in a self-constructed ghetto. I don't like that kind of thinking. I know some of it exists, and some of our best friends are part of it. It's not for me. Progressive rock was the enemy in 1976. And it still is. And it has many, many faces. This beast is lurking everywhere. It can describe itself as indie rock. It's the same [blanking] thing. It's misery. I have seen so many great minds struck down by it. . . . When you suggest we're betraying ourselves by doing TV shows and promotional stuff, to me the Super Bowl was our Ed Sullivan moment. It just came 25 years later. I didn't expect it. But it is the moment I'm most proud of in my life.

Q: Why is the idea of associating a song with a product a good idea?

A: I accept that that is alarming. I really do. Our being on TV, I don't have a problem with that—we should be on TV. But OK, associating our music with a product. You've got to deal with the devil. Let's have a look. The devil here is a bunch of creative minds, more creative than a lot of people in rock bands. The lead singer is Steve Jobs. These men have helped design the most beautiful object art in music culture since the electric guitar. That's the iPod. The job of art is to chase ugliness away. Everywhere we look we see ugly cars, ugly buildings . . . [he pauses, and looks out the window at the Chicago skyline]. . . . You're lucky here in Chicago on that front. But you see ugly objects in the workplace. Everywhere. And these people are making beautiful objects. Selling out is doing something you don't really want to do for money. That's what selling out is. We asked to be in the ad. We could see where rock music is, fighting for relevance next to hip-hop. And I love hip-hop. It's the new black entrepreneur. It's about being out there, loud and proud about what you're doing. Selling it on the street corner if you have to. From penthouse to pavement. Advertising the new song in another song. Taking on the world. Meanwhile, a bunch of white, middle-class kids are practicing in Daddy's garage, saying [adopts fake Midwestern whine], "No, man, that is just so un-cool." As hard as it is, as ghetto as it is, hip-hop is pop music. It's the sound of music getting out of the ghetto, while rock is looking for a ghetto. We never wanted to be a garage band. We wanted to get as quick as we could out of the garage. The people who say they like the garage usually have two or three cars parked outside. Rock music is niche. We want people who aren't in our niche listening to our music. If you pour your life into songs, you want them to be heard. It's a desire to communicate. A deep desire to communicate inspires songwriting. Rock music was most exciting when it was in the 45 [rpm single], when it was disciplined into a single. Whether it was the Sex Pistols, Clash, Buzzcocks, Nirvana, The Beatles, the Stones. The 45 is the pure rock to me. That is why I wanted to be in a band.

Q: I understand that, but I've seen some of my favorite songs corrupted because of that attitude. [Iggy Pop's] "Lust for Life" is now a Jamaican vacation commercial. I don't know if I want to listen to that song anymore.

A: If I love the song, I love the song. We looked at the iPod commercial as a rock video. We chose the director. We thought, how are we going to get our single off in the days when rock music is niche? When it's unlikely to get a three-minute punk-rock song on top of the radio? So we piggybacked this phenomenon to get ourselves to a new, younger audience, and we succeeded. And it's exciting. I'm proud of the commercial, I'm proud of the association. We have turned down enormous sums of money to put our songs in a commercial, where we felt, to your point, where it might change the way people appreciated the song. We were offered $23 million for just the music to "Where the Streets Have No Name." We thought we could do a lot of good with that money. Give it away. But if a show is a little off, and there's a hole, that's the one song we can guarantee that God will walk through the room as soon as we play it. So the idea that when we played it, people would go, "That's the 'such-and-such' commercial," we couldn't live with it. Had it been a cool thing, or didn't have a bad association, or it was a different song, we might've done it. But we have to start thinking about new ways of getting our songs across, of communicating in this new world, with so many channels, with rock music becoming a niche. I hear so many songwriters describe their songs as their children, that they have to look after them. [Nonsense!] They're your parents, they tell you what to do. They tell you how to dress, how to behave when you're playing them. They tell you what the video looks like. If you listen to them, they manage you. And if you get it right, they pay for your retirement [laughs]. Because songs demand to be heard. "Vertigo," which you didn't like, is deceptively simple. That riff, you can think, "Aw yeah, another rock song." It doesn't become great the first time you hear it. It becomes great the thousandth time you hear it. And that's true of a lot of rock riffs. So we have to get the density of exposure for that to be a hit.

Q: You told me the other day that U2 had "Kid A'd" itself to death [a reference to Radiohead's 2000 progressive-rock album "Kid A"]. It was a funny line, but I'm disappointed to hear that.

A: I want to hear Radiohead, extraordinary band that they are, on MTV. I want them setting fire to the imaginations of 16-, 15-, 14-year-old kids. I was 14 when John Lennon set fire to my imagination. At that age, you're just [angry], and your moods swing, and it's an incredible time to be hit with something like that. Our last two albums are essentially about the combo. We used the limitations of the combo. We had 10 years of experimentation. We decided to rope it in, and tie ourselves to only one thing. And that's the only discipline. Is it a great song? Is it fresh? Experimenting in rock is at its best when you dream from the perimeters and bring it back to the center. All my favorite innovators disappear into the woods and bring something back, and you get to hear the songs distilled from those experiments. I used "Kid A" as an example, because I love the album. We did our "Zooropa," we did our "Passengers," even our "Pop" experiment. There were great ideas on that album, but we didn't have the discipline to screw the thing down and turn them into magic pop songs. We'd become progressive rock! Ahhh!

Q: You're killing me now. I thought those '90s albums were great. I didn't understand "Achtung Baby" right away. But after seeing the tour, I realized it was your best album. I still feel that way. And I loved "Zooropa" in that way, and "Passengers." I even liked "Pop." To me, you guys were showing us how it should be done. You were [screwing] with our heads and making great music. You were doing those weird ballads from "Pop" as an encore at Soldier Field [in 1997]. I loved that you were so far out on a limb with saw in hand, and you were trying things, pushing things. And now you never play songs from those albums anymore. What happened?

A: We have ideas that we want to communicate [in a concert], not just a bunch of songs. If we get it right, it feels like one song. What band at our level would play 10 songs, seven from the new album and three from our first album? The reason we do that is because this album and our first album have very similar themes. The first is an ode to innocence, as it's being held onto. The latest is an ode to innocence, as it's been remembered, with the thought that you can get back to it. There's nothing in U2's catalog that sounds remotely like "Vertigo." It's completely fresh. "Vertigo" is actually quite a gem, contrary to what you say, and it's very new. For the second half of the show, we take on this notion of the journey of equality. This is our generation's challenge. So we thought about using flags as a backdrop during "Where the Streets Have No Name." I remember singing it the first night: It's not a very good lyric, but it has really great ideas suggested in the lyric, the idea that you could go on a journey to that other place. That lyric was written in a dusty field in northern Ethiopia, and I can finally make sense of it because of what we're talking about in this show. And then we go into "One," and we could do a new arrangement of "One" as you might want us to, but you see, I'm only one member of this band, and Edge is three. And if he thinks an arrangement is perfect, why mess with it? He says, "I'm not jamming here. That's a guitar melody. I've written it. I can't improve on it." Adam and I are the jazz men in the band. But the Teutonic Larry Mullen and the Presbyterian Edge always demand, "No fat. Back to the original arrangement. We're not going to change the bass line just because we feel like it."

Q: It helped when you put "Original of the Species" in the set last night. It made me want to hear what I missed on the record. That's what was lacking in the first show [at the United Center].

A: It's a classic, especially on the album. We have to figure out how are we going to get that song on MTV. Those songs do not come around easy. The melodies of most songs are A-B, A-B, and this is A-B-C-D. The construction of it is unique. And I want you to want us to have that song out on the radio. Because it's about other bands [who value songwriting] coming through. It's not just us. Rap-metal nearly put the white race in jeopardy [as a creative force]. It's a travesty. Those [rap-metal] people should just take suicide pills and go away. What we have to offer, if we're lucky, are lyrics, some interesting arrangements and beautiful melody. That's what rock music can do right now. To be relevant, to set the imagination off on a new generation coming up. Songs that up the ante.

Q: It sounds like "Pop" didn't work for you because it didn't sell. To my mind, it worked because it was a good, daring album. There's no shame in not selling.

A: It didn't communicate the way it was intended to. It was supposed to change the mood of that summer [1997]. An album changes the mood of a summer when you walk out of a pub and you have those songs in your head. And you hear them coming from a car, an open window. It changes the mood of the season. Instead it became a niche record. And I know you're a man who appreciates the niche. And I'm glad you appreciate that one, but that's not what it was intended to be. It's not about sales; we don't need the cash. It's about your ambition for the song. With "Pop," I always think if we'd just had another month, we could have finished it. But we did a really bad thing. We let the manager book the tour, known in this camp as the worst decision U2 ever made, and we had to wrap up the album sooner than we wanted. You don't need an album to communicate for you to enjoy it, you don't need it to be trimmed of fat to enjoy it, because you're enjoying the ideas, the textures. But for me to enjoy it, I need it to do that [communicate on a wider level].

Q: The last two albums look back. With "All That You Can't Leave Behind," I thought you made your retro record, you'd made your [version

of the Stones' 1978 album] "Some Girls," an album that sums up all your best moves in a concise way. You're allowed to make that album, once. Now you've made "All That You Can't Leave Behind," and you're looking back and I think, whoops, you really are turning into the Stones. I expected more; I expected you to break out of that box.

A: Hey, there are some amazing songs on [the Stones' 1994 album] "Voodoo Lounge." But what you're missing is that each time [in history] has a mood. You think it's looking backward; I think it's looking forward. I think to be in a studio, tied to the four-piece band setup right now is

---

Greg Kot on U2

A look back at the U2 reviews written by Tribune music critic Greg Kot:

2005 UNITED CENTER CONCERT

May 9, 2005: It appears U2 is falling into the same trap as the Rolling Stones: Charging big money for a stadium show obligates the band to turn into a hits jukebox. But especially in a city such as Chicago, where U2 has been embraced like few other bands, the quartet can afford to take more chances. The promise of U2 has always been big music tied in with conviction, imagination and innovation. Now the band sounds like it believes less in its ability to surprise and dazzle with its new music, and more in the necessity to recycle its past. If that trend continues, U2's avid concern for social justice won't be enough to keep it relevant.

U2'S MIDLIFE CRISIS

Feb. 13, 2005: In recent years, their business practices have become more suspect, their attention-seeking more transparent, their principles more readily compromised, and their music less challenging.

"HOW TO DISMANTLE AN ATOMIC BOMB"

Nov. 21, 2004: Fans who embrace this album will undoubtedly be comforted by how closely it hews to the band's trademark sound. But U2 carries weight and meaning because it has always challenged its fans as much as embraced them. "How to Dismantle an Atomic Bomb" shrinks from that high standard by offering U2 by the numbers.

2001 UNITED CENTER CONCERT

Oct. 17, 2001: After the events of Sept. 11, the stakes have been raised for touring rock bands. . . . U2's songs have always addressed the big

Greg Kot on U2, cont.

subjects: war and peace, love and betrayal, sin and faith. And those themes—once so easy to take for granted only a few months ago—resonated more deeply than ever for an audience clearly starved for some sort of spiritual sustenance.

"ALL THAT YOU CAN'T LEAVE BEHIND"

Oct. 31, 2000: Still, for all its lack of bold experimentation, "All That You Can't Leave Behind" cuts deeper than any mere rehash of old glories. In reclaiming the indelible, wall-to-wall tunefulness that first won the band a home on commercial radio, the new album recalls the Rolling Stones' last great release, "Some Girls."

1997 SOLDIER FIELD CONCERT ("POP MART" TOUR)

June 30, 1997: They needed all the personality they could muster not to become a mere soundtrack for their special effects. . . . The most resonant moments were the most intimate, such as a haunting "If You Wear That Velvet Dress" performed as an atypically hushed encore. . . . Those who came looking to hear only the old U2 missed the beauty of the new as it soared quietly, in the shadow of its own monster.

"POP"

March 2, 1997: U2 has done its share of falling down. Now they sit off to the side trying to sort out the mess. Their subject is the illusion of instant gratification, the discovery that what they "thought was freedom was just greed," and fittingly they make music that is often slippery and enigmatic.

"ZOOROPA"

July 4, 1993: The lack of preciousness about preserving what once was thought of as the group's signature sound is refreshing. In the most convincing manner possible, "Zooropa" has finished the job started by "Achtung Baby!"

1992 "ZOO TV" TOUR OPENER IN FLORIDA

March 2, 1992: Once architects of a black-and-white world, the band was now feeling and stumbling its way toward some new, undetermined destination with exhilarating force.

"ACHTUNG BABY!"

Nov. 17, 1991: Although no one will mistake it for the latest Nirvana release, "Achtung Baby!"—from its fanciful title on down—shows the band in a grittier light: disrupting, rather than fulfilling, expectations.

a very modern thing to do. And to use that mystery and power to write songs, we did two records like that. This one goes even further than the last one in that direction. You get beauty like "Original of the Species" that you can play on a piano. Just put piano and voice on that song, and it's special. That's not retreat. That is progressive. That is progress.

Q: The strength of your band has always been that you build a case for your new music on the road. And it's my job to say when you don't.

A: As a writer who cares deeply about music, you're right to give rock bands a kicking when they deserve it. And we have deserved it at times. But you also need to explain to us how rock can progress. And I would like it if writers would step back and look at what we've done . . . [apart from] the codified rules and regulations that are suffocating rock music right now. Great groups were broken up, like the Clash, because of ridiculous concepts like not selling out. It's the cultural revolution in China all over again: Let's rid rock music of thinkers; let's rid rock music of big ideas. I saw it destroy great groups like Echo and the Bunnymen, extraordinary talents who crashed and burned on these things. You tell me about the hundreds of e-mails you got, well I got them with every single turn this band has made. I got them when we made the "War" album. I got them when we made "Joshua Tree." I got them when we made "Achtung Baby." Of course we're going to lose fans along the way who don't like what we're doing. But you need to understand what we're actually trying to do, and that's why we had to have this talk.

Q: I had to laugh, because at last night's show you said that "some really annoying people are standing up" for what they believe in, "and God bless them." That reminds me of you, including the annoying part.

A: [Laughs] Yes, you're right.

Q: But you do have the courage of your convictions. You don't care what people think of you for having those convictions. You sparked a weeklong debate in this town about music, and what kind of social role it should play, and why people care about it, and why they should care about it.

A: We've always annoyed people. Around the time of "Zoo TV," we were in danger of being cool, but we fixed that [laughs]. Now there are loads of people who would love to murder me on a daily basis. Stirring it up, it's good. Our definition of art is putting your head above the parapet, and be ready for the custard pie. I happen to love the taste of it.

....

Bruce Springsteen reborn in smaller venues

AUG. 14, 2005

This month, Bruce Springsteen is quietly wrapping up a solo tour of North America. In the wake of an acoustic album, "Devils and Dust," that has already drifted off the charts, he is playing to audiences one-fifth the size that would normally see one of his arena tours with the E Street Band.

But Springsteen is making some of the best music of his career this summer, and he hasn't been this engrossing and unpredictable on a concert stage since the '70s. There are none of the rituals, jokes and choreography that have dusted recent E Street tours with shtick and nostalgia. As he sweated buckets leading Clarence Clemons, Steve Van Zandt and the rest of his loyal clan in another chorus line on the last E Street tour, at least some longtime Springsteen watchers had to feel a little sad. Most of the fans loved it, and the band members stuffed away their retirement money, but Springsteen the artist had settled into routine. Here was one of the greatest rock performers living out one of his best-known lyrics: "Glory days, they'll pass you by . . . in the wink of a young girl's eye."

*[I]*n a solo concert at the Bradley Center in Milwaukee *[Aug. 7, 2005]*, where he gave a performance that eclipsed even his fine show three months earlier at the Rosemont Theatre, it was Springsteen doing the winking. The singer walked the line between loose-limbed self-confidence and iron-willed purpose; he was smiling and laughing like a man completely at ease with himself and his audience. He was clearly having a ball rummaging around in the back alleys of his extraordinary songbook.

Bruce Springsteen at the Rosemont Theatre in September 2005.
CHRIS WALKER

Better off

It prompts a heretical conclusion: At this point in his career, the singer is better off without the E Street Band. He may not sell as many concert tickets or albums. But he's a more daring artist: darker, stranger, more at liberty to challenge himself and surprise his audience.

He opened with a rarely performed B-side from the early '80s, "Shut Out the Light." The arrangement was little more than a droning handful of chords on a pump organ, and it foreshadowed the adventure to follow. "Reason to Believe" arrived next, a swamp blues with Springsteen howling into his harmonica microphone while stomping the floorboards with a boot heel. He would build on these musical ideas for the remainder of the two-hour-plus concert, using trancelike patterns to evoke dreams, reveries, hallucinations.

Throughout, he tinkered with arrangements, tempo and melody, as if to slap the songs out of their comfort zones. On electric guitar, he used a modified "Theme from Peter Gunn" rhythm to evoke the feverish paranoia of "State Trooper." On acoustic guitar, he barely touched the strings as he knocked out a syncopated backdrop for a desolate "Promised Land." His electric keyboards drifted woozily as he shivered through the betrayals of "Point Blank."

What's startling to realize is that Springsteen is still growing as a musician and a singer. His piano playing has improved markedly in the last few months, as he built undulating patterns beneath the sparse chords of "Racing in the Street." The richness also resonated on the electric keyboards for the lovely "All That Heaven Will Allow," which he connected to the pocket symphonies of '70s power-pop group the Raspberries. And he surrounded "Darkness on the Edge of Town" with ringing, rapidly strummed overtones on an acoustic 12-string.

As a vocalist, he's using his voice not just to convey lyrics, but to shade them in new colors. His high, eerie, feminine cry sounded like a cross between Roy Orbison and a wind-whipped musical saw on the ghostly "Leah." Dropping to a whisper, or pulling away from the microphone and letting his voice fade, Springsteen used his voice to orchestrate mood as skillfully as he did with guitars and keyboards.

Family and religion

As resonant as individual moments were, they accumulated power in the way they played off one another. This was a show built around twin themes: family and religion, and, as Springsteen said, "The poetry, the mystery, the terror . . ." inherent in both. He said he was moved by the "images of transcendence and belief" in his Catholic upbringing yet constantly at war with what the church's unwavering authority represented in his life.

This conflict underscored many of the songs, from "My Father's House" to "Jesus Was an Only Son," in which Springsteen ruminated on what might have been had the world's most renowned martyr lived long enough to have a family. It went unspoken, but Springsteen has been cast in the role of a rock 'n' roll savior a few times in his career. With the American flag as a backdrop and the E Street Band at his side, he has played the superhero who could rock any stadium to its knees. It was with him in this role that Springsteen's songs became miscast as arena anthems, the anxiety and turmoil coursing through them flattened by the need to entertain 20,000 fans a night.

But Springsteen the solo performer doesn't have to play to the back row of the arena. He can shrink the songs back to a more human dimension, and they can breathe again. Their finely tuned details change shape on any given night, depending on how Springsteen wants to perform them. His songs haven't sounded this adaptable, mutable and alive in decades.

It's why the singer's interpretation of "Dream Baby Dream," the eerie hymn by New York electro-punk duo Suicide, has closed many of the concerts on this tour. It allows Springsteen to end the show as he began it: singing over the undulating drone of the pump organ. The words are almost childlike: "Dream, baby, dream . . . we gotta keep the light burnin' . . . C'mon, baby, dry your eyes . . . I just wanna see you smile." But as Springsteen sang them with gradually escalating fervor, they took on a hypnotic power.

With eyes closed, he was as riveting as drag queen Dean Stockwell serenading Dennis Hopper with a Roy Orbison song in the David Lynch movie "Blue Velvet." It was a type of intimacy rarely seen from Springsteen before. The words were reassuring, but the music was not, and the effect was electrifying.

Liz Phair takes to stage as her once-controversial classic 'Exile in Guyville' is reissued

JUNE 22, 2008

Now that Liz Phair's "Exile in Guyville" is being repackaged on its 15th anniversary as an indie-rock landmark, it's easy to forget what a ruckus it caused when it first came out.

Though instantly acclaimed for its songwriting, "Exile" also had its share of detractors. Phair pressed a lot of buttons because she was a child of privilege, a North Shore kid educated at New Trier High School and Oberlin College in Ohio. When she drifted into bohemian Wicker Park to make a go of it as a visual artist and songwriter, she was regarded as an interloper who hadn't paid her dues.

At the Vic [*June 24, 2008*], Phair will return to the scene she left behind for California years ago to play "Exile" in its entirety. She is a far more assured performer today; back then, she hated to perform live, and rarely did. But she received attention from national magazines while scads of local rockers who had been toiling for years remained anonymous. This made her "the most hated woman in Chicago," according to her producer, Brad Wood, when interviewed shortly after "Exile" was released.

The singer also dared to compare her debut to rock's Holy Grail, "Exile on Main Street"; she said it was a song-by-song response to the Rolling Stones' 1972 classic. She also brought the wrath of feminists and the leers of Neanderthals by posing on its cover partially nude.

The "Who does she think she is?" outrage was exactly the point. The songs were a volatile mix of invective, humor, sex and sexual role-playing, laced with explicit language. They were Phair's unfiltered portrait of life in "Guyville," the Wicker Park haunts where her expectations about life and relationships were thrashed in long nights of dreaming, drinking and flirting.

"I've been taken for everything I own," she sings on "Johnny Sun-

Chicago native Liz Phair at the Vic theatre June 24, 2008.
ALEX GARCIA

shine." Yet for all its anger, "Exile" is also a darkly funny album. And it rocks. For all the talk about the content of Phair's songs, it wouldn't have mattered if they didn't stimulate the hips as much as the mind.

Many of the "Exile" songs first appeared on three homemade cassettes dubbed "Girly Sound" in 1991–92: One voice, one guitar and a whole lot of issues. Phair sang in a deep, deadpan voice, and tried to play intricate rhythm and lead lines simultaneously to make up for the lack of a backing band. The songs dealt with the toxic consequences of intimacy in a way that was rare for indie-rock: with an explicitness that suggested the bawdy R&B of Millie Jackson. But unlike Jackson's brassy tone, Phair's voice was small, narrow. It belonged to a girl who sounded as if she had "access to expensive grooming products," as Phair herself once said of her upbringing in tony Winnetka. It was a voice that seemingly had no business saying the things it did. And yet there it was, a bundle of contradictions: smutty yet literary, funny yet sad, smart yet impractical.

Dressed-up 'Girly Sound'

"Guyville" took the "Girly Sound" songs and dressed them up slightly. Producer Brad Wood preserved the songs' core: Phair singing while playing her guitar. Around that he arrayed drums and other rock instruments, but kept the proceedings relatively sparse. Its release in 1993 on the highly respected independent label Matador Records brought a flash flood of mostly laudatory reviews; at year's end it finished atop the Village Voice's nationwide poll of music critics and enabled Phair to land a major-label deal.

In a DVD accompanying the album's re-release, Phair looks back on its difficult birth, and with few exceptions, doesn't sugarcoat. Among the people she interviews is John Henderson, a longtime behind-the-scenes player in Chicago who hooked her up with Wood and helped shape the record in its early stages, only to abandon the project when he saw where Phair wanted to take things. Henderson wanted a smaller record that preserved the intimate tone he heard on "Girly Sound"; Phair veered toward a more rock-oriented approach.

A talent betrayed?

"I'm reminded of the famous Greil Marcus quote about Rod Stewart, something about how he wanted to be a rock star and all that entailed—sitting by the pool, having sex with groupies and snorting coke—and if he had to write great songs to do it, he was perfectly willing to write them," Henderson said of Phair when interviewed in the mid-'90s. "I think she betrayed her talent in much the same way."

He pretty much confirms that viewpoint, in less colorful language, on Phair's DVD, and to her credit, she includes his less-than-charitable comments. She also admits that she was willing to lie and "take advantage of people" to get her music heard and her bank account fattened.

And that's exactly what happened after "Exile" became a hit. Phair's records became increasingly blander and slicker as she played out the string at the major labels. Now she's back on an indie, ATO, and told Billboard that "for the first time in 15 years, I feel creative."

It's another way of saying that "Exile in Guyville" set a standard for Phair's music that she's been hard-pressed to match ever since.

The DVD illustrates why, but not until its conclusion. Until then, it's a pretty standard talking-heads commentary about the making of an album. What's odd is that all the talking heads are male. It would have been illuminating to hear from some women who helped define the Chicago scene as Phair was emerging.

On her way

Some excerpts from Greg Kot's reviews and stories from 1993, when Liz Phair and "Exile in Guyville" were bursting onto the national music scene:

"This Wicker Park artist's debut has been weighed down with all sorts of baggage: It's a feminist manifesto; it's a response to that most sacred of rock albums, the Rolling Stones' 'Exile on Main Street'; it's a big kiss-off to the local boys club of musicians in Wicker Park, a.k.a. 'Guyville.' None of that really matters, however. What does is the immediacy of these 18 songs, the spare yet inventive production enhancing a voice that dares to be intimate about intimacy."

"Lacerating, explicit, and yet laced with humor—listen for the moment in 'Girls! Girls! Girls!' when Phair turns a background vocal into a dead-on Ethel Merman imitation—'Exile in Guyville' strives to engage the listener on multiple levels. It prompts comparison to such emotionally frank, pop-savvy records as P.J. Harvey's 'Dry' and 'Rid of Me' and the Pretenders' self-titled debut."

"'Exile in Guyville' packs a giddy wallop all its own. Phair writes sturdy riffs that make her rudimentary guitar technique beside the point, and her largely mid-tempo material cuts through the surf like a shark fin. Above all, it's her singing, wispy one minute, feral the next, that makes 'Guyville' sizzle."

Phair was largely a token female artist in a male-dominated business and scene, and the DVD (perhaps unintentionally) reinforces that notion of otherness. She wasn't speaking for, or to, the men in the DVD; her audience was disenfranchised young women like herself. And Phair's multifaceted songs spoke to that audience with a frankness and empathy that still resonates.

For all the sensationalism that surrounded explicit songs, the album was defined by its sense of loss. The characters in "Exile" couldn't be easily categorized; they weren't just playing the stereotypical roles of victim, vixen or the angry female. They were all of those things and more. And they all yearned for something better, something that always seemed out of reach. Phair says in the DVD that when she listened to the album again recently, she cried.

"That girl was so sad," she says.

As the DVD winds down, about a half-dozen women chime in with their views on "Guyville." Unlike the male figures in the video, they aren't immediately identified because they aren't even semifamous. They are just listeners who were going through many of the same issues as Phair. Their stories are in her songs. And their faces eloquently express just how much those songs still mean to them.

....

If Shellac can play the Pritzker Pavilion, anything's possible

AUG. 12, 2009

There was a surreal moment of theater that broke out in the middle of Shellac's concert at the Pritzker Pavilion in Millennium Park [*Aug. 10, 2009*].

Singer-guitarist Steve Albini was embodying the last radio announcer playing the last song on Earth. To his left, Bob Weston played a funeral-dirge riff on bass. Behind them, Todd Trainer roamed the vast expanse of the Pritzker stage with a snare drum, a Puck-like muse for the announcer broadcasting into nothingness.

Shellac at The Hideout Dec. 14, 2007.
KAMIL KRZACZYNSKI

Albini signed off by invoking Studs Terkel, Ken Nordine and
Jimmy Piersall, Chicagoans who defined their city through strength of
a personality that could have been forged nowhere else. Shellac shares
a few qualities with those greats, not the least of which is its individu-
ality as a band. Love or hate them, Albini, Trainer and Weston sound
like no one else.

All the more reason to hail their debut at the crown jewel of Chicago outdoor venues. The city has been notoriously averse to booking
rock bands at Pritzker in past seasons, but that trend is slowly changing (thanks to enlightened thinkers such as Michael Orlove of the
city's Department of Cultural Affairs and independent promoter Mike
Reed), and this summer there has been a groundswell of not only rock
music, but cutting-edge rock music at the venue. Shellac's appearance
drew an audience that filled the lawn and about half the pavilion, a
landmark moment for the city's vast independent music scene.

For 17 years, Shellac has been releasing albums at a leisurely pace
and playing concerts in between the members' day jobs. (Albini and
Weston are world-class recording engineers.) Their music is rigor-
ously orchestrated. Rather than creating a hierarchy separating lead

and rhythm instruments, Shellac puts drums, guitar, bass and voice on equal footing. These elements drop in and out of the mix, with dramatic swings in volume and density. Albini manipulates sound and texture on his guitar rather than playing traditional "leads," Trainer orchestrates the drums as much as he swings the tempos, and Weston's bass sounds as if it could double as a bulldozer.

The band worked through songs spanning its career, from early single "Wingwalker" to new, as-yet-unreleased material such as "Czar of All Czars," with lyrics drawn from a workers union songbook. There were dramatic set pieces laced with bitterly comedic lyrics ("Prayer to God"), propulsive stomps ("Steady as She Goes") and a lament about home wreckers who live in trees ("Squirrel Song"). There were Shellac stage rituals (Weston's question-and-answer sessions with the audience; the three-drummer, cymbal-bashing finale of "Watch Song") and a few surprises, including a guest vocal by poster artist extraordinaire Jay Ryan.

The fans, massed against the stage rather than confining themselves to their seats, loved it. The band, known for its combative personality, seemed to revel in the moment. And why not? Chicago has not always been kind to its music community, treating it with indifference or outright hostility. But, hey, if Shellac can play the Pritzker, anything's possible, right?

"Let's let the city of Chicago know that they didn't make a mistake," Weston cracked. Amen to that.

....

Billy Corgan's mission statement for 'Oceania': Do or die

JUNE 17, 2012

Billy Corgan calls "Oceania," the Smashing Pumpkins' first studio album since 2007, "an anti-midlife crisis album."

Whatever it's called, the new album represents Corgan's best work since the '90s, when the Pumpkins were among the most successful bands of their time. The band broke up in 2000, and to hear Corgan

Smashing Pumpkins at the Riviera Theatre Oct. 14, 2011.
CHRIS SWEDA

tell it, he's spent most of the last decade figuring out how to create fresh music out from under the shadow of that legacy without fully letting go of it. He says that after reuniting with original Pumpkins drummer Jimmy Chamberlin in 2005, he realized that he was holding on to an idea of the band caught between unrealistic expectations (repeating the success and sound of the Pumpkins' 1993 breakthrough, "Siamese Dream") and his own nostalgia-loathing intentions.

He's in the midst of writing what he describes as a "spiritual memoir," and it's causing him to "dredge up stuff from the past I wish I had forgotten. This album is basically my way of saying I don't want to carry this stuff anymore. I don't want to carry (original Pumpkins members Chamberlin, James Iha and D'Arcy Wretzky) forward anymore. It's done. I couldn't have made 'Oceania' if I didn't let go of that band."

Chamberlin and Corgan parted ways in 2009, soon after a tumultuous tour that found the singer verbally tussling with his audience. For a 20th anniversary Pumpkins tour, many fans were expecting a greatest-hits retrospective. Corgan instead presented a deep dive into his music, in which the beloved '90s singles were balanced by deep cuts and plenty of new tracks. The often-hostile reaction led him to "blow up the band" so that he could start fresh.

Corgan rebuilt the Pumpkins with young guns: guitarist Jeff Schroeder, bassist Nicole Fiorentino and drummer Mike Byrne. The imperative was not only to re-energize the audience, but "to reconnect with that part of me that made me want to make music in the first place." In an interview, he described the process:

Q: A few years ago, you said the album was dead, and you began releasing your music song by song online. What changed your mind?

A: We did a radio tour, one of those BS things—if you go play a radio station's party with seven other terrible bands, they'll play your record. We're playing and we're looking out at 18- and 20-year-olds and they don't care. What is this? How do you win this? You don't. We basically sat down and said, 'This is it. This is boring.' So what do we do to actually change this? Only thing that made sense was to make an album. Can you make an album that is so strong that it reignites the flame within you and the audience? Is that even culturally possible? We went to (a studio in Sedona, Ariz., with longtime producer and engineer Bjorn Thorsrud) for a while to work. It was small steps. I can write songs, I can always write songs. That's been part of the problem. Maybe I write too many songs and put them out loosey-goosey. So let's get down to it and challenge ourselves. It takes so much psychic energy to do this. I did this album for a year, 12 hours a day. I understand how it gets tough for people when they reach a certain age and you just don't want to work that hard because it's easier not to. We could've made a lot of money playing the nostalgia shows. I cut that road off. It was do it this way or die.

Q: So you want to get the feeling of 1995 back, but you want it to do it with new music?

A: I want the new feeling. Picasso did some of his best work in his 90s. Neil Young is making some of his best music now. I don't want to be 25 again. There are people out there who are older who are cool. I want that. Music is your guide. At the heart of Jimmy Page is the 14-year-old playing skiffle and trying to figure out Scotty Moore licks in his bedroom. The year 1995 for me was miserable in some ways. I just dream of having a voice in the conversation. Not being written off by the bloggers as some grandpa who keeps showing up at the buffet table.

Q: How'd you rediscover that feeling?

A: I've found peacefulness in myself where I found I didn't have to be more than or less than. Be yourself moment to moment. Go left, right, and in between. You like keyboards, guitars, loud stuff, quiet stuff. Just go with it. Stop overthinking it. It's very similar to the way I worked in the '90s.

Q: So you're saying you lost that in the last decade? Why?

A: I got away from that to teach myself a few things. I'm a bit weird. I'm the guy who would be bored with two-on-two basketball, so I'd play against four guys to make it interesting. I've done a lot of that in (2005 solo album) "The Future Embrace," (2003 band project) Zwan—working within concepts of limitation. Can I box my way out of this corner? I think this is the first time I've made a record where I didn't box myself in. If it sounds like Frank Zappa one minute and Vangelis the next, OK.

Q: How were your earlier records boxed in? Whatever people say about them, the Pumpkins were definitely their own thing through much of the '90s.

A: I said this to the current band the other day. The "Siamese Dream" band didn't exist. I created that band and then we learned how to be that band after the record. I expressed to (producer Butch Vig) an idealized vision. A beautiful, silver version of the Smashing Pumpkins that did not exist. It was a movie. The videos, the success enhanced and filled in the gaps. (The 1995 album "Mellon Collie and the Infinite Sadness") is a much more accurate portrayal, it's the band as we really were—mean, dark. (The 1991 album "Gish") is me trying to be somebody, "Siamese Dream" is me trying to create something, "Mellon Collie" is the band unvarnished. "Siamese Dream" was me working within my own and Butch's straitjacket. (Nirvana's Kurt Cobain) went through it, with the idealized version of Nirvana on "Nevermind" and the unvarnished version on "In Utero" with (Steve) Albini. Finally you reach a point where it's over, the game doesn't work, Smashing Pumpkins is dead. I couldn't just flip the switch and be great. So is there nothing in this for me? You walk away or try to make it for you. The difference for me is that at 45 I feel I have to deliver or you don't get another chance. Our axiom for "Oceania" was you have one chance. Don't expect anyone to listen seven times. They'll listen one time if you're lucky.

Q: You spent a lot of time in the last decade working to get a band up to speed. But people feel it's you who call all the shots. How much a part of this album is the band?

A: The album tells the best version of the story. People have a general misunderstanding of what I do, like I'm standing in the back directing things. The behind-the-scenes pace of the way we work is different. It's hard to translate. But they're playing on the album. This is not one of those things where in 10 years I'm going to say I actually played all the instruments (laughs).

Q: What's the main difference between this album and (2007 Pump-kins comeback album) "Zeitgeist"?

A: "Zeitgeist," in retrospect, is the death album—the last album of the Smashing Pumpkins era. It just took seven years to come out. I went in with a very naive idea. Everyone wants me to make "Siamese Dream" again, which equated in my mind to a bunch of loud guitars, with that as a transition into a new era. It was like "Indiana Jones" Part 3. You play to an expectation. The smart move when we got back together would've been to do a greatest-hits album, a greatest-hits money tour, then do a new album. I didn't do that—much to the consternation of Jimmy (Chamberlin) and my management, because I left millions of dollars on the table. But my plan didn't work either. When I made "Siamese Dream," I was taking LSD, crashing on people's couches, brokenhearted over a girl who later became my wife. You can't be that again. It's disrespectful to your own past to think you can relive your own past. I kept saying to Jimmy, where is the psychedelia? Because I always felt that was the heart of our sound. So I got rid of things, until it became this very primal music, one angry guitar and one angry drummer. I tried to build on that. But my relationship with Jimmy was broken. I didn't want to admit it. He would've been happy to keep it going, and I had the blinders on and was marching forward. I just stepped in the wrong mudhole. But I learned some things. I came across an apathetic audience, and it ignited something in me. It brought back that old "(expletive) you."

Q: Things got hostile during that 2008 tour. You were pretty abusive toward the audience, and some people still haven't forgotten that or forgiven you. It reminded me of some weird, uncomfortable Andy Kaufman skit.

A: It's (pro) wrestling (laughs). I'm in character. Even Jimmy Chamberlin believed it. All he saw was money going down the drain. I'm a weirdo like Wayne (Coyne) from the Flaming Lips. He'll be the guy in the bubble floating above the audience, and I'll be the guy in the black dress on stage. There's a saying in wrestling where you start to live your gimmick. On the road, I'm in character, at home I'm with my cats playing Xbox. Is it smart? No. Is it compelling? At times. But I needed to do it.

Q: It was your way of blowing it up?

A: It's an unconscious expression. I still remember standing on that stage in Chicago (in 2008). The band and the audience are getting more uncomfortable, and there's little Billy in the center with his microphone. I want to be in the moment. If that had been a super-warm crowd I wouldn't have reacted like that. The show we did at the Riviera last year *[2011]*, that was one of the warmest crowds I've ever played for in 25 years. It's irksome for me as an artist for my life to be reduced to a song, or a moment, a performance. That's not me. I've left a lot of money on the table by being a weirdo, but I'm still here.

Q: There's inherent tension between the guy who's weird, the outsider willing to alienate your audience, and the one who also wants to be part of the conversation, at the center of the culture. How do you resolve that?

A: I wanted to be from the normal "Leave it to Beaver" family and wasn't. I was being singled out about my birthmark, I was too tall, too weird. From the start I was on the outside. Maybe everyone goes through it. But I turned it into a narrative that is in my DNA. All the local bands were talking (expletive) about us when we started to get big. We were very isolated. We go to New York for the first time in 1990, it's Sonic Youth land. Again we don't fit. We go in with an adaptable sense of if we don't belong, we're going to storm your stage. You really want to be accepted, but you do this pose to get through.

Q: So how do you measure this album, whether it's successful or not? Through sales, or something else?

A: "Oceania" I think is going to turn the corner, and we're going to be positive for a while. I have to fight the temptation to blow it up. Maybe it's self-destructive. But if reaction so far can be a gauge, we've done something good. Hard-core hater fans are liking it. People default to what they know when you don't give them something powerful. But if you give them something powerful, they all crawl back. We're all going through this collective identity crisis. We're online forming new personalities. The systems of things we used to count on, are breaking down, and it's a free-for-all. Success is how do we survive that. Success isn't record sales, it's street cachet. The temperature of the Pumpkins right now is pretty good. Six months ago, not so good. Two years ago, it was down the tubes. With this group we've rebuilt the credibility with the fan base. People were hearing the songs on YouTube a year ago, and I would get messages from fans, "Don't (mess) it up, Billy." They liked the songs and were worried I was going to mess up a good thing.

Q: You've decided to release the album through a major label, EMI, even though you've long said the traditional record-industry model is broken and beyond repair. What happened?

A: I still think that. But I thought naively that by becoming an entrepreneur and putting out my own music, that my fans would rally and help me market it. They didn't. I got, "This is the worst, retire," from some blogger. As a music fan of artists with a certain longevity like Tom Waits, Van Morrison, Neil Young, I want to hear all of it. The good, the not so good, everything. They've earned it. But that's not the way our country works. We're the absolute worst at appreciating that sort of thing.

Q: So social media is not the democracy we thought it was?

A: It's just allowed the most narcissistic among us to amass more power. But a lot of people in my generation are avoiding it. It's just not interesting. Chat boards chase away people who want to be positive, and they get shot down, so they retreat from it.

Q: So at what point did "Oceania" take shape as an album? Was there a turning point song or moment?

A: I'm in Sedona, the band is taking a break (in February 2011). I'm there by myself working with Bjorn. There is a message from the ex-wife of (former Electric Prunes bassist and recent Corgan collaborator) Mark Tulin. She's crying, he's dead of a heart attack, just 62 years old. I'd seen him two days before. His death hit me hard. It made me think, "What am I doing?" There were 400 people at his funeral. It was a joyous, joke-filled dinner, because that was his spirit. I went back to Sedona and went through all our music. We'd done 30 demos. I heard his bass parts and would cry. The band was in limbo. And it hit me, "If I'm gonna do this, I'm gonna do it right." Stop (messing) around. You're

44 at the time, get off your pity party. You know how to make records, stop being a baby, just do it. It was like, I had a sense of purpose. I went into my old mode. I was ruthless in the '90s. I did whatever I had to do to get the band where it needed to be. There was one destination. It had to be big. And when I got there I realized it wasn't so great. The band went boom. I didn't have any more bullets in the round. I didn't want to have to justify anything. I had to let go of the band, the legacy, a new chapter. Better suit up. I got very sober, serious, very deliberate. I'm much kinder than I used to be, but I'm still ruthless. . . . For a while there, I didn't want to be at the center of every decision when I was making records. But the best music I ever made I was at the center of every decision. I don't make any apologies about that anymore. I don't want to be in a windowless room poring over musical details. But that's the lesson I learned. I wasn't going to fail because I didn't go for it. (Chicago Cubs slugger) Dave Kingman was my idol as a kid. He was a .220 hitter. He struck out a lot. But when he hit the ball, it went way over the fence and through the window across the street.

Q: When things are working, great artists say they reflect their audience. Do you feel you're still in touch with your audience?

A: I feel I'm reflecting the part of the audience we don't hear from. There are a lot of people out there who love music but don't have a place in music culture as it exists. I meet these people all the time. Soccer mom, 34, has good taste in music. They are your average rock fan who isn't part of the Pitchfork culture. They don't follow the train. They're the difference between 40,000 sales and 400,000. We've disenfranchised that part of the culture by playing to the (snobby, snarky) crowd. The Internet has swelled that (expletive) crowd. The crowd that trashes what you do instantly and writes you off. It's like the '90s indie-rock crowd all over again: Don't look this way, don't dress this way, don't play long guitar solos, whatever. But there are people out there in their teens who found Led Zeppelin and Pink Floyd, they don't care that those bands don't exist anymore. They exist in their computer. They're finding this other value system that isn't contemporary. It's a wider scope. The unspoken audience, the stragglers, and this new audience who isn't snarky or cares much about modern record business, that's our audience.

....

Nick Cave's influences: Bowie, Cash, failing at art school

MARCH 13, 2013

N ick Cave has written novels, movie scripts and a few dozen of the greatest songs of the last 30 years. Yet for him, it never gets any easier.

The problem with finishing a song, Cave said as a featured speaker at the 27th annual South by Southwest Music and Media Conference [*March 12, 2013*], is that then you have to start over again. "There are all these nasty births" that are like "pushing burning watermelons out of a tiny orifice."

The raven-haired, rail-thin singer looked back on a life devoted to music that began by accident. Growing up in Australia, his ambition was to become a painter, but he failed art school in his second year, a devastating blow.

Fortunately, "I had a band on the side."

Johnny Cash's "Man in Black" was an early, outlaw influence, and so was David Bowie. "I didn't do sports, so it was assumed I was homosexual," he said. "It toughened us up." He dressed in drag to provoke the macho boys, and then fought back with the rocks he packed in his handbag.

The violence followed him to London, where he moved in 1980 with his first great band, the Birthday Party. "People came to the gigs to beat the (expletive) out of us," Cave said. "It was like being back at school."

The physical bumps and bruises eventually healed, but a few psychic scars still linger. The bass player in the band referred to Cave as "the unmusical one," the guy who couldn't play, so he became the singer by default. "I still feel very much an impostor in the whole music scene," he said, a role he now accepts. Over time, he came to trust his voice, learned how to sing softly, and opened up his songwriting to include a more "feminine" perspective that a girlfriend, singer-songwriter Anita Lane, helped him discover and refine.

He kept moving—to London, then Berlin, then Brazil—each time, he said, to start over and, in one case, to find out how to live without heroin. During drug rehab in London, he said, "the idea was to break you down, which they do quite well, but they didn't do the building you up part very well."

Brazil brought him out of a long period of depression and started a new creative burst, punctuated by a 1996 hit duet with pop singer Kylie Minogue on "Where the Wild Roses Grow." Not all of his fans loved it, he acknowledged, but for him it was "a moment that resonates positively with me. . . . Maybe it was a little camp, but it didn't feel that way at the time."

With "The Boatman's Call" in 1997, his songwriting took another major turn, presenting a more personal perspective. It became part "of a world I've been building, a Cave-ian world: an absurd, magical, transformative world that is different than the real world." Through it, he said, he has come to know himself and the people he loves better. "My wife (Susie Bick) dances in and out of the songs. I feel I know her better in songs than I know her in real life. It makes me feel closer to her. I weld myself to her in those songs."

Grinderman, a smaller, punkier version of his main band the Bad Seeds, was created when he and co-conspirator Warren Ellis "wanted to reduce the music to its core elements," Cave said. "Rather than sack the band members, we just used a few. It was absolutely (screwed-up), passive-aggressive behavior." Ellis' motto for the band was "no God, no love," and lyrics were "basically ad-libbed."

"My writing had become quite congested," Cave says. "It broke things open."

Phone rings . . . and it's Mick Jagger

APRIL 4, 2013

A few hours after the Rolling Stones announced another North American tour [*April 3, 2013*], Mick Jagger called and answered a few quick questions.

Q: After the Stones came off the road the last time, did you think another tour was inevitable?

A: They're never inevitable. Everyone had a really good time in the five shows before Christmas (in London, New Jersey and New York). We wanted to see how the band was playing, how people were reacting. We didn't get too much moaning or complaining. What was quite good is that we set a small goal. We rehearsed for a long time, as if we were doing 100 gigs. But it's helpful to do these things in bite-size pieces, so you're not feeling there's this dreadful endless thing of being on the road. You knew it was going to be done. Similarly, this tour has modest demands. At the beginning of the summer you're done. We're not going crazy, so everyone was up for that.

Q: Why did you book arenas instead of stadiums?

A: The Christmas shows were arena shows. We got that going, and we're content with doing that. We're doing a few outside festival shows in England, but we just feel more in the groove doing arenas.

Q: Your old guitarist, Mick Taylor, will be touring with you for the first time since the '70s. How did that come about?

A: He played very well as a guest in the shows last year *[2012]*, though he only played on one song. We had a lot of guest guitarists. It was fun trying to keep track of all of them. I was scared of announcing the wrong guy, like introducing Jeff Beck instead of Eric Clapton or something. I had to have cue cards in front of me with so many guests. Ronnie (Wood) would stand behind me saying, "You've got the wrong one!" But Mick Taylor played well, and he's going to do a guest spot on this tour. I don't know how many songs it will be.

The Rolling Stones, at the United Center June 3, 2013.
NUCCIO DINUZZO

Q: What about your old bass player, Bill Wyman? Was he asked to rejoin?

A: He played with us in London last year, but he's not keen on touring. He made that very clear to us.

Q: Any surprises on the set list, or will it be mostly greatest hits again?

A: Well, we have quite a lot of songs. We will swap around somewhat. I'm interested in feedback and learning what people want. It's a tricky thing for me when I do a set list. You get bored doing the same songs.

Let's say we do one ballad in two hours, and it's "Wild Horses." If you say, I'm tired of that, let's try something less well-known, and then you're out there stumbling through this song you just relearned at sound check, and you realize people probably want "Wild Horses" instead of this. (Laughs.) You do need to do some songs that aren't so well-known. The question is how many? I'm open to people posting their requests. (Jagger has solicited songs on his Twitter account, @mickjagger).

Q: I've heard from many people today who say they would like to go to the shows but can't afford a ticket. What do you say to them?

A: If you really can't afford a ticket, it's sad. I feel bad about that. But there are seats at different prices. We have some cheap ones that are quite good too. There's a price for everybody I think.

Q: People are already fretting that the secondary ticket market will gobble up most of the best seats and resell them at several times face value. What is your attitude toward these secondary-market sellers and are the Stones participating at all in those profits?

A: I'm very much against the secondary ticket market. I don't know anyone who isn't. We have a lot of secondary-market problems in the U.K., it's really bad there. And lots of artists are starting to participate in it, because they put the tickets up at a certain price, then the tickets get marked up by the secondary sellers and someone else gets twice as much as you. Personally, we don't participate in it. That's the view we take. I think it should be illegal, and in the U.K. it would be very easy to stop it. It's a very concentrated operation you could stop immediately. It's a bigger problem in the U.S., more difficult to contain, but they don't even try. It should be made completely illegal. If people don't like it, don't complain to the artists. Each state should make secondary reselling illegal.

Q: Is there any new Stones music or an album in the works?

A: I have a lot of songs and I'd love to do some more recording with the band. But we're going to get through the tour first and then see what happens.

If you've just paid hundreds of dollars for a Rolling Stones ticket, what kind of a set are you paying to see? Hits, all the hits, and nothing but the hits? A deep-cut festival of connoisseurs' favorites with a couple of crowd-pleasers at the end? A sensible if somewhat conservative mix of classics, a few (very few) recent tracks and one or two surprises?

Based on the first dates of the North American tour that arrives at the United Center for concerts May 31 and June 3, 2013, the Stones believe that their deep-pocketed customers are choosing Door No. 3. They're playing a majority of hits, one or two wild cards, plus two new songs, recorded for a 2012 greatest hits collection.

Over the last couple of decades, Mick Jagger and Keith Richards have both weighed in on the "ideal set list" question, with Jagger leaning toward crowd-pleasers while Richards advocates mixing it up more. From the singer's perspective, it's understandable why he'd want to stick with familiar stuff; he's the point person for an audience's adulation or disdain. He's also a former student at the London School of Economics, so he understands there is an unspoken contract involved: Consumer pays big bucks, consumer expects to hear big songs.

Richards would have you believe that he doesn't pay attention to such mundane monetary matters, but nor is he much for routine. He has made his living as a guitarist by mixing riffs with a rhythm-lead style that ensures no song will be played exactly the same way twice, especially as he practices the "ancient art of weaving" with his chain-smoking co-conspirator, Ronnie Wood.

If it were up to Richards, he'd probably play a different set each night. But on the current tour, even pirate Keef has become a slave to routine; he usually sings lead on the same two songs, "Happy" and "Before They Make Me Run," each night when Jagger briefly exits the stage.

Such late-career conservatism isn't a surprise. Even Stones heroes like Muddy Waters and John Lee Hooker were pretty much playing the same songs each night as the grew older. But some '60s peers (Neil Young, Bob Dylan) avoid predictable greatest hits tours, and veteran artists such as Prince, Bruce Springsteen and Tom Petty mix it up nightly. The Stones may feel they have to play certain songs to please their audience, but as a fan my fondest wish is for my favorite artists to play what excites them. I'm sorry, but I don't believe the Stones are invested in performing "Satisfaction" or "Start Me Up" for the zillionth time.

Given that this is shaping up as the Stones' last go-round as a touring band, they want to hit all the obvious high points. But for me, those high points maybe aren't so obvious. My dream set list would go something like this:

1. "The Last Time": Because we know this just might be the last time on a major tour for the Stones. Plus, it makes for a nice Chicago homage—Richards' riff mimics the version that the Staple Singers recorded in 1961.

2. "Tumbling Dice": Love it when all the instruments drop away and it's just Richards laying down that indelible riff.

3. "Stray Cat Blues": The Stones at their nastiest; Jagger creates one of his most sinister narrators over a droning guitar-piano combo that the Velvet Underground would love.

4. "Out of Time": The Stones approximate the British Invasion cool of the Zombies, but who would play Brian Jones' indelible marimba part?

5. "Emotional Rescue": The Stones broke this one out for the first time on this tour, and it's a weirdly great slice of rocked-up disco.

6. "Sway": Time for a "Sticky Fingers" twofer, beginning with this bleary embrace of the "demon life."

7. "Moonlight Mile": Haunted, poetic road song with Charlie Watts' orchestral drumming and Jagger on acoustic guitar.

8. "Time Waits for No One": With Mick Taylor, the guitarist during the Stones' mostly brilliant 1969–74 run, touring as a special guest, it's time to break out this lead-guitar showcase from the "It's Only Rock 'n' Roll" album.

9. "Can't You Hear Me Knocking": The second half of this "Sticky Fingers" track is another opportunity for Taylor to cut loose over a Latin groove.

10. "You Don't Have to Mean It": Richards opens his solo spot with a reggae vibe, one of the Stones' best from the last two decades.

11. "You Got the Silver": Richards' second solo piece, a forlorn country-blues.

12. "2000 Light Years from Home": The Stones at their trippiest from the underappreciated "Their Satanic Majesties Request" album, their warped, cynical response to The Beatles' "Sgt. Pepper's Lonely Hearts Club Band."

13. "Hand of Fate": One of Richards' best riffs, from the just about totally forgotten "Black and Blue" album (1976).

14–20. Parade of hits: "Jumpin' Jack Flash," "Gimme Shelter," "Street Fighting Man," "Rocks Off," "Paint it Black," "Sympathy for the Devil," "You Can't Always Get What You Want" (with choir).

Encore:

21. "Rip This Joint": Can Richards play this hard and fast anymore? Would love to see him make the attempt.

22. "When the Whip Comes Down": Savage guitars from 1978; the Stones out-punk the punks.

23. "Torn and Frayed": A country lament that would make a great final encore. Picture it: Jagger, Richards and Wood on bar stools with acoustic guitars, Watts on brushes. "Just as long as the guitar plays, let it steal your heart away."

....

Replacements reunion bucks history

JULY 14, 2013

A Replacements reunion? If you had mentioned the possibility to the band's primary songwriter and singer, Paul Westerberg, over the last couple of decades, he'd have come this close to cracking you over the head with his guitar.

Tommy Stinson of The Replacements at Riot Fest Sept. 15, 2013.
ARMANDO L. SANCHEZ

But now Westerberg and original Replacements bassist Tommy Stinson have announced that they're playing at least three reunion shows this year *[2013]*, including a date at Riot Fest, Sept. 13–15 in Humboldt Park. The pair got together last year to record a benefit EP for ailing Replacements guitarist Slim Dunlap. Now, after years of resisting big-money offers to reunite at major festivals such as Lollapalooza and Coachella, they've decided to play a few shows at a festival with a punk pedigree.

Once upon a time, anything could happen at a Replacements gig—and often did. The quartet teetered between genius and idiocy each night, their anarchic spirit buzzing around some of the best rock songs of the past 30 years. For all his seemingly slapdash attitude, Westerberg crafted songs that could be achingly vulnerable and sweetly melodic one minute and hit like an out-of-control bus the next. Part of the fun was not knowing which Replacements would show up on any given night. Even the disastrous shows played into the myth: a night entirely composed of covers because the band was too drunk to play its originals, an appearance by Bob Stinson in a tutu, the onstage fistfights, the outrageous and often self-deprecating heckling. Can a band heckle itself off the stage? The Replacements often tried.

Then there was the time they ended a show by handing their instruments to their roadies and walking off, apparently for good. The Replacements broke up on stage July 4, 1991, in Grant Park. For many fans, it was the perfectly imperfect ending to a career defined by spontaneity and surprise. Anything else—a choreographed farewell tour, a formal announcement, a tearful final bow after being showered with gifts from the fans—would've been a letdown.

The only swan dive that rivals it in rock annals was the Sex Pistols' supposed final concert in San Francisco to cap their first North American tour in 1978. "Ever feel you've been cheated?" Johnny Rotten sneered and walked off into the night, sealing the Pistols' place in rock infamy.

But even the Pistols eventually came back, in 1996, dubbing their return the "Filthy Lucre Tour." In typical Rotten fashion, it was a brutally honest assessment of a comeback that allowed tens of thousands of fans to see the band for the first time and the Pistols to fill their pockets, an opportunity they never got the first time around. It's difficult to begrudge any revered band the opportunity to finally cash in, but it did put a dent in the quintessential punk outfit's outlaw credibility. Now that even the anti-everything Sex Pistols had "sold out," anybody could.

The purists who believe that once a rock band breaks up, it should stay broken, have been having a rough go of it lately. The thinking goes that no band is ever as good the second time around, and that reunions only tarnish the legacy. It's impossible to name more than a few reunions where the music made during a band's cash-in phase rivaled, let alone surpassed, what it did during its prime. But, as the Pistols proved, the idea of one last go-round, or several, is often too difficult to resist.

In 1976, American promoter Sid Bernstein offered The Beatles the then-staggering sum of $1 million to reunite, which they resisted. But that's chump change by today's standards. The Police made an average of more than three times that amount per night on their 2007–08 comeback tour, as they replayed 30-year-old hits for customers willing to pay more than $100 a ticket for the privilege. The Eagles patched up their differences to hit the road in 2008–11 after more than a decade off and raked in more than $250 million in revenue.

The Eagles and the Police were hugely successful the first time around, but the reunion circuit has allowed a number of bands to have second acts far more lucrative than their first, even without the benefit of great music, or any music at all in some cases. The Pixies were widely considered one of the most influential underground bands of the '80s and early '90s but didn't really start raking in revenue until they came back together in 2004 after a decade apart. In its first incarnation, the band's peak audience in Chicago as a headliner was 2,500 at the Riviera. In 2004, the band played to 23,000 fans in five straight sold-out concerts at the Aragon. The quartet consistently played to audiences five to 10 times the band's original peak and made more than $9.5 million in revenue that year.

The Pixies' reunion train has been rolling ever since, even though the band has clearly been at a creative impasse; it only announced plans to release a new studio album, its first in two decades, after founding bassist Kim Deal departed. A few years ago, songwriter-guitarist Black Francis acknowledged he was reluctant to release new Pixies music because he didn't want to screw up the band's legacy. He knew anything he did would be compared to his classic material. "You want anything you do to be at least as good as what people remember you by, but how many bands have been able to (do) that?" he said.

Like the Pixies, the Replacements are a band with an off-the-charts cool factor, a trove of indelible songs and the potential to draw from an expanding fan base. They'll not only attract many of the original followers nostalgic for the '80s but also subsequent generations eager to see a legendary band perform live for the first time. But as Black Francis suggested, "legendary" can be a double-edged sword.

When last seen more than 20 years ago, the Replacements were selling out 4,000-seat theaters.

By then, founding members Bob Stinson and Chris Mars were long gone, and only Westerberg and Tommy Stinson remained from the original lineup. The ramshackle charm of the early days had long since been replaced by a steady professionalism, until that one final shot of chaos in Grant Park.

Any great band deserves a victory lap after a few—or, in the case of the Replacements, 22—years off. A brisk, spirited sprint through the hits and almost-hits is what's in demand. But the Replacements have never been much for meeting expectations. So how will they confound and delight their fans this time? How will they simultaneously undercut and live up to their myth? It may prove to be the band's greatest challenge.

Reunions that clicked

• MISSION OF BURMA: The Boston indie-rock trio left behind an obscure but hugely influential studio album and an EP in the early '80s, then picked up right where they left off with an excellent 2004 comeback, "OnOffOn."

• LED ZEPPELIN: It's not Zeppelin without drummer John Bonham, whose 1980 death broke up the band in the first place. So it was fitting for Robert Plant, Jimmy Page and John Paul Jones to play one final gig (a 2007 benefit concert in London) with Bonham's son, Jason, sitting in on drums, and bring down the hammer of the gods one final time.

• THE FEELIES: The New Jersey post-punk quintet would probably assert that it never reunited because it never actually broke up. But the 2011 album "Here Before" was its first in 20 years, and it found the band sounding as sharp and buoyant as ever.

Reunions that flunked

• THE WHO: After a series of "farewell" shows in the early '80s with the band running on fumes in the wake of Keith Moon's death, Pete Townshend, Roger Daltry and John Entwistle regrouped a few years later. Moon, unfortunately, was still dead, and the band turned into a karaoke caricature of itself.

• THE DOORS OF THE 21ST CENTURY: The Doors without Jim Morrison? Yes, Ray Manzarek and Robby Krieger apparently thought that would be a good idea. Even drummer John Densmore sued his former bandmates to try to stop this travesty.

• INXS: Michael Hutchence died in 1997, which should have ended the band forever. It didn't. The Australian group decided it would be a wonderful idea to reconvene in 2005 with a new lead singer, J.D. Fortune, winner of the band's own reality TV series. It wasn't.

Black Sabbath goes back to vibe of early days to recharge sound

AUG. 16, 2013

t looked like an impossibility a few years ago, but three-quarters of the original Black Sabbath lineup finally got around to recording and releasing a new studio album several months ago and then launching a world tour.

For founding members Ozzy Osbourne, Geezer Butler and Tony Iommi, the reunion was decades in the making; the Rick Rubin-produced "13" (Vertigo/Universal) is their first Sabbath album together since 1978. Still, it was nearly derailed by Iommi's struggle with cancer and a legal tussle with founding drummer Bill Ward, who eventually pulled out of the reunion. He was replaced on the album by Rage Against the Machine's Brad Wilk and on the current tour by Tommy Clufetos.

Iommi, who along with his bandmates is one of the primary architects of heavy metal, talked frankly about the turmoil as Sabbath was beginning a tour that arrives at the First Midwest Bank Amphitheatre in Tinley Park [*Aug. 16, 2013*]. An edited transcript follows.

Q: How's your health?

A: Not so bad, dare I say. I'm still under treatment. That's not going to go away. I work our tours around my treatments. Each time we get a break, I go back to England and have another treatment. It will be ongoing till next year. It's an antibody treatment, intravenous, and makes you feel the same way as chemotherapy does. It's an awful feeling for a few days.

Q: Has it affected your ability to perform?

A: The shows have been good. I just have to work out my days so I don't exert myself too much. It's important for me to get rest. Unfortunately, I'm in the wrong job to get rest. There are times when I get

Ozzy Osbourne and Black Sabbath at Lollapalooza Aug. 3, 2012.
BRIAN CASSELLA

really exhausted. You just have to push through. Once you get onstage, the adrenaline takes over.

Q: The Black Sabbath album seems like it had been in the discussion stage for 10 years. Did you ever think it would come out?

A: We wrote some songs about 10 years ago, but it never went any further. Ozzy was doing (his reality TV show) "The Osbournes." Nobody was into it properly back then. It was just too casual. The only way to do an album is that everyone would really want to do it, everybody had to be 100 percent into doing an album, and it took a while to get there. Once we did, we worked quickly. I don't like to sit around pondering things. The actual recording time was only a few weeks.

Q: How did you get involved with Rick Rubin?

A: Rick has always been a fan. He always wanted to do a Black Sabbath album. When it came to doing an album, I said to the guys: We do need a producer. I knew I didn't want to do it, and I thought the band shouldn't be doing it. Rick was the obvious choice because he had expressed interest.

Q: The music has a bluesier hard-rock feel with some jazz elements, similar to the way Sabbath sounded in its earliest days. Was that intentional?

A: When we sat down and talked to Rick, he played us our first album at his house (the 1970 release "Black Sabbath"). We thought, "This is weird." But it was his idea to create that vibe of the early days. You haven't got 10 guitars and five vocals on a track. It's all basic. He said, "I'd like you to look at this as a follow-up to your first album 40 years out." Which is bloody hard to do! You get into a way of recording, and it's hard to change. But it was good to do that, because you got the raw band, the raw sound. We wanted Ozzy to sing like he did in the early days, in a lower register, so we could do all the songs onstage.

Q: Why didn't things work out with Bill Ward?

A: We went in full-heartedly, the four of us, and then Bill changed his mind. It threw us a lot. We weren't expecting it. Lawyers got involved; he didn't talk to us personally. It was a big shock when he pulled out. Between him and his lawyers, they wanted a certain thing, and we couldn't do it. There may have been other issues, but I don't know. I don't know if he was worried about playing the songs, but it just seemed weird that he backed out. We couldn't come to an agreement to get him back, and I said to Bill, "We have to get on with it. We can't sit around waiting for you."

Q: Did anything surprise you about working with Rubin?

A: A lot of things surprised us about Rick. He has a very different way of working from what we're used to. He'd leave us to it. We'd write songs; he wasn't involved with the writing at all. We thought, well, this is strange. He just pops in now and again. He left it all to us, until we got into recording, then he'd start to make suggestions. He had his reasons for waiting. . . . Over the last 40 years, we got into a pattern of putting in the backing track, then working out the solo, then adding the vocals. We'd do it in pieces. This time, Ozzy was singing in the booth in back while we were playing. Everybody was in there all the time and involved. Over the years it got to the stage where everyone would do their parts, and I'd be in there on my own, doing the guitar parts. It was never a joint effort, until now.

Q: A lot of bands used to working a certain way for so long would've been upset. Were there disagreements with Rubin?

A: At first, Rick wanted 30 songs, and I told him, "You got no chance of that." Sabbath has never done 30 songs for anybody. We'd never done more than eight or 10 an album. But in the studio, he kept pushing us. Rick put Geezer under a lot of pressure: "We need lyrics for this tomorrow." Bloody hell, but we needed that. We went in with 10 songs, but other ideas came up in the studio—(the acoustic track) "Zeitgeist" and the blues jam ("Damaged Soul"). We ended up with 16 to choose from at the end. We recorded the album in Malibu (Calif.), in Rick's studio. We'd have weekends off, and one Friday evening he emailed me, "Do you think you could come up with an acoustic track with Ozzy?" On Saturday I came up with the idea for "Zeitgeist," and on Monday I played it in the studio for Rick and the other guys, and we recorded it. It was that off-the-cuff.

....

Alt rock lives (self-doubt intact)

SEPT. 15, 2013

"Alternative rock," a music-industry term that encapsulated the '90s rise of bands such as Nirvana and Nine Inch Nails, never really went away. In some ways, it's as lucrative as ever, and getting humorously zinged by Mudhoney, the Stooges-loving rabble-rousers who helped birth the Seattle music scene from that era.

"I like it small," singer Mark Arm declares, in a typically self-deprecating new song on Mudhoney's first studio album in five years, "Vanishing Point" (Sub Pop). And the video—which appears to have been shot on a $25 budget—works as a sardonic commentary on Nirvana's iconic if equally low-rent 1991 video for "Smells Like Teen Spirit."

The Nirvana hit marked the unofficial birthplace of alternative rock—the wave of music inspired by punk and post-punk that crashed the pop charts for a few years in the early '90s. The era included bands who at least paid lip service to the idea that they were marginalized outsiders (some even actually were). They spoke loudly to a generation that felt left out, and bands such as Nirvana, Soundgarden, Pearl Jam, Nine Inch Nails, Smashing Pumpkins, Green Day, Offspring and Primus ended up playing arenas and selling millions of albums. Even lo-fi artists such as Beck, Pavement, Guided By Voices and Liz Phair became stars.

Now, many of them are back with new music or repackaged versions of the albums that shaped their legacies. Nirvana and the Pumpkins are in the midst of a series of boxed-set releases celebrating their '90s heyday. Pearl Jam has a similar archival dig underway but has also scheduled an album, "Lightning Bolt," for release in October 2013. Soundgarden returned in November 2012 with its first album of new material in more than a decade, "King Animal" (Seven Four/Republic). And after launching a "farewell" tour in 2009, Trent Reznor resurrected Nine Inch Nails for the recent comeback album, "Hesitation Marks" (Columbia).

Nine Inch Nails at Lollapalooza Aug. 2, 2013.
ALEX GARCIA

Demand for these bands never really went away; their names have become "brands" beloved by an audience that is now in its 30s and 40s and willing to pay big money to see them.

Nirvana's "In Utero: 20th Anniversary Deluxe Reissue" (Geffen), due out Sept. 24, revisits the Seattle trio's third studio album, the 1993 follow-up to the 30 million-selling "Nevermind." "In Utero" was a pricklier album than its predecessor. Recorded by Steve Albini in two weeks, it represents a clearer picture of how singer Kurt Cobain tried to integrate two contradictory impulses: punk mayhem and bubble-gum-pop melody. Whereas "Nevermind" smoothed the rough edges, "In Utero" underlined them. The album presents the band at extremes: vulnerable and chaotic. It was in many ways an affirmation of the '70s and '80s underground and the notion that guitar-bass-drums rock 'n' roll still could inspire and upend.

Unfortunately, that is not the case with the overstuffed 70-track "In Utero" boxed set, which adds little in the way of revelatory new material that might justify its hefty $100-plus price tag. As souvenir items go, it's a nice reminder of what once was. But the idea all along was that "alternative" was an engine for change, that Rock Inc. was being shoved out the door while bands like the Jesus Lizard, the Melvins, Sonic Youth, the Flaming Lips and Ween signed major-label deals and ransacked the palace. It didn't quite work out that way. Within a few years, the movement had become a commodity, spawned Lollapalooza, a commercial radio format and a bevy of sound-alikes on the charts (Bush, Seven Mary Three, Stone Temple Pilots).

"In Utero" saw it coming. Cobain understood how quickly things would come undone as the cash flowed. "I am my own parasite," he barked on the scorched-earth "Milk It." The album's second half is a series of noisy screeds, finally descending on the heart-breaking "All Apologies."

"What else should I be? . . . What else could I say? . . . What else should I write," Cobain sang, as if interrogating himself about what it all meant and whether it was worth it. His music was part of a soundtrack made largely by and for the 82 million Americans born between 1965 and 1984, the so-called Generation X as defined in Douglas Coupland's 1991 novel, "Generation X: Tales for an Accelerated Culture."

This was the generation that came of age after the mostly prosperous, post-World War II baby boomers. A segment of this community—including Cobain, Mudhoney's Mark Arm and Pearl Jam's Eddie Vedder—found its voice on the 7-inch singles available only at independent record stores and heard only on college radio stations, a world in which Husker Du and the Melvins mattered as much or more than huge '80s hit-makers such as Michael Jackson and Bruce Springsteen.

Their music questioned everything, including itself. That's why "All Apologies" still resonates. On the latest Pearl Jam single, "Mind Your Manners," Vedder also grapples with big questions: of faith, doubt and the purpose of rebellion. He does it over a scratchy guitar riff and furious drum volleys that hold up well next to the music Pearl Jam made during its '90s heyday.

On Nine Inch Nails' new "Hesitation Marks," Reznor is loaded with uncertainty, almost to the point of inertia. Cobain and many of his peers were rock-music fans who understood the pitfalls of stardom and nostalgia and how that could undermine everything they valued. Reznor, who used keyboards and computers to fashion some of the most aggressive rock music ever made in the early '90s, figured out how to sound just as disturbing in the quieter terrain of his 1999 masterpiece, "The Fragile." After that creative high point, what was left for him to do?

"Hesitation Marks" wrestles with how to reconcile Nine Inch Nails' corrosive sound and attitude with where Reznor is now: a well-rewarded, middle-aged rock star with a wife and family. "Everything I say has come before . . . I am never certain anymore/I am just a shadow of a shadow of a shadow," he sings.

Cobain, Vedder, Reznor and many of their peers were rock stars who had swagger but were always self-conscious about it. They were their era's answer to a lineage that went back to The Beatles and Elvis Presley but was shaded by punk-rock guilt and skepticism. To quote Mudhoney, which never climbed as high as many of the alternative bands it influenced, on "I Like it Small": "Limited appeal! . . . Dingy basements! . . . No expectations!" Kurt Cobain felt exactly the same way in 1989, and it ticked him off. Then everything changed.

Cobain became a bigger deal than he ever could've imagined. Even after he died, Nirvana just kept on selling: Far more Nirvana music has been released after the singer killed himself in 1994 than in the band's relatively brief lifetime. No wonder that for nearly every Gen X hero of the '90s, Cobain's flippantly acerbic opening line on "In Utero" must sound prophetic: "Teenage angst has paid off well."

PART 3

RAP

Common
Chicago native remains a South Sider at heart

MARCH 31, 2000

He calls Erykah Badu his "buddy" and has dueted with Lauryn Hill. He hangs with Roots' philosopher-percussionist Questlove, and he's embraced by hip-hop veterans such as De La Soul and A Tribe Called Quest. D'Angelo calls him "a great guy . . . part of a positive movement in music." If measured solely by the company he keeps, Chicago-born rapper Common has arrived, and his new album, "Like Water for Chocolate," confirms his prowess as one of the best emcees in hip-hop.

Such recognition seemed a pipe dream not long ago, when the phrase "Chicago hip-hop" was an oxymoron. In a city built on blues, gospel and house music on the South and West Sides, rap never flourished as it did in New York, Los Angeles or even Miami, Houston and Atlanta. But as artists such as Twista and Crucial Conflict broke into the national charts with their rapid-fire linguistics, and Do or Die sold hundreds of thousands of records with their "Po Pimp" gangsta rap, Chicago hip-hop began to assume a national identity in the mid-'90s.

No artist has done more to give the scene credibility than Common, a.k.a. Rashid Lynn, 27. Though the rapper moved to Brooklyn to further boost his career, he remains a South Sider at heart and the spiritual leader of a Chicago underground that includes such verbally and socially enlightened artists as All Natural and Rubberoom.

"Whatever success I do achieve, I am going to bring back to the crib," says the rapper, who has founded the Common Ground foundation in his hometown to raise funds for community centers, summer camps and scholarships. "There's just a lot more opportunities to help my career progress in an entertainment capital like New York."

His debut, "Can I Borrow a Dollar?" (1992), which came out under the name Common Sense, marked him as a clever, playful emcee (he later changed his nom de rap when a company claimed the copyright).

Chicago born hip-hop artist Common at the House of Blues June 1, 2005.
NUCCIO DINUZZO

But it was the follow-up, "Resurrection" (1995), that established him as a hip-hop visionary. That album's "I Used to Love H.E.R." was an instant classic, an allegorical history of the music that suggested the beauty of hip-hop had been corrupted by greed—a subtext of virtually every recording Common has made since.

"One Day It'll All Make Sense" (1997), steeped in philosophical and moral conflict, raised the bar: "Retrospect for Life" found Common apologizing to an aborted child while "G.O.D. (Gaining One's Definition)" struggled with issues of faith. The album's guest stars bespoke his rising status: De La Soul, Badu, Hill, Q-Tip of A Tribe Called Quest.

Despite the respect and critical acclaim, Common remained an underground artist, his record sales dwarfed by less ambitious rapper-entrepreneurs such as Master P and Puff Daddy. He left his old label and moved to Brooklyn to try to bring his career to the next level.

"When the industry is saturated with a certain kind of music, it makes it harder for people with my sound and stance to get a chance,"

Common says. "At the same time, I'm not going to compromise my music and spirit to get on the radio, because I wouldn't be happy looking in the mirror. I want radio play and the success of the mainstream, but I won't change my music to achieve that."

Proof that Common lives by his words is "Like Water for Chocolate" (MCA). The Chicago native doesn't succumb to gangster posturing or raps about gats, blunts and 'ho's. Instead, he fuses the playful street sensibility of his debut with the more thoughtful stance of the last two albums to create his most fully formed portrait of the artist yet. On "A Film Called Pimp," Common poses as a street hustler who maintains a stable of politically correct whores, satirizing gangster imagery while poking fun at his image as the rapper for "backpackers, white dudes and coffee-shop chicks."

"I keep on pushing, man, I keep on pushing," he says. It's no accident that he alludes to Curtis Mayfield's soul classic as he describes his determination to create multilayered art, connecting the work of Mayfield, Donny Hathaway and Marvin Gaye to the lyrically deft, sonically dense hip-hop of A Tribe Called Quest, Gang Starr and De La Soul. "My past taught me to help elevate people. At the same time, you have to acknowledge that you're not there yet, you have faults and you indulge in things that may not be good for the spirit. Even revolutionaries want to have a good time once in a while."

Working with the Roots' Questlove as producer, and artists such as D'Angelo, Mos Def, jazz trumpeter Roy Hargrove and Femi Kuti (the son of Nigerian jazz-soul giant Fela), Common has added to the recent canon of deeply personal records that blend hip-hop street grit with old-soul instrumentation and spirituality.

"D'Angelo having a No. 1 album opens some doors for all of us," Common says, referring to the singer's recent "Voodoo" opus. "That somebody could do something fresh and innovative . . . and be successful with it, that's inspiring to me."

....

The rap that Dre built

JULY 2, 2000

Dr. Dre, the architect of some of the nastiest hard-core hip-hop albums of the last decade, knows his pathology. But even he laughs in disbelief at the audacity of his latest find, Eminem, a.k.a. Marshall Mathers.

"I am always shocked by the stuff that comes out of his mouth," Dre says of Eminem, whose stage name is a play on his initials, M&M. "I can't censor or stop him from saying anything. In fact, I encourage him. Together we do stuff that nobody else can even think of doing, that nobody else has the guts to do or say."

Dre turned music with a limited underground fan base in the late '80s into a mainstream formula for platinum albums. Whereas rock has largely shed its rebel skin, Dre-driven hip-hop is the music that scares parents, horrifies the politically correct and brings suburban teens flocking to record stores by the millions. And perhaps no one represents that better than Eminem.

On his latest Dre-produced disc, "The Marshall Mathers LP" (Aftermath/Interscope), Eminem trashes everyone from gays to pop star Christina Aguilera and indulges macabre fantasies in which he kills his wife, his mother and even Dre himself. The content is dire, frequently hateful, delivered in a cartoonish, sing-songy voice that suggests it's all a sick joke.

Reaction has been mixed: Many critics have given the album a guarded endorsement, decrying some of its content while praising Eminem for his verbal skills and his transgressive humor. Aguilera proclaimed in Rolling Stone that she's "offended and really disgusted" by the rapper's explicit putdown of her in his latest single, "The Real Slim Shady." More significantly, the Gay and Lesbian Alliance Against Defamation calls the album's lyrics "the most blatantly offensive" it has ever seen. And even Eminem's mother doesn't see the humor in her son's screeds; she has made him the target of a $10 million defamation

Eminem in the Up In Smoke concert at Allstate Arena June 8, 2000.
KEVIN TANAKA

suit for lyrics targeting her on the rapper's previous album, the multi-platinum 1999 release "The Slim Shady LP."

No doubt spiked by all the controversy, Eminem's sales have made him a superstar, "arguably the most compelling figure in all pop music," Newsweek says. "Marshall Mathers" has been the No. 1 album in the country for several weeks and in a month has already sold more than 3 million copies—an 'N Sync-size success by an 'N Sync fan's worst nightmare.

Last weekend *[June 23 2000]*, Eminem stood in baggy shorts and a flipped-back golf cap at the lip of the stage of Memorial Stadium in Seattle. More than 20,000 fans responded to his call.

"My name is . . . !" the pale, blond-haired imp shouted, a hand cupped to his ear.

"Slim Shady!" came the deafening response.

Slim Shady is Eminem's alter-ego, a pet name he has for his temper. Suddenly, he cut the tune short.

"I hate that [expletive] song!" Eminem snarled. "How many of you ever get angry?" Again, the crowd roared.

"So mad that you could just kill somebody?" The crowd cheered again. "Next time you get mad, I want you to play this song."

And he ripped into a diatribe called "The Way I Am," in which his high, nasal, Pee-wee Herman voice became a low, high-speed growl. Here was the rap icon of the moment telling the whole world to crawl in a hole and die. The crowd ate it up. Later came "The Real Slim Shady," in which Eminem minced across the stage over a loopy rhythm while declaring that "there's a million of us . . . just like me . . . who dress like me, walk, talk and act like me."

Eminem is indeed not alone in his musical taste, his sense of humor or his prejudices. He grew up in Detroit, a lower-class kid from a single-parent home who was a 9th grade dropout, had a child out of wedlock, and latched desperately onto hip-hop as a way out of a dead-end life as a short-order cook. He is one of many youths of all races who grew up in the '90s dressing, walking, talking and acting like an inner-city rapper, a generation for whom Dr. Dre provided the soundtrack.

Initially, Dre's first major group, NWA, spoke primarily to inner-city blacks with its mix of West Coast party raps and raw, ribald protest music. The group's 1989 album, "Straight Outta Compton," ranted against police harassment and described Los Angeles street warfare in explicit detail; the band members grew up in Compton, one of the city's worst neighborhoods, and some ran with gangs and dealt drugs, lending an authenticity to the scenarios that only enhanced the group's reputation with record buyers.

But soon after the FBI fired off a warning letter to the group's label protesting the content of the song "[Expletive] Tha Police," which protested shakedowns of ghetto blacks, NWA exploded in popularity, reaching a new audience of young suburban whites fascinated with the group's outlaw image. The next NWA album, a far inferior effort called "Efil4zaggin" released in 1991, became the first hard-core rap release to reach No. 1 on the Billboard pop chart.

"Our stuff is like drugs," Dre said in an interview with the Tribune at the time. "People can't get enough of what we do. They have to buy it, even though they know they shouldn't."

NWA's sparse funk grooves and eerie synthesizer textures established Dre, a.k.a. Andre Young, as a first-rate producer, and his subsequent solo projects, such as "The Chronic" (1992), and the work of proteges such as Snoop Dogg and Eminem have made him the most important figure in hard-core hip-hop.

Dre's latest album, "Dr. Dre 2001" (Aftermath/Interscope), has sold 4 million copies and remains in the top 20 eight months after its release. Eminem's two Dre-produced albums have turned the rapper into a staple on top-40 radio; the track "The Real Slim Shady" is being played 80 times a week on some pop stations, in between hits by Britney Spears and Sisqo.

Todd Cavanah, program director of WBBM-FM 96.3, which has been playing the track "The Real Slim Shady" every 90 minutes, says he had "problems" with the song's lyrics. Some of its most explicit content is edited out, but the song's graphic attack on gays remains audible. "We held off on it, because it's definitely on the edge," Cavanah says. "But it was the No. 1 most requested song, the song is everywhere on other stations and MTV, and in order to stay in business we have to play it."

A track by NWA, "Boyz-N-The Hood," has been covered by a Texas rock band, Dynamite Hack, and is a fast-rising hit on modern-rock stations, despite an explicit description of a woman being beaten. "This is humor, this is novelty," says Dave Richards, program director of Chicago rock station WKQX-FM 101.1, which has been playing the song dozens of times a week. "We thought it was offensive, but it has become the most requested record of the last three weeks."

Can an NWA reunion be far behind? The key surviving members of the group founded by the late Eazy-E—Dre, Ice Cube and MC Ren—have joined a national tour that also brings Snoop Dogg, Eminem and Dre's brother, rapper Warren G, to the Allstate Arena.

Together, these rappers have defined hip-hop's outlaw fringe for the last decade, and have the houses and sports cars to show for it. Dre and Snoop are hip-hop's most notorious hedonists; Dre's insistent mid-tempo funk beats underpin tales of gin-and-juice drinking, pot-toking, women-baiting "players" and pimps. The producer is pictured on his new CD with his head in a bag full of chronic, a potent strain of marijuana. If there's an overriding agenda, it's to throw a party and rake in the cash.

According to Dre, he has two goals: "I want people to say Dr. Dre is the best hip-hop producer that ever went into the studio, and also to feed my family." And if hard-core hip-hop no longer paid the bills? "I'd find something else to do. We're in this for the money."

Only a few years ago, Dre sounded like he was sick of hard-core rap's more noxious subject matter. He left his Death Row record label under acrimonious circumstances, vowed to cut down on his hard-partying lifestyle and got married. On the 1996 song "Been There Done That," from the album "Dr. Dre Presents . . . The Aftermath," he chastised rappers who "talk that hard-core [expletive] 'cause that's all they're worth."

"I felt because I had just gotten married I couldn't go around making music like I had" with its disparaging references to women, Dre says. But when "Aftermath" didn't sell, the producer had a change of heart.

"It was temporary insanity. I found myself attracting the wrong audience. People in their 40s and 50s were coming up to me saying, 'I like that "Been There Done That" song.' I had to get back and grab the audience that put me where I am today."

Dre says it was his wife, Nicole, who encouraged him to return to the hard-core style. "She knows what I do best," the producer says. "She knows when I talk about 'ho's' and 'bitches,' it's strictly for entertainment and body bumping."

Yet Dre's casual misogyny sounds almost mild next to Eminem's more virulent assaults. There's no denying that Eminem's wordplay can be clever and that his verbal attack has moments of true inventiveness. On "Stan," the best track on "The Marshall Mathers LP," he constructs a riveting cautionary tale about an obsessive fan. In the tradition of the most extreme rock and rap, from the Rolling Stones' "Under My Thumb" to Nine Inch Nails' "Closer," Eminem's strongest tracks pack a wicked transgressive thrill.

"Half of the satisfaction that I get from releasing music comes from the look on people's faces when they hear it," Eminem said in a recent Internet chat hosted by AOL.

But following closely in the blood-stained footsteps of its multimillion-selling predecessor, "Marshall Mathers" sounds more exploitive than subversive. Though anger and hate can be powerful fuels for great art, using them as a calculated formula for selling records is inexcusable. Whereas Eminem could pass himself off as an equal opportunity offender on his first album, he sounds almost desperate to shock on the follow-up. It's the difference between a risk-taking personal statement and crass, lowest-common-denominator commercialism.

Dre disagrees. It's about "entertaining our audience by any and all means necessary," he says. "Five-year-olds should not be listening to our records. I'm doing records for people who want to roll down their windows, bang some [expletive] and live on the wild side a bit."

But it's a party to which gays, self-respecting women and the people who love them aren't welcome. "It's not up to me to make the world kinder," Eminem said in the AOL chat. "I can't parent every kid in the country."

For that, at least, we can be grateful.

Time to be real
Will rap and R&B get their due at the Grammys?

FEB. 16, 2001

Will the Grammys get in touch with commercial reality at the 43rd annual awards [*Feb. 21, 2001*]? And, if they do, will this gang of industry professionals be able to look at itself in the bathroom mirror the morning after?

The National Academy of Recording Arts and Sciences, the 16,000-member organization that allegedly rewards "artistic excellence" when it votes on the Grammys, has traditionally treated rappers and R&B singers like misbegotten strays in a kennel full of meticulously groomed poodles named Sting and Celine. It wasn't until two years ago that a hip-hop album was even nominated for Album of the Year, but that was a doozy—Lauryn Hill's "The Miseducation of Lauryn Hill." Its triumph hinted that the academy was finally willing to broaden its definition of the mainstream to include a woman of color who rapped rather than sang like a Whitney wanna-be. Last year's sweep by Carlos

Macy Gray at the Aragon Ballroom June 10, 2000.
PETER THOMPSON

Santana was a no-brainer—Santana made a classic crossover album that appealed to listeners of all ages—but *[2001's]* show will truly test the academy's efforts to fit Generation Hip-Hop into one of its tuxedos.

The numbers don't lie. More than 197 million R&B records were sold last year, the most of any genre and a 12 percent increase from the previous year. In addition, hip-hop sales climbed 20 percent to 105 million. Most other major genres of music took a big hit in 2000:

album sales of classical, jazz, country, Latin and Christian music all declined. Only alternative rock challenged the rap-R&B stranglehold with sales of 131 million, up 8 percent.

If the Grammys follow that pattern, it'll be a big year for multiple nominees such as Destiny's Child, D'Angelo, Macy Gray, Dr. Dre and Eminem. But that's a big "if." None of this year's nominations in the big four categories—song, record and album of the year, and best-new artist—has the broad appeal of Santana or even a Lauryn Hill. The album-of-the-year category in particular dramatizes the deep divisions within Grammy country: the futuristic rock of Radiohead ("Kid A"), the ultra-hip pop of Beck ("Midnite Vultures"), the solid craftsmanship of two veteran performers with critically lauded but modest-selling comeback albums (Paul Simon's "You're the One" and Steely Dan's "Two Against Nature") and the explicit multiplatinum hip-hop of Eminem ("The Marshall Mathers LP").

Eminem's nomination in particular leaves the academy in a bind: Though "The Marshall Mathers LP" was easily the biggest rap record of the year, selling more than 7 million copies, and Eminem was praised by critics and fellow rappers alike for his nimble delivery and outlandish imagination, the record was marred by its profane lyrics, which liberally bash gays and women. If Eminem wins album of the year, the Grammys can say they're in tune with the marketplace, but at what price? If they reward one of the other albums, they'll be accused of playing it safe (anointing respected old pros like Steely Dan and Paul Simon for albums that don't rank with their very best work) or killing their TV ratings with obscurity (it's likely that many viewers will be hearing the names "Radiohead" and "Beck" for the first time).

The Grammys could have solved the problem by nominating D'Angelo's "Voodoo" for album of the year—a multimillion-selling hit that set a new standard for R&B. It's a work that even older Grammy voters would love for the way it draws on classic soul, funk, jazz and gospel, while charming hip-hop heads with its snaking bass lines and atmospheric arrangements. D'Angelo is nominated in some lesser categories, but his omission from the major awards is another glaring example of why, despite their best intentions, the Grammys seem to come up short every year.

Nonetheless, the Grammys continue to influence record-buyers like no other music awards show. Here's a look at which artists in some of the major categories will be celebrating:

- RECORD OF THE YEAR: The Grammys blew it last year *[2000]* by bypassing Macy Gray for best new artist. They'll make it up to her by tapping her terrific single "I Try" over entries from Destiny's Child, U2, Madonna and 'N Sync.

- ALBUM OF THE YEAR: Eminem is too controversial to win, and Beck and Radiohead are relatively unknown to the Grammy voters and should cancel each other out (though Radiohead's experimental dreamscape, "Kid A," is clearly the best of the nominated albums). That leaves old pros Paul Simon, who has won 12 Grammys previously, and Steely Dan, who have yet to win a single statue. Expect Simon to win on the strength of the good but not great "You're the One."

- SONG OF THE YEAR: Macy Gray's evocative, lyrically deft tunes have started to show up on other artists' albums, from Wynonna to Rod Stewart, and in a category honoring song-writring she should be a lock for "I Try."

- NEW ARTIST: This category is a perennial joke, because nominees often put out albums long before hitting the Grammy radar screen. Shelby Lynne is on her fifth album, and Sisquo was a member of the best-selling R&B group Dru Hill before making his solo debut. Lynne's country-soul sound has plenty of advocates, but Jill Scott matched critical acclaim with healthy sales for her simmering soul debut, "Who is Jill Scott? Words and Sounds Vol. 1."

- POP ALBUM: Don Henley and Steely Dan represent the Baby Boomers. 'N Sync and Britney Spears dominate the listening habits of teens. But Madonna's "Music" speaks to both audiences and should win.

- ROCK ALBUM: Bon Jovi? Matchbox Twenty? No Doubt? Was the year in rock really that ugly? At the Drive-In might have something to say about that, but they weren't nominated. Of those albums that made the cut, Rage Against the Machine's "The Battle of Los Angeles" is the clear standout, but the now-splintered group has made plenty of enemies with its sometimes muddled left-of-Castro politics. That leaves the door open for the Foo Fighters' "There is Nothing Left to Lose."

- ALTERNATIVE ALBUM: Radiohead and Beck duke it out again. Radiohead's "Kid A" is the stronger work, but Beck ("Midnight Vultures") may have better name recognition among the voters.

- R&B ALBUM: If D'Angelo's "Voodoo" doesn't walk away with this award over Boyz II Men, Toni Braxton, Joe and Sisquo, the Grammy voters ought to set up an after-show dunk tank for themselves in the parking lot.

- RAP ALBUM: The five nominees (DMX, Dr. Dre, Eminem, Jay-Z, Nelly) all had major commercial impact, but they represent a narrow sliver of the hip-hop world with their gangsta bravado. Too bad Common's "Like Water for Chocolate" or De La Soul's "Art Official Intelligence: Mosaic Thump" didn't make the cut, or that Outkast's "Stankonia" was released after the Sept. 30 eligibility deadline. In lieu of that, look for "Dr. Dre 2001" to beat out Eminem, because Dre's party raps don't have quite the nasty edge of his blue-eyed protege's.

- COUNTRY ALBUM: Lee Ann Womack ("I Hope You Dance") and Trisha Yearwood ("Real Live Woman") are two of the finest Nashville singers of the last decade, but they're no match for the overhyped sex pot Faith Hill, whose "Breathe" will win on the basis of her steamy videos, if not the quality of her tissue-thin voice or the triteness of her lyrics.

- CONTEMPORARY BLUES: The revered Koko Taylor should win her second Grammy for "Royal Blue," though the North Mississippi Allstars did more than any single act to shake up the genre with the fierce trance-boogie of "Shake Hands With Shorty."

Wreck in Honduras kills TLC's sizzling rap artist

APRIL 27, 2002

Lisa "Left Eye" Lopes, the rapper who put the sizzle in TLC's best-selling pop soap opera, was killed in a car crash [*on April 25, 2002*] while visiting Honduras.

Lopes, who would have turned 31 on May 27, was visiting the Central American country, where she has a condo on the northern coast. The tragedy marked the second accident-related death of a major R&B star in the last year. Last summer the singer Aaliyah died in a plane crash in the Bahamas.

TLC was one of the most successful female pop groups of all time and sold 21 million albums. The Atlanta trio bridged the Supremes and Destiny's Child with a mix of socially conscious, feminist lyrics and rap-inflected pop melodies that earned it four Grammy awards and a string of hits: "Baby-Baby-Baby," "Creep," "Waterfalls," "No Scrubs" and "Unpretty." But Lopes' musical contributions often were overshadowed by her volatile relations with her bandmates, record label and boyfriends.

"We had all grown up together and were as close as a family," surviving bandmates Tionne "T-Boz" Watkins and Rozonda "Chilli" Thomas said in a statement. "Today we have truly lost our sister."

L.A. Reid, president of the group's Arista Records label, called the loss "devastating."

Eight other people, including one of Lopes' sisters, were in the Mitsubishi Montero when the crash occurred near Jutiapa, about 10 miles west of La Ceiba, on Honduras' northern Atlantic coast.

La Ceiba Police Inspector John Cole said Lopes was trying to pass a car on the highway when a truck approached from the other lane, forcing her to veer sharply to the left. Her vehicle struck two trees and flipped several times, Cole said.

Lopes was killed instantly. Several other people in the car were taken to a hospital in La Ceiba for non-life-threatening injuries, Cole said.

Born in Philadelphia, Lopes joined Watkins and Thomas to form TLC in 1991 under the direction of Reid's wife at the time, singer-songwriter-producer Pebbles. The group members established strong individual personalities that appealed to MTV-era fans, while a host of up-and-coming producers crafted the trio's songs and shaped its sound.

Lopes may not have been the most musically talented member of the multiplatinum group, but she easily was the most watchable. She earned her nickname by wearing a condom taped over the left lens of her spectacles, and brought a tough-minded if squeaky-voiced rap sensibility to the group's sound, dubbed "new-jill swing" for the way it blended R&B sophistication with hip-hop attitude. The group's street-wise songs addressed safe sex, AIDS, black-on-black crime and self-esteem, and packaged the messages in glossy pop-crossover arrangements crafted by top-name producers such as Dallas Austin, Babyface and Organized Noize.

On TLC's last concert tour, the word "Crazy" was etched on Lopes' baggy wardrobe, a tongue-in-cheek affirmation of her volatile private life.

In 1994, she admitted to setting fire to the mansion of her boyfriend, pro football wide receiver Andre Rison, after the couple quarreled. She pleaded guilty to arson and was sentenced to a halfway house, 5 years' probation and a $10,000 fine. The two later broke up, only to reunite and break up again. However, last year they announced plans to marry.

In 1995, TLC filed bankruptcy, claiming $3.5 million in liabilities and less than $1 million in assets, even as its second album, "CrazySexy-Cool," was released and sold more than 10 million copies. The group squared matters with its creditors and acquired new management, but it would be four years before it could release another album. Despite the gap—an eternity in the fickle pop market—the group returned with the multiplatinum "Fanmail" in 1999 and two No. 1 singles, "No Scrubs" and "Unpretty," which enhanced TLC's artistic credibility.

Yet the group's comeback was blighted by infighting. Lopes canceled or missed interviews and television appearances, and sent a letter to the group's label threatening to quit TLC. Fed up with their bandmate's erratic behavior, Watkins and Thomas described her as "evil" in an interview. Lopes shot back by saying she was the group's true creative force, even though she received only a handful of co-writing credits on "Fanmail." She challenged the band members to put out solo albums and let fans determine who was most popular. But her own solo album, "Supernova," flopped commercially overseas last year and was not released domestically.

In recent months, Lopes reportedly signed a solo deal with Suge Knight's Death Row label to put out another solo project under the pseudonym "N.I.N.A." (New Identity Not Applicable). She also helped start the group Blaque, an R&B trio that had the hit "Bring It All to Me."

Yet TLC had reportedly reconvened in the studio to work on a new album.

"Every group goes through stuff," Thomas said in an interview last year. "You have to agree to disagree. . . . I can't see a breakup. If there is one, it's far away."

....

The beats that changed music
Jam Master Jay's spinning created blueprint for rap

NOV. 3, 2002

When Run-DMC disc jockey Jason "Jam Master Jay" Mizell was shot to death [*Oct. 30, 2002*] in his hometown of Queens, N.Y., hip-hop lost one of its greatest ambassadors, a deejay whose mastery made him the Jimi Hendrix of the turntables.

Hip-hop wasn't invented by Run-DMC, but the New York City trio did more than any single group to bring the new sound of urban America to the rest of the world. Without them, the current popularity of such hardcore rappers as Jay-Z and Eminem, or rap-rockers Kid Rock and Limp Bizkit, would be unimaginable. Before that, they set the stage for the mainstream acceptance of such breakthrough acts as the Beastie Boys and Public Enemy.

"Run-DMC is our [hip-hop's] Beatles," said Public Enemy's Chuck D. Jam Master Jay "was the glue that makes Run-DMC click. Jam Master Jay is directly responsible for Public Enemy."

Run-DMC co-founders Joseph "Run" Simmons and Darryl "DMC" McDaniels traded call-and-response rhymes like hip-hop's answer to soul duo Sam and Dave. While they would often finish each other's sentences with a fiercely urgent style that brought a new dimension to the rap MC's role, Jam Master Jay became a postmodern master of rhythm on the turntables, or "wheels of steel." Just as The Beatles and the Rolling Stones provided the blueprint for how a rock band should look and sound, Run-DMC were the template for all the hip-hop acts that followed their 1983 debut single. That hip-hop, rather than rock, is the voice of youth culture is unquestioned today, a transformation set in motion by Run-DMC's revolutionary music.

Jam Master Jay played a crucial role in blazing the new sound and sensibility. He wasn't the first deejay to fashion monster grooves by scratching a needle back and forth on vinyl records, but he became the first hip-hop deejay to be widely heard across America because of Run-DMC's success in translating what was essentially party music into million-selling albums that were perceived as artistic statements on par with the most ambitious rock releases. Jay blended crushing beats—packing all the wallop of the hardest heavy metal or punk records—with an uncanny feel for arrangement and space. He popularized the "break beat," prolonging the most danceable parts of old funk and soul records, and his prowess was celebrated on several of Run-DMC's finest works.

"Jay's like King Midas, as I was told/Everything that he touched turned to gold," the group declared on its 1986 hit "Peter Piper."

Rapping on records

"He was one of the best deejays as far as interacting with the rappers on record," said Chicago deejay-producer the Legendary Traxster. "Until him, and even after him, I never heard anybody be so much of a part of the records as he was. You'll have deejays scratching on the records, but with him, it was like he was rapping almost."

Indeed, Jay's turntables were like a third voice on Run-DMC's albums, and it was Jay's beats as much as Run-DMC's rhymes that revolutionized rap music in the '80s.

"We never liked R&B because it was soft," Jay once said in a

Tribune interview. "I used to scratch [Aerosmith's] 'Walk this Way' when I was deejaying in the parks. We had routines off that guitar riff, just repeating it over and over. It had nothing to do with the vocal, and everything to do with the beat, that guitar riff. We loved it because it was hard—harder than anything Michael Jackson was doing at the time."

Turntables became avant-garde instruments in the hands of deejays emceeing outdoor parties in public parks during the late '60s and '70s, particularly in the Bronx in New York.

These party maestros would plug a sound system into a streetlight power box, play records and rhyme over the beats while people danced.

Deejays such as Kool Herc, a native of Jamaica, began manipulating the beats on old funk records, extending the breaks and driving crowds into a frenzy out of which break-dancing was born.

By the early '80s, hip-hop began blasting out of the ghetto and reaching a wider audience in the form of 12-inch vinyl singles: the Sugarhill Gang's "Rapper's Delight," Kurtis Blow's "The Breaks," Grandmaster Flash and the Furious Five's "The Message." But the music was still regarded as a fad without the staying power of "real music" made on "real" instruments.

A fresh perspective

Run-DMC changed that perception. It was part of hip-hop's second-generation from Hollis, Queens, a black, working-class neighborhood of New York that gave the group a fresh perspective on the music that had started in the Bronx housing projects. Just out of high school, Simmons and McDaniels enlisted their younger, basketball-playing pal Mizell and cut their first single.

Despite an upbringing more privileged than many of their predecessors, their image was more "street" than anything the hip-hop world had seen before; just as punk had stripped rock of filigree a few years before, Run-DMC redefined hip-hop by cutting away its excesses.

Whereas the early hip-hop crews saw themselves as inner-city dandies (the Treacherous Three sported matching red leather outfits, the Furious Five resembled the Village People), Run-DMC members were "b-boys," with their unlaced gym shoes, warm-up suits and black fedoras. The music was just as tough: street-level reportage supported by mega beats that fused James Brown funk with Led Zeppelin metal.

The trio's first double-sided single, "It's Like That"/"Sucker MCs," was released in 1983 and signaled the start of a new era in hip-hop: These were masterpieces of minimalism, beats erupting from chasms of silence, unimpeded by the cheesy synthesizers and disco accoutrements that had cluttered previous hip-hop tracks, the rappers not just reciting rhymes but shouting them at each other.

If Run-DMC had made only that one single, their place in hip-hop history would have been assured. But they were only just beginning. Their self-titled debut album, released in 1984, was another landmark. Its accomplishment forced everyone to take notice, as Chuck D once said. "People didn't make hip-hop albums before then," he said. "It was a singles medium, and because of that it was never taken seriously. Then Run-DMC came along and put out an album with one great track after another. They made everything legit."

After that, Run-DMC knocked down one wall after another: first hip-hop group to go gold (500,000 copies sold), then platinum (1 million), then triple platinum. First to release three platinum albums in a row. First to appear on MTV, "American Bandstand" and the Grammy Awards. First on the cover of Rolling Stone and first to star in their own movie ("Krush Kroove," 1985).

Their 1985 album title, "King of Rock," proved prophetic. By the end of the decade, Run-DMC was as big and hard-hitting as any rock group in the land, and rappers would soon usurp rock 'n' rollers as the voice of youth culture. Run-DMC's 1986 masterpiece, "Raisin' Hell," laid the groundwork for rap-rock and resurrected Aerosmith's then-moribund career with the crossover hit "Walk This Way."

If there is a more powerful opening sequence in '80s rock or rap than that album's initial burst of "Peter Piper," "It's Tricky," "My Adidas" and "Walk This Way," I have yet to hear it. "Raisin' Hell" turned Run-DMC into hip-hop's first arena act, the toast of not just inner-city b-boys, but frat rats and suburban high schoolers across the land.

It was to be the trio's last major moment; they had brought hip-hop into the mainstream, then watched as new innovators exploited their breakthrough for commercial gain. "D.J. Jazzy Jeff and the Fresh

Prince got our pop audience, N.W.A. got our hardcore audience, so we got stuck in the middle," Jam Master Jay said in a 1990 interview. "But that's OK, because we're not restricted in what we can do anymore. We flow through everyone, every style."

Formidable live act

The albums became more sporadic, yet Run-DMC continued to be a formidable live act; they joined Aerosmith and Kid Rock on a major amphitheater tour last summer that played at the Tweeter Center in Tinley Park, but were at their best headlining in clubs, where their string of hits were slammed out with a still-joyous glee.

Throughout, Run-DMC resisted the commercial trend toward coarser imagery and rhymes that extolled violence or put down women and gays. Part of the timeless brilliance of Run-DMC's music was its inclusiveness; it spoke to both headbangers and hip-hoppers, blacks and whites.

That's why Jam Master Jay's violent death is more of a shock than the shootings of two other hip-hop giants, Tupac Shakur and the Notorious B.I.G.

"In the case of Tupac and Biggie, their music was so engulfed in violence that you would think that it just spilt over into reality," Traxster said. "But in Jam Master Jay's case, it just seemed like their music was so happy and positive, as far as reflecting the true nature of hip-hop entertainment, that it seems far more tragic for him to die in such a violent way."

Jam Master Jay left behind his wife, three children and a series of recordings that defined hip-hop as a force for positive change. His innovations left an indelible groove on the hip-hop world's consciousness. As Run's brother and hip-hop mogul Russell Simmons said: "For nearly 20 years, Run-DMC has been the closest thing to gospel artists that the contemporary music community has had. They talked about God and their higher selves, the importance of staying away from drugs, and generally inspirational and uplifting subject matter. They represented everything good and positive about hip-hop."

....

Kanye West's rise: From South Side to top of charts

FEB. 11, 2004

t wasn't enough for South Side native Kanye West to emerge as one of the hottest, most respected producers in pop music in the last few years. He was determined to become a rapper and star in his own right, as well, and not even a nearly fatal accident could stand in his way.

In October 2002, he was in a car crash in Los Angeles that shattered his face. With his jaw wired shut, his veins saturated with pain killers and infection-fighting drugs, West recorded the vocals for "Through the Wire," the song that set him on the path to recovery, and to his first solo album, "College Dropout" (Roc-A-Fella), out this week.

"I was mad because I was not being taken seriously as a rapper for a long time," says West, who headlines two concerts at House of Blues [*Feb. 11, 2004*]. "Whether it was because I didn't have a larger-than-life persona, or I was perceived as the guy who made beats, I was disrespected as a rapper. I was making good beats before I made good raps, but I've been rapping for longer. It's hard to rap, man. You can't accidentally rap well, but you can accidentally make a good beat. Accidents—weird, right? An accident changed my life."

As West regained consciousness in a Los Angeles hospital, "lines started coming into my head," he says.

> *How do you console my mom or give her light support*
> *Telling her your son's on life support*

For West's mother, Donda West, an English professor at Chicago State University, the call came at 5 a.m. that her son had been in a terrible accident. She was on a plane to Los Angeles three hours later. "I never thought he'd die," she says. "I had to push those thoughts out of my mind."

She stayed with him in Los Angeles while he recovered. "He came up with a healthy respect for God, but the accident had a profound im-

Kanye West raps at the House of Blues Feb. 11, 2004.
E. JASON WAMBSGANS

pact on him," she says. "He particularly knows that by the grace of God he was spared, and spared for a particular purpose. I've never witnessed him as a card-carrying Christian—he's just too hip-hop for that—but I think he has an appreciation for the fact that he could have been dead, and he feels there are angels watching him and protecting him."

For the producer-turned-rapper, "Through the Wire" was a turning point. "That song made all the difference," he says. "It opened up people to hearing what else this guy could do. I thought even if the song didn't blow up, it would go down in history as one of the best hip-hop songs ever because it was real."

More than a year later, Donda West says her son is still recovering from his injuries. "The initial healing process took about two months, and it was excruciatingly painful," she says. "The process since has been slow. But he couldn't be kept down."

Until the success of "Through the Wire" and the release of "College Dropout," West was best known as a beats maestro whose imprint is on hits by Jay-Z, Britney Spears, Mos Def, Talib Kweli and Alicia Keys, among dozens of others. The hit he wrote and produced for Chicago rapper Twista, "Slow Jamz," was in the top 5, and Twista's album, "Kamikaze," debuted at No. 1. "College Dropout" is expected to follow suit.

Product of South Side

West was born 26 years ago on the South Side to Donda and Ray West, a Black Panther who became an award-winning photojournalist and a pastoral marriage counselor. West's parents separated when he was 11 months old, and were divorced when he was 3, but the boy maintained a relationship with his father and often spent summers with him. Donda West nurtured her son in myriad ways, encouraging his gifts as a visual artist, for which he eventually earned a college scholarship, and budding poet.

"We were coming back from a short vacation in Michigan when he was 5 and he composed a poem in the back seat," she says. "The one line that sticks with me is 'the trees are melting black.' It was late fall, and the trees had no leaves. He saw how those limbs were etched against the sky, and he described them the way a poet would."

Young Kanye spent a year with his mother in China while she was teaching English at Nanching University. The 10-year-old would make money by break-dancing on the streets for the locals. "He was an entrepreneur even then," she says.

While attending Polaris High School on the South Side, he struck up an acquaintance with the producer No I.D., who was then working with a future star named Common Sense (who later shortened his name to Common). Kanye would have his mother drive him to No I.D.'s house, where he'd soak up knowledge at the producer's basement studio. At 15, Kanye acquired his first sampling keyboard. Between the tutorials from No I.D., whom West would refer to as his "almost stepfather," and incessant tinkering, rapping and beatmaking in his bedroom, West developed his skills as a producer and rapper. His first break came in 1998 when he sold a beat to Atlanta producer Jermaine Dupri for his "Life in 1472" album, and West's life as a college student who would follow in his mother's multiple-degree footsteps became an afterthought.

"It was drummed into my head that college is the ticket to a good life," Donda West says, "but some career goals don't require college. For Kanye to make an album called 'College Dropout,' it was more about having the guts to embrace who you are, rather than following the path society has carved out for you. And that's what Kanye did."

Soon the non-stop traffic in the fledgling producer's apartment studio in Chicago became too much for his landlord, and in 2001 West packed his bags for the East Coast, first settling in Newark, N.J., and finally a $3,000-a-month apartment in Hoboken, across the river from New York City.

The man with the beat

There he began supplying beats to some of the biggest names in hip-hop, including Jay-Z, who pried open the door for a deal at the Roc-A-Fella label. "I was definitely intimidated, because Jay-Z is a superstar, and one of my idols," West says. "But even if he told me one of my beats stinks, it wouldn't have crushed me. I still got real high self-esteem."

The mix of a down-to-earth Midwestern work ethic and a self-confidence bordering on arrogance is what makes West such an arresting new figure in rap. "College Dropout" is his warts-and-all story, told from an outsider perspective, the street-smart kid who doesn't pretend to be a gangster, gangbanger or high roller flaunting his diamonds and luxury cars. Instead, he works for minimum wage at a retail store, the would-be ladies man who dares to "talk about God" even though it might mean his "record won't get played." And when he sinks into the world of "crunk" (southern, bass heavy style) funk, he does it with a sense of humor, belittling himself for succumbing to temptation: "Always said if I rapped I'd say something significant but now I'm rapping about money, hoes and rims again."

He's a deft wordsmith, a rapper with the ability to change the direction of his flow at the drop of a pun. "College Dropout" blows out hip-hop borders with string sections, gospel choirs and the speeded-up old-school beats that have become West's production signature. "I saved the best tracks for my own album," West says with a chuckle. "Rap is my first love, but there are so many other facets of rapping that I wanted as part of this record. The main thing is message and melody, even more so than rapping. I do as much singing on this record as I do rapping."

In tracks such as "I'll Fly Away," "Two Words," "All Falls Down" and "We Don't Care," West offers a critique and celebration of a world defined by hip-hop values. "College Dropout" is the portrait of a young African-American struggling with new responsibilities in the guise of an ambitious and vividly arranged album that invokes hip-hop excess, soul beats, gospel hosannahs, classical orchestrations and pop sizzle. It's a world where "Jesus walks" alongside frustrated crack dealers, a world more real, in other words, than that portrayed in many hip-hop records striving for chart dominance.

"It was important for me to rap about a real person, instead of a cartoon," West says. "I grew into this person, and that's who I am as a rapper. It's like everybody in the room is wearing gold jewelry, and I walk in with a suit on. That's the best way to get noticed."

....

Meditation in progress: Producer Rick Rubin on working with Johnny Cash, Beastie Boys and more

JULY 4, 2004

The sign greeting visitors at Rick Rubin's mansion in Hollywood Hills advises, "Meditation in progress . . . Silence . . . Please remove shoes."

Something doesn't add up. What's with the becalmed message from a producer who is no stranger to mayhem, at least on record? Rubin cut a swath through the '80s by producing some of the most explicit and confrontational rock, rap and comedy records ever made by Slayer, Danzig, Public Enemy, the early "Fight for Your Right to Party" Beastie Boys and Andrew "Dice" Clay. Even Rubin's much-acclaimed work with Johnny Cash kicked off in 1994 with a song called "Delia's Gone," in which the narrator calmly kills his lover.

From a distance, the media-shy producer can cut an imposing figure with his shaggy, ZZ Top-length beard, ubiquitous shades and burly frame. But reclining on a couch in his vast Mediterranean-style villa that overlooks Sunset Boulevard, Rubin comes off as a gracious rock 'n' roll Buddha: bare feet, soft blue eyes, and a tan the shade of a lightly toasted English muffin.

Incense from a candle wafts through a vast array of books, videos and compact discs in the sun-drenched library where he sits. In the next room is the grand piano that Benmont Tench played when Rubin recorded Cash's jaw-dropping vocal performance of Nine Inch Nail's "Hurt" in the mansion's recording studio. The only even marginally intimidating feature of the house is a slightly surly black Hungarian sheep dog, the same mop-haired species featured on the cover of Beck's "Odelay" album.

Born on Long Island in 1963, Rubin grew up the only child of upper middle-class parents who encouraged his preoccupation with music.

No obstacles

"I've never taken any drugs in my life, I've never been high," Rubin says, his voice as mellow and measured as a yoga instructor's. "So music has always been my other world, the way I've connected to other realms. If the balance in music feels good, it's the same feeling you get from a sunset, or a beautiful piece of architecture, or a cloud formation that takes your breath away. That's really the job: To touch that through music."

Rubin was studying philosophy and then film and television at New York University when he began playing guitar in a punk band and producing hip-hop records out of his dorm room. At a party in 1984, he met Run-D.M.C.'s manager, Russell Simmons, and the rising rap mogul was taken aback.

Rubin had produced "It's Yours," a hot-selling independent rap single by T. La Rock and Jazzy Jay, and "Simmons couldn't believe it was a white guy who produced it," Rubin says with a laugh. "He said, 'That's the blackest sounding record I'd ever heard.'" The pair formed Def Jam Records, soon to become the most powerful imprint in hip-hop. Rubin's productions for LL Cool J ("Radio"), Run-D.M.C. ("Raisin' Hell"), the Beastie Boys ("Licensed to Ill") and Public Enemy ("Yo Bum Rush the Show") began rap's two-decade-long dominance of the pop mainstream.

LL Cool J at Allstate Arena in October 2002.
ANTHONY ROBERT

"Rap records in those days were very slick—typically disco records musically with a guy rapping over the top," Rubin says. "But when Run-D.M.C. came along, it was black punk rock. They didn't invent that sound—it was what you heard at the clubs if you went out. Our approach to record-making was to document that sound. Our inexperience helped. We didn't know how to make slick records. But pretty soon everyone in hip-hop wanted to do what we were doing."

Rubin remains oblivious to engineering concerns but he did create the brutally terse, testosterone-charged musical beds on these early records with his limited knowledge of keyboards, drum machines and sampling. Later, as he began working with self-contained rock bands such as the Red Hot Chili Peppers and Slayer, he served as more of an adviser and song guru.

"The key to every record I work on is the songs," he says. "I spend a great deal of time in rehearsal with bands. Before we go into the studio, we sit around just talking about songs and working on songs, and shaping them and molding them and going over the lyrics and melody—what happens if this part were shorter? or if it were cut? or if

it were longer?—and really playing around with the music. We're starting from this foundation that is really unshakable."

Taboo topics

He produced albums rife with explicit imagery: Slayer sang about serial killers and Nazi torturers, Danzig dabbled in Satan worship, Public
Enemy extolled militant black power. But Rubin didn't engage his artists in moral or political debates.

"My relationship with the artists is that I fall in love with the art,"
he says. "The content doesn't matter so much to me. I will say that I
am drawn to edgy content because it entertains me. But there have
been examples of bands saying things that I am radically opposed to,
but I have no trouble producing or supporting them. I believe in free
speech, and I believe people should say what they want to say. How
successful they are artistically is my only concern. And bands like
Slayer or Public Enemy, no matter who they upset, I thought were
extremely good at what they did. I was a fan, otherwise I wouldn't
have worked on their records."

Early in his productions, Rubin had very specific ideas about how
songs should sound, and clung stubbornly to his beliefs. Along the way,
he alienated bands like the Beastie Boys, who never worked with Rubin
again, despite selling millions of copies of their "Licensed to Ill" debut.
He parted ways with the equally headstrong Simmons, and moved to
California in 1988 where he started his own label, Def American (later
known as simply American).

Rubin learned from his missteps and began focusing on creating a
space where artists could feel secure enough to take risks. When the
Chili Peppers came to his home studio in 1991, they were still perceived as punk-funk party band. Because of that reputation, singer Anthony Kiedis was reluctant to show his bandmates the more personal
songs he had written, such as "Under the Bridge," a wrenching ballad
about his struggles with heroin addiction.

"They were a narrowly defined band, and my job was to break down
those walls, to show them that a song didn't have to fit inside a box to
make the record," Rubin says. "Once Anthony felt comfortable enough
to play that song, to sing those words for the rest of the band, the

band loved it. That's when I realized a big part of my job is creating an environment for an artist to feel safe enough to be really vulnerable. Because those are the compelling moments, the moments that touch us and resonate with us."

"Under the Bridge" became the Chili Peppers' breakthrough hit, and set the stage for the band's string of commercial successes through the last decade. Since, Rubin has helped path-breaking bands such as System of a Down and Mars Volta establish their sound.

"We discovered that Rick's not only this enigmatic figure with a beard, but an actual gentle human being who likes a lot of things we do," says Mars Volta singer Cedric Bixler. "Most producers will tear you to shreds to the point where you don't want to play your instru-

---

Rubin's greatest productions

- LL COOL J, "Radio" (1985)
- RUN-D.M.C., "Raisin' Hell" (1986)
- SLAYER, "Reign in Blood" (1986)
- BEASTIE BOYS, "Licensed to Ill" (1986)
- DANZIG, "Danzig" (1988)
- SLAYER, "South of Heaven" (1988)
- TROUBLE, "Trouble" (1990)
- RED HOT CHILI PEPPERS, "BloodSugarSexMagik" (1991)
- JOHNNY CASH, "American Recordings" (1994)
- TOM PETTY, "Wildflowers" (1994)
- JOHNNY CASH, "Unchained" (1996)
- TOM PETTY, "Echo" (1999)
- RED HOT CHILI PEPPERS, "Californication" (1999)
- JOHNNY CASH, "American III: Solitary Man" (2000)
- SYSTEM OF A DOWN, "Toxicity" (2001)
- SAUL WILLIAMS, "Amethyst Rock Star (2001)
- JOHNNY CASH, "American IV: The Man Comes Around" (2003)
- MARS VOLTA, "De-Loused in the Comatorium" (2003)

ment. But Rick knows how to criticize constructively and tell you when things aren't working. He's a great communicator."

Along the way, Rubin had his share of failures. Worthy bands such as Trouble and the Four Horsemen were commercial stiffs. One album that he cherishes—Tom Petty's "Wildflowers"—coincided with Petty's decline as a major radio force. And Mick Jagger's 1993 solo album, "Wandering Spirit," still makes Rubin cringe. "Just about any time something would start sounding good, it would make him uncomfortable," Rubin says of the Rolling Stones singer. "I guess because anything good reminded him of the Stones, and he wanted to shy away from that on his own record."

Union with Cash

Rubin's experience with another iconic figure—Cash—was far more satisfying, and in many ways a career peak for both men. When Rubin met the singer, Cash was on the verge of quitting the recording business, convinced that his music no longer had relevance.

"I asked him before I signed, 'What would you do with me that was different from anybody else?'" Cash told the Tribune in 1996. "And he said, 'I want to hear your best songs. I want you to sing every song you ever wanted to record.' So I started showing up in his living room with my guitar, and he had a microphone set up. I brought a list of songs and he brought a list. There was no clock on the wall to watch, no red light telling us this was a 'take.' I did 80 songs I love, and week after week we just recorded them all. I remember after a few of those sessions, I did [an adaptation of the traditional songs] 'Cowboy's Prayer'/'Oh Bury Me Not' and he said, 'I want it exactly like that.'

"And it was a revelation, because I had always wanted to do an album with just my guitar. I remember 25 years ago telling Marty Robbins I wanted to do an album called 'Late and Alone.' But it never felt right. Doing that record was a dream come true."

That record, "American Recordings," was the first of four Cash-Rubin collaborations released over the next nine years. A boxed set of outtakes, "Unearthed," was released last winter, and a fifth and final studio album—much of it recorded in the months between the death

of Cash's wife, June Carter Cash, and the singer's own death last year—
is expected to be released this year *[2004]*.

"He was in a funny place," Rubin says of meeting Cash. "I know
he was thinking that recording didn't feel important to him anymore.
That change, of all of sudden making music that seemed vital to people
again, got him excited about writing songs, and making records, and
taking things forward."

The sessions also put the once-notorious Rubin in a new light.
T Bone Burnett, the renowned producer who is working on the
soundtrack for a forthcoming movie about Cash, says, "When Nashville and the industry weren't interested in him at all, Rubin recorded
this guy like he'd never been recorded before. I thought it was a great
way to go, the idea of sitting around in a living room, Cash playing
tunes with people listening. Rick performed a great service for all of us."

If there's a tinge of surprise in Burnett's voice as he says this, it's
perhaps because such empathy wasn't expected from the producer
who shaped the early careers of Public Enemy and Slayer, and who
just worked on the most recent album by new-metal rabble-rousers
Slipknot.

"To me, most of the things I've worked on fit together not necessarily in a genre, but in how far left of center they are," Rubin says. "That's
the kind of music that really excites me. Johnny Cash was out on the
fringe when I began working with him. He's this lauded figure, but he
didn't fit anymore. The early days of hip-hop didn't fit with what else
was going on in music. And Slayer was a category all its own. They are
all fringe artists who are so good at what they do that they transcend
the fringe."

From Lupe Fiasco to Kanye West, Chicago rappers shun thug themes to explore religious faith, paying the rent and . . . skateboarding?

JULY 2, 2006

Lupe Fiasco's 122 pounds swim inside his baggy t-shirt and even baggier jeans. He is wire-rimmed, smooth-faced, small-boned and 24 years old, though he could pass for 18. Yet he walks on the Metro stage poised to pounce, and it's no pose: This seemingly bookish pushover is actually a 4th-degree black belt in karate. And he is an even more accomplished verbal combatant; he has what the hip-hop heads call great "flow," an ability to improvise complex rhymes with an astonishing dexterity that suggests a jazz soloist in flight.

The capacity Metro audience, which has been primed by a long weekend of Grade-A hip-hop as part of the annual Chicago Rocks festival, greets Fiasco's arrival with its loudest cheers of the night. Among dozens of striving underground hip-hop artists, Fiasco is the star-on-the-verge, a West Side kid whose debut, "Lupe Fiasco's Food & Liquor," is one of the summer's most anticipated albums.

When he performs his recent single "Kick Push," it plays like an anthem, even though its subject matter is unconventional by hip-hop standards. It's not about hustling in the 'hood, but about skateboarding, of all things. In the first verse, the rapper talks about busting a lip after a fall and talking with a lisp. But soon a broader theme emerges: a tale of escape and freedom. "Just a rebel looking for a place to be," Fiasco chants, the sampled horns swelling like a cool breeze blowing at his back. "So let's kick . . . and push . . . and coast."

It's immediately evident why Fiasco, born Wasalu Muhammed Jaco, is the fastest-rising new voice in Chicago hip-hop. Along with Rhymefest and a handful of other up-and-coming rappers, he represents the next wave in a new era defined by the multimillion-selling

Che Smith, aka Rhymefest, in the Chicago Tribune studio on Aug. 5, 2010.
NANCY STONE

albums of Kanye West. No matter how one regards West's outspoken-ness, his cockiness, there is no denying his impact. His records not only sell, they have changed the way mainstream hip-hop looks and sounds.

West grew up middle-class on the South Side, and he's made his mark not by rhyming about guns, gangs, hookers and drugs, but about his real-life experiences working minimum-wage jobs and his con-flicted feelings about God. By blending cannily chosen samples with an orchestra of instruments, he has made some of the most sumptuous and groundbreaking pop records of the new millennium, and given Chicago hip-hop something it has never had in the mainstream: a sound, a sensibility, an undeniable presence.

Hip-hop has been pop music's universal language for at least a decade. But Chicago has struggled to make itself heard, a bench-warmer in a musical game dominated first by New York, then Los Angeles and lately Atlanta, New Orleans and Houston. Though there have been flashes of commercial success from the Chicago rap scene in the past, most notably in the mid-'90s with Common, Da Brat, Twista, Crucial Conflict and Do or Die, it wasn't until West's "The

College Dropout" arrived in 2004 that the city produced a true commercial heavyweight.

West has a reputation for arrogance that belies how generous he
has been in sharing the spotlight. Even though he moved from the
South Side to the East Coast in 2001 to establish himself as a top-
tier producer for Jay-Z, Alicia Keys and other pop and rap acts before
starting his solo career, West continues to work with Chicago artists
and rejuvenate or kick-start their careers.

"I did move to New York to make it, because that's where the music
industry is," he told the Tribune after his debut album was released.
"If you want to be the best basketball player in the world, you can't stay
in Europe, China or South America. You've got to move to the United
States and open the doors, possibly. That's what I'm trying to do: open
doors for Chicago. But I had to go to New York to find the key."

In the last two years he played a major role in the biggest commercial successes yet for two stalwart if underappreciated denizens of the
local hip-hop scene: He wrote and produced Twista's 2004 hit "Slow
Jamz" and he collaborated on Common's acclaimed 2005 album "Be."

"Kanye took something we were all doing and he did all the right
things to make it popular," says the longtime South Side producer Dion
"No. I.D." Wilson, who produced Common's first three albums and is
the executive producer on Rhymefest's forthcoming album, "Blue Collar" (J Records). "His view was from the perspective of a middle-class
or lower-middle-class guy, and he proved it can work, it can be popular.
It doesn't have to be all about the 'hood. Common and I pushed that
pile, and then we ran into a few obstacles, and Kanye took over and
pushed it even further. Now the door is wide open for people like Lupe
Fiasco and Rhymefest, who are talking about some of the same things
in their own way."

Rhymefest, born Che Smith 28 years ago on the South Side, became friends with West long before he was a star. Rhyme-fest co-
wrote West's transcendent 2004 single, "Jesus Walks," and West had
a hand in producing Rhymefest's "Blue Collar." Yet the relationship
wasn't always smooth.

"Me and Kanye almost had a fight when we first met," Rhymefest
says. "I thought he was the most arrogant [jerk] ever."

But the two eventually became friends and collaborators. "I help Kanye with rhymes, Kanye helps me with rhythm and catchy choruses," Rhymefest says. "We have two different missions, but the same challenge. We blend."

Rhymefest's first album, an independent release in 2001, was produced by West. It was the work of promising, if callow, artists still searching for a distinctive identity. Rhymefest had won free-style competitions, including a now legendary conquest over a then-unknown rapper named Eminem at Cincinnati's Skribble Jam in 1997, but he wasn't much of a songwriter yet. West had skills as a producer, but still wasn't taken seriously as a rapper.

"Jesus Walks" changed those perceptions, though not immediately. It first showed up as a Rhymefest performance on a demo tape he was shopping to record labels. Then he performed it at Metro at the first Chicago Rocks concert in 2003 and eventually was signed to a record deal because of it. A year later, the song became the centerpiece of West's first album, and in the summer of 2004 shattered boundaries at commercial video channels and radio stations. Here was a gospel-stoked anthem that wrestled openly with questions of faith, a conversation with God set to music. West had to fight to get the song on his album and spent $1 million of his own money to craft three distinct videos for it. His faith in the song paid off: It became a pop hit. Though the song established West as a star, he did not take for granted Rhymefest's role in it.

On the set for one of the "Jesus Walks" videos, Rhymefest and West found themselves sharing a quiet moment on a hill overlooking Los Angeles. "He wanted to race up that hill, and after we got to the top, we sat down, just two brothers on a hill overlooking the lights of L.A.," Rhymefest recalls. "And he said, 'I'm so thankful where I'm at, and I'm so thankful to have you in my life, and to have good people around me. We should bow our heads and thank God.' And we prayed. That was the first time I ever saw him humble himself for anything."

The moment still resonates with Rhymefest because he himself had a spiritual awakening when he was a teenager. Unlike West and Common, who grew up the sons of educators in stable homes, Rhymefest as a boy knew only a life of chaos in the notorious Jeffrey Manor projects.

He was born a day after his mother turned 16. He saw his father three times while growing up, and his mother struggled with drug addiction and abusive boyfriends.

"No one knows how it feels when you're in 8th grade and a girl comes up to you and says, 'My brother sold your mama crack,' in front of the whole class," Rhymefest says. He was lured by gangs, but a concerned member of the Vice Lords took him to an Islamic temple before he could join. "I heard the imam speak, and it made me cry," the rapper says. "He was speaking of community and brotherhood and love, and I saw men all around me who had their boys with them. I saw these men in this holy place, with their shoes off, prostrated before God. I said, 'That's the kind of father I want to be.'"

Now he shares a house in Indianapolis with his mother, who has been clean for years; a teenage sister; and his young son from a brief marriage, Solomon. Rhymefest worked countless jobs to support them, eventually becoming a teacher and youth counselor. He could have easily written an entire album about his close proximity to the gang life where he grew up.

"Discovering God was my way out," he says. "You know why some rappers glorify drug dealing? They don't tell the whole story. They don't talk about the lives destroyed by it. The children left at home who eat paint chips off the wall, that go to school hungry. They aren't telling the whole story, and I hate that."

Instead, Rhymefest seeks what he calls a "balance" on his first major-label album. "Blue Collar" is a tour of a complex personality and his struggle to rise above his upbringing. Humor is its most potent weapon. "I'm ahead of my time/But behind on my rent," he raps on "Devil's Pie." "Asked Kanye for money/Just to pay for my gas bill."

Struggling to pay the rent is not a subject often encountered in a Top-40 song, but "Devil's Pie" has a few things going in its favor—a smart if unlikely guitar-based sample culled from a song by garage-rockers the Strokes, a snappy chorus and Rhymefest's undeniable charisma. The rhymes are detailed, seductive and witty. Most of all, they ring true.

"It's a tough sell, because you know how narrow radio can be," says Carolyn Williams, vice president of urban marketing at Rhymefest's record label. "He doesn't fit a particular format. But what he's doing isn't a novelty; it's genuine, from the heart. It hit home when he said to me, 'In my neighborhood, there may be three guys on the corner selling drugs, but across the street there'll be six other people at the bus stop going to work.' His music gets that idea across, and people will be able to relate."

Lupe Fiasco certainly can. Like Rhymefest, he grew up in an urban war zone; his West Side home at Madison Terrace was surrounded by drive-bys and drug deals. An older brother ran with a gang. His father, an engineer and former Green Beret, made sure young Wasalu Jaco learned how to defend himself before moving his son to south suburban Harvey.

"I was throwing grenades and firing AK-47s [at shooting ranges] when I was 5," Fiasco says. "My father told me to respect weapons. I learned to respect them so much that I never wanted one. I did martial arts. If I had to fight, I could defend myself. But it also taught me how to see when a fight is coming and how to defuse it. I learned how to think. That's the most important thing my mother and father taught us."

Fiasco's intellect served him well. He studied classical music and jazz, and initially disdained hip-hop. But his ability to string words together into long, stream-of-consciousness poems eventually became undeniable. He and a high school friend jerry-rigged a recording studio in his father's basement. "My junior year in high school, we decided we were going to be rappers or nothing," he says. After a series of talent contests and showcases, Fiasco and his crew were briefly signed to a major-label deal fresh out of high school. When it came time to cut a record, they struck a gangsta pose. Fiasco wore chains, bracelets and expensive watches, the "bling" bought by record-deal money.

Then came a personal reckoning.

"We had a song out about cocaine, guns and women, and I would go to a record store and look at it and think, 'What are you doing?'" he says. "I felt like a hypocrite. I was acting like this rapper who would never be judged, and I had to destroy that guy. Because what Lupe Fiasco says on this microphone is going to come back to Wasalu Jaco. When the music cuts off, you have to go home and live with what you say."

Fiasco had been around Islam all his life, but now he began to take its tenets seriously. Four years later, the only jewelry he wears is a $50 wristwatch. Along the way he also lost the fake gangsta attitude and vowed that any deal he signed would maintain his creative integrity. He wanted to make records that reflected his vision and views, not those of record-industry insiders trying to manufacture a hit for an unknown act.

Making the rounds of East Coast labels after his first record deal imploded, Fiasco forged a relationship with West and Jay-Z, the renowned rapper and hip-hop mogul. A deal with Jay-Z's Roc-A-Fella label fell through at the 11th hour, and by the time Fiasco turned 22 in February 2004, another major-label contract (with Arista Records) went down the tubes when label President Antonio "L.A." Reid was ousted. But that same month West's debut album arrived, on Roc-A-Fella, and eventually changed Fiasco's fortunes.

Last summer, he released a song called "Conflict Diamonds" on his Web site, and it quickly passed into hip-hop lore. The song's hook was based on West's then-current Shirley Bassey-sampling single "Diamonds Are Forever," but Fiasco's version was harder-hitting in every way. Rather than a benign ode to precious gems, he turned it into a protest song reflecting his own beliefs about the high price of bling. He raged about the way the diamond trade satisfies materialist Westerners, including himself, while financing bloody civil wars in Africa.

The track stirred a minor Internet sensation. West, coincidentally or not, later added a politically charged verse of his own to his remixed version and the song appeared as "Diamonds From Sierra Leone" on his multimillion-selling 2005 album, "Late Registration." He also invited Fiasco to perform on another song from the album, "Touch the Sky," an even bigger hit than "Diamonds."

By then, Fiasco was neck-deep into recording his debut album for Atlantic Records via a deal with his label, 1st and 15th. It's an extraordinary work, a showcase for a lithe rapper intent on pushing the boundaries of how a hip-hop song can sound and what it can say. The album's executive producer was none other than Jay-Z, but he was more of an overseer than a hands-on decision-maker. The bulk of the tracks were recorded with Fiasco's homegrown producers, Soundtrakk and Pro.

"I don't record in New York, and I have no lust to be there or in L.A.," Fiasco says. "I'm from Chicago, and I'm meant to tell the Chicago experience. You can't tell that experience if you don't absorb Chicago, if you don't know what Chicago is about. I ride around the city with a bunch of beats [pre-recorded rhythm tracks] and I write."

Like the albums of West, Common and Rhymefest, "Lupe Fiasco's Food & Liquor" creates its own world, one that sounds like the city that inspired it.

"If you just reach back to what Chicago's roots are-jazz, blues, soul-you can hear that in the rap records that have come out of here," Fiasco says. "Kanye and Common definitely have that. And I think I have that. New York is fast, fast, fast. And if you record there, you're going to get caught up in that. And then before you know it, your music becomes something else and it has no longevity. People can't relate to it."

But it's more than just a sound. It's also sensibility, a feeling—regular guys rapping about everyday life.

"They were trying to make Lupe do club stuff back when he signed his first deal," says the producer Juvenal "PNS" Robles Jr. of the long-time Chicago production team the Molemen, which put together the Chicago Rocks hip-hop showcases. "But what's his big success? A motivational song about skateboarding."

"And look at Kanye's success," says PNS' Molemen collaborator, Edward "Panik" Zamudio. "He represented something new at a time when guys who got shot nine times were getting signed to record deals. Kanye starts rapping about Jesus, and people were like, 'Wait a second,' until the song blew up."

Robles and Zamudio express concern that, if the Rhymefest and Fiasco albums become hits this year [2006], the Chicago scene will be mined by the mainstream music industry for sound-alikes and copycats rather than original talent. But for now, they're pleased that after all these years, Chicago hip-hop has forged a distinctive international identity.

Fiasco nods in assent. "There's a certain vein in Chicago, these regular dudes who are really, really skilled MCs, who can talk about the most abstract or mundane subjects and still make it fit. It competes against what would come out of the mouth of a Nas or a Young Jeezey for entertainment value, and it's cool. We definitely have the ability and talent to make the uncool cool."

At the Chicago Rocks concert, the wire-rimmed nerd is a star. "So let's kick . . . and push . . . and coast." Hundreds of voices shout the words at him. Lupe Fiasco's eyes are lethal slits, his muscles taut, like he's about to break out some martial-arts skills. It's just a setup. Like any great MC, he knows how to build anticipation and deliver a punch line that speaks volumes about who he is and where he's from.

"Hip-hop is back!" he declares. "It wears glasses."

....

Kid Sister grows up

Hanging with stars or rewiring music genres, Melisa Young holds onto her suburban roots

DEC. 30, 2009

Melisa Young—better known in the pop world as Kid Sister—has just gotten off a plane and stepped inside her North Side apartment for the first time in weeks.

"It's nice to be home," Young says with a laugh as she picks up the phone to start this interview, her last bit of business before she goes to sleep. She says her apartment is cold, so the interview is done under the covers of her bed with her coat on. She's just completed an exhausting month of promoting her debut album, "Ultraviolet" (Downtown/Universal), one of the most talked-about albums of the year with its cutting-edge merger of hip-hop, dance music and pop.

"Last night I had dinner with Questlove of the Roots, and he played a little DJ set in the meatpacking district (in New York)," she says. "It was very yuppie, but a lot of fun. I danced around in my underwear."

For some performers, an underwear dance might connote something provocative. But Young makes it sound anything but, more like a bunch of girlfriends enjoying themselves at a slumber party. "I am a nerd," she says. "I'm not a celebrity. Being a celebrity is an attitude, but Chicago is way more low-key about that. People don't grow up here thinking they're going to be the next big star."

Melisa Young, aka Kid Sister, in her Chicago apartment in December 2009.
NANCY STONE

Yet in the last few years she's become one of the brightest new faces in club music. She's collaborated with artists such as Kanye West, Pharrell Williams and Gnarls Barkley's Cee-Lo Green, all of whom requested to work with her. She made her first network TV appearance a few weeks ago on "Late Night With Jimmy Fallon," showing not a hint of stage fright as she frolicked in the audience while performing an energetic version of her single "Right Hand Hi." Already a veteran of main-stage appearances at festivals such as Coachella in California and Lollapalooza in Grant Park, she is now preparing for a new year of heavy touring worldwide.

Through it all, Young remains unfazed, a budding pop star who still remembers very well where she came from: a blue-collar upbringing in south suburban Markham and years of trying to squeeze music making between shifts clerking at retail stores. At one point she was holding down three jobs and catching catnaps on breaks while fending off warning notices from utility companies because she couldn't keep up with her bill payments.

"I don't think I realized this was my full-time job until about nine

months ago," says Young, 29, of her music career. "I was going to release my album last year, and then I took it back to work on it some
more because it wasn't exactly the way I wanted it. That's when it sunk
in: This is what I do. It took a long time. I'd always played it off as,
'These are my little songs; it's not a big deal. It's just a hobby.'"

Young was born in 1980 to parents of different races: her mother
of Irish and German descent, and her father African-American. Her
brother Josh was born three years later. Both parents worked various
day jobs and kept the family fed and sheltered but could afford few frills.

A relative of Young's mother made sure the kids were exposed to
the arts.

"Our parents instilled a work ethic in us," Josh Young says, "and our
Aunt Rose, my mother's aunt, was a big supporter of us going to plays
and concerts and paid for Melisa to attend Piven Theatre workshops"
in Evanston.

Melisa Young played a number of lead roles in school musicals
while attending Rich South High School in Richton Park, and she
briefly lived out her childhood dream of becoming a performer. Those
plans were deferred as she studied film while attending Columbia College in the South Loop. She worked behind the scenes on a couple of
Hollywood movies, doing everything from fetching coffee for Sigour-
ney Weaver to building props. She didn't have enough money to move
to New York to find steady work, and she found the movie industry
even less lucrative in Chicago. A "tedious and repetitive" stint as an
assistant on an ill-fated reality TV show for $100 a day convinced her
she was in the wrong business.

Meanwhile, her brother was ripping it up on the DJ and dance scene
in Chicago with his friend Curt Cameruci. Their inventive mash-ups
of hip-hop, pop, rock and electronic music brought a measure of underground fame in the duo Flosstradamus. Melisa Young started tagging
along to their parties, bringing her friends to dance the night away.

"I was broke, and my brother was making money doing music, doing
something fun," Young says. "I took notice of that."

"She was always the artist in the family," her brother says, "whereas I
was more the jock, the kid who played sports in school. She took piano
lessons, she sung in the school plays, she took voice lessons, and when

she was in college, she would always send me mix tapes that got me started into the style of DJ-ing I'm doing now, so for her to start writing her own songs, it wasn't out of the blue. She always had it in her, but being around people she knew who were actually doing it made her want to take the next step."

Melisa Young started rapping and became a regular presence at Flosstradamus shows. In 2006 she met one of her brother's friends in the business, Alain Macklovitch, aka A-Trak, who was the DJ for rising star Kanye West.

"I was working on some new sounds, moving from hip-hop productions to messing around with a lot more clubby, up-tempo tracks with synths and electronic influences," Macklovitch says. "She was just starting out, but that was her background: house and hip-hop. She had an understanding of new sounds bubbling up in club music that a lot of rappers were not aware of. But she also had the potential to be a real rapper, not just someone who raps over tracks just to make her friends laugh, so it was cool to test out my stuff with a new artist who didn't have any preconceptions about what this could be. She just did it naturally."

Macklovitch launched his record label, Fool's Gold, with Kid Sister's debut single, "Damn Girl." The follow-up, "Control," began to establish her sound and persona. In her lyrics, Young used her girl-next-door upbringing as inspiration rather than mimicking the extravagant fantasies and boasts of mainstream hip-hop.

"When my old friends hear my lyrics, they say, 'Girl, that sounds just like you,'" she says. "That's because those lyrics come from conversations I've had or little phrases I'd use in everyday life."

Her 2007 breakthrough hit, the sassy, instantly catchy "Pro Nails," was homemade too. "A-Trak made that beat in my kitchen that smelled of hot dogs when I was living with six people," Josh Young says with a laugh.

The hot-dog-flavored beat—even Melisa Young found it "a little weird at first"—was a turning point, especially when Kanye West paid it the ultimate compliment.

"Kanye heard it on the tour bus, and he really liked that hook and the chord progression," Macklovitch says. "He was really into the idea of the indie club scene and electronic music before anyone else in hip-hop, and he saw the potential. He'd go to my parties while we were on tour, and he'd see the kids reacting to this music, and he'd say, 'I need in on this.'"

West added a rap verse to "Pro Nails" and participated in the low-budget video shoot. The song, launched off Young's MySpace site, became an Internet hit, and the video aired on MTV. Pretty soon Melisa Young was fielding calls from record-label executives offering deals. She eventually signed with New York-based Downtown Records, home of Gnarls Barkley, Santigold and Mos Def.

An album, "Dream Date," was pieced together for release in 2008, but Melisa Young and A-Trak, the executive producer, decided against releasing it.

"No one could agree on a single; that was a sign that it wasn't ready," Macklovitch says. "We started questioning how well-rounded the album was. We took out three hip-hop-sounding songs and added five that felt more like Kid Sister songs: clubby, futuristic. We wanted something more conceptual, a listening experience. The album as a way of promoting music is almost outdated, but the albums that do work in recent years are more focused and conceptual; they're not just a collection of songs. If even Beyonce is now making concept albums, we should be at the cutting edge; we should be making the album with more of a vision, more depth.

"I wanted to put my stamp on this movement," she says, "one that we helped start with 'Pro Nails.'"

That almost passes for bravado in Young's world. For a performer who was shy about making music a couple of years ago, her determination is proof she has no doubts now.

"I've always been different, sometimes for good and sometimes for not so good," she says. "You can be glittery, and you can also be a regular person. I wear sequined underwear and cover myself in glitter because it's fun, a part of my personality. But you don't have to be a total freak; you can be down to earth and approachable. I want to be the girl who makes it who's not a jerk, who still goes bowling and drinks PBRs. I'll prove it to everyone—and I'll do it in high heels."

....

Kanye West, Jay-Z trade off, collaborate in Chicago show

DEC. 2, 2011

With Kanye West at his side, Jay-Z removed his cap about halfway through their bursting-with-hits "Watch the Throne" concert, the first of two at the jampacked United Center.

Like just about everything Jay-Z does, it was a small gesture that spoke volumes. The MC glides with stealthy grace and spent the first hour of the show with his head bowed, his movements minimal. Like a gangster or poker player who doesn't want anyone to read his next move, his eyes were constantly shaded by a dark Yankees baseball cap. His power was in his voice, an instrument that betrayed no outsize emotion, made pronouncements in a coldblooded monotone, chose words with surgical exactitude.

Only his lips and left hand moved as he leaned into his verses, finding endless ways to rhyme about his favorite subjects: the business of power, and the power of business. Or, as Jay-Z himself would put it, "I'm not a businessman, I'm a business, man."

He had no patience for soul-searching or self-revelation; his is a world in which everything is defined by commerce, and he is a self-made master. A CEO dressed in black with an American flag scarf dangling from his jeans, he delivered chorus after chorus that allowed everyone to share in his good fortune.

And then the hat came off. There they were, Yeezy (West) and Hova (Jay-Z), just a couple of multimillionaires sitting on the front stoop of their stage trading verses about their future, yet-to-be-born children on "New Day." It was a rare moment of vulnerability for Jay-Z, who allowed himself a slight grin, and in the close-up videos on the big screens, his eyes appeared to glisten with something approximating warmth.

For West, such moments of introspection are standard. "This is the realest (stuff) I ever said," he announced, though that could apply to

Jay-Z and Kanye West at the United Center Nov. 30, 2011.
SCOTT STRAZZANTE

almost any of his songs. Pouring it out and pouring it on are the only speeds he knows.

Whereas Jay-Z's movements were all confined to that articulate left hand, slicing and dicing imaginary syncopations and syllables in the air, West was like a child in a toy store amped up on chocolate and soft drinks. He darted from one end of the large stage to the other in a leather kilt, dancing spastically, dropping to his knees, thrusting a fist or a leg as if fending off an imaginary Bruce Lee attack. Jay-Z gives off the aura that nothing can faze him, Kanye acts and sounds as if everything does. At one point, he started and stopped "All of the Lights" three times, demanding more lights each time, and tossing off an aside that the song had just been nominated for a Grammy Award—all in a night's work.

The big and little brother routine has been playing out since West moved east from Chicago to New York in the late '90s to drop some beats on Jay-Z tracks, and both artists have only gotten bigger ever since. At the moment, they preside over hip-hop like twin king-pins, collaborating on an album earlier this year [2011], "Watch the Throne," in which they compared notes on their bank accounts, jets and luxury cars.

Here, however, the pair obliterated the bad taste left by that self-aggrandizing album with a furious string of hits and jacked-up perfor-mances. The show played out amid spidery laser lighting, in shadows and silhouettes on a stark, vast stage, with only a small, anonymous backing band lurking in the background for accompaniment.

The duo entered on risers at the opposite ends of the arena, tower-ing over their audience as they spat out the rhetorical question, "Who Gon Stop Me?"

The sound and fury were accompanied by hackneyed images of jun-gle predators baring their teeth and hunting their prey. But the music was undeniable, the pair coming together and then splitting off for mini solo sets, West blasting out "Flashing Lights" and "Jesus Walks," Jay-Z counterpunching with "Public Service Announcement" and "Run This Town."

Their differences were made explicit by another mini-set: Jay-Z de-livered big, rousing anthems such as "Izzo (H.O.V.A.)" and "Empire State of Mind," making it look so easy as he brought cheers crashing down from balconies full of fans. West, in contrast, stood on a riser, bathed in blood-red lighting, tied to the whipping post of regret in "Runaway" and "Heartless." He's without doubt the first and probably last pop star to call himself a "scumbag" and worse in the chorus of one of his hit songs.

When the two got together to bring the 21/2-hour concert to a close, even Jay-Z got caught up in West's energy—blowing an air saxophone solo during "Gold Digger." The show wrapped up anticlimactically with the throwaway hits "Lift Off" and multiple versions of a party ditty with "Paris" in the title. By that point, though, the duo had earned the right to act like a couple of old pals blowing off a little steam in their private club.

Danny Brown's long road to brilliance

MARCH 30, 2012

Rapper Danny Brown's rise to excellence runs contrary to the usual pop music notion, which is to hurry, hurry, hurry.

In a hurry-up culture, Danny Brown says taking his time was the key to the depth and off-kilter resonance of his 2011 breakthrough album, "XXX" (Fool's Gold).

By hip-hop standards, the 31-year-old Brown is practically an elder statesman—or a late bloomer, take your pick. After a series of mix tapes and a wayward decade of drug dealing, jail time and record-deals-gone-bad, Brown summed up his chaotic life on "XXX" and ended up on numerous year-end best-of lists.

"When I started, I tried to write like Nas all the time," Brown says. "I didn't know how to write like me. I had the talent to write words and work out rhythms. I had melodies, but I didn't have my style. I had to grow into that. Nas was like Rakim at the start. But you can't predict the number of years it will take for someone to find themselves, to mature into their own voice. When I got to be 30, I was finally writing like Danny Brown."

Brown grew up in Detroit, and at an early age was stringing together rhymes with astonishing dexterity—a byproduct of immersing himself in the collected works of Theodor Seuss Geisel, aka Dr. Seuss. "I remember the first time I rapped, the expression on my cousin's face was, 'What the (expletive)!'" Brown says. "I was 5 years old, in kindergarten. Everybody has a talent. Mine was not basketball. From an early age, music was my only thing. You come from Detroit, you learn how to make the most of what you can do best."

Brown's dad, a house DJ, encouraged his son's passion and took him to hip-hop concerts, including a memorable outdoor show by Run-DMC and LL Cool J in the late '80s. "Hearing and seeing it, it was like a way of life. Everybody in the audience looked like a rapper too," he says. "It was a no-turning-back moment."

He spent a lot of time alone in his bedroom, as his parents tried to shelter him from the gang-banging and drug dealing in their neighborhood. "I had a lot of time on my hands," Brown says. "The only good thing about being alone like that is that I studied great music. I'd read best-of-all-time lists, and I'd get the records and study them to figure out what made them work. I remember being in 11th grade trying to listen to (the Beach Boys' 1966 masterpiece) 'Pet Sounds.' I couldn't tell my friends about stuff like that, because they wouldn't get it. I adapted this private side of bedroom music that was known only to me. I knew about all the top rap music with my friends, then during my alone time I would study everything else."

Did he appreciate "Pet Sounds" when he first heard it?

Brown laughs. "As a kid, I thought it was boring as (expletive). But once my ears started to get adjusted and trained, I went back to it in my early 20s and started to appreciate the transitions they were making, and how that album influenced (The Beatles' 1967 album 'Sgt. Pepper's Lonely Hearts Club Band')."

He focused on writing as much as performing, teaching himself how to craft songs by studying the work of older, more accomplished peers already trying to break into music.

His success with underground mix tapes led to some flirtations with the mainstream business, but his quirkiness—his high-pitched voice, his sometimes discomforting or explicit subject matter, his flamboyant dress—made him a tough sell.

50 Cent was briefly interested in signing Brown but took a pass "because he didn't like the way I dressed. He tried to get me to tone down my look. My pants were too tight. I wear pink sometimes. He wasn't into it."

The clothes fit the unconventional personality Brown brings to his songs. They blend humor and bleakness, sex and poverty; they disconcert as much as entertain. They reflect a life in which dope deals helped pay the rent, interrupted by a brief jail term for violating probation in 2007.

On "30," the final song on "XXX," he raps about using his kitchen stove and oven to stay warm in winter. "Die Like a Rock Star" details enough bad choices that "it's a miracle I'm livin.'"

"The most popular rap artists aren't supposed to be rapping about being broke," he says. "They're supposed to be rich and popping Cristal and hanging out with models."

Yet Brown says he didn't consider compromising to sign with 50 Cent. "I'm so old," he says with a laugh. "I can't go to bed at night with (expletive) like that. I was 28, 29 when that happened. If I was 20, sure, I would've considered (changing his style). But now, I'm like, 'Nah, I know what I want to do with my life.'"

The music of his latest obsession, Joy Division, helped him cope.

"I watched a documentary about them, got sucked into their story and then listened to their albums," he says. "(1980 Joy Division album) 'Closer' is my favorite album of all time right now. All the metaphors in there could relate to what happened between me and the music industry. 'Atrocity Exhibition'—man, that about sums it up."

Boundaries made to be broken in Big Boi's world

APRIL 26, 2013

Big Boi is a serial collaborator, one of those endlessly curious artists who's always thinking "what if?" when he charges into a new project. As one-half of OutKast, Big Boi helped expand the language of hip-hop. As a solo artist, he's gone further out in playing musical mix-and-match on "Sir Lucious Left Foot: The Son of Chico Dusty" (2010) and his latest, "Vicious Lies and Dangerous Rumors."

For as long as he can remember, Big Boi, born Antwan Andre Patton 38 years ago in Savannah, Ga., didn't discriminate against musical styles.

"Growing up, my grandmothers and aunties listened to all types of music," he says. "They were never biased about it. We didn't have a lot of money, so I didn't see a lot of shows, other than free ones in the park. But my grandmother would send us to the record store every week to buy 45s (7-inch singles)."

He remembers two records in particular that had a big impact: "Bob Marley's 'Buffalo Soldiers'—my grandmother played the (expletive) out

Big Boi at the Congress Theater Sept. 17, 2010.
CHRIS SALATA

of that record. I loved the horns and Bob's voice, and the vibe from the bass player. That was a real calm, laid-back, dope record with a powerful message. And then there was Kate Bush's 'Running Up That Hill.' My Uncle Russell was a very eclectic guy in terms of the kinds of things he'd listen to and appreciate, and he gave me one of her records. I'm riding my bike, and it was like a movie listening to Kate Bush."

Big Boi began collaborating with a like-minded high school friend, Andre Benjamin (aka Andre 3000), and the two ended up recording six genre-busting albums as OutKast from 1994 to 2006.

"The two of us were listening to Fleetwood Mac, N.W.A., the Isley Brothers, The Beatles, Kool and the Gang, James Brown—there were no boundaries," Big Boi says. "When we started out, there was a lot of back and forth. On the early albums, we sat in the studio and wrote together, traded bars. It was a full-on collaboration. By the time we got to (the 2003 double album) 'Speakerboxxx'/'The Love Below,' we were in different spaces—he was at his house in Atlanta, and I was at Stankonia (OutKast's studio), but we still came together at the end to piece it all together."

As brilliant as that double album was, it signaled that the duo was starting to drift apart. After a movie and soundtrack, "Idlewild" (2006), Big Boi and Andre 3000 put OutKast on hold.

"I just kept going," Big Boi says. "I record year-round. Dre and I have owned Stankonia for 15–16 years; it was previously owned by Bobby Brown. Basically, I live there. There's a loft upstairs, and sometimes I sleep with the music. On a typical day I'll get there around 4 or 5 (p.m.) and record all night until the juice runs out, around 4 or 5 in the morning. I'll go to sleep, catch me a little Waffle House and get back to work."

He has dozens and dozens of notebooks dating back decades containing all his lyrics, poems and musical ideas.

"An iPad? Hell, no! I'm not into that," he scoffs. "I write it all down, scribble-scrabble style. I'm working on many songs simultaneously, and each one has its own page."

Big Boi also works just as tirelessly on finding new collaborators. While on tour for "Sir Lucious Left Foot," he bonded at festivals with artists such as garage-rockers Wavves, indie-pop duo Phantogram and Swedish electronic band Little Dragon. All ended up contributing to tracks on "Vicious Lies and Dangerous Rumors," along with rappers Ludacris, T.I., Kid Cudi and B.O.B.

"In the A," with Ludacris and T.I., conjures classic Southern G-funk, and "Apple of My Eye" could be a close cousin of OutKast's "Hey Ya." But the murky space ballad "Descending" with Little Dragon and the whistled interludes on the scrappy "Shoes for Running" with Wavves push Big Boi's music into new territory.

"It doesn't matter who's hip-hop or not. I'm only interested in working with the dopest, most creative artists I can find, because it can create something bigger than hip-hop," he says. "I want to make music that's global. I'm an MC first and foremost, and hip-hop is my home, but I don't want to be pigeonholed. I'm more interested in making great music, regardless of what genre people call it."

Does he have a dream collaboration that he'd like to see happen? "Oh, yeah. Me and Kate Bush could do something. I spoke to her on the phone, and she said she was flattered that I love her music. When I go to Europe next, we're gonna have some tea and maybe chop up some beats."

....

Adam 'MCA' Yauch
From Beastie Boy to Buddhist

MAY 5, 2012

Adam "MCA" Yauch was co-leader of the Beastie Boys, a New York City trio that transformed hip-hop. But just as significantly, the group and especially Yauch transformed themselves, providing a model for how artists can mature and grow as people without losing their credibility or relevance.

"Role model"—Yauch, who died at age 47 after a three-year battle with throat cancer, would have hated that term. But he became one almost in spite of the Beastie Boys' early reputation as foul-mouthed innovators.

"To become this gentle Buddhist soul who literally would not step on a fly was something else," said his friend, Rage Against the Machine guitarist Tom Morello, shortly after news of Yauch's death was announced. "His commitment to social justice and especially to Tibet's freedom put it on the map for an entire generation of people."

Michael "Mike D" Diamond, Adam "Ad-Rock" Horowitz and Yauch were in their midteens when they formed a hardcore punk band during the early '80s, before crossing over into hip-hop.

Adam "Ad-Rock" Horovitz and the rest of the Beastie Boys at the Riviera Theatre Sept. 26, 2007.
TERRENCE ANTONIO JAMES

At the time, it wasn't exactly commonplace for white kids to be rapping, but the cultural implications "didn't really occur to us at the time," Diamond once told the Tribune. "The early rap shows we did were in front of all-black audiences. We'd be in small clubs in Queens or Brooklyn, opening for Kurtis Blow or somebody like that, and they'd look at us like we were nuts."

They hooked up with Rick Rubin, a New York University student who would start the Def Jam label out of his college dorm room. Their first full-length album, "Licensed to Ill," was issued in 1986 and met with a mix of acclaim and derision, equal parts Led Zeppelin, Grandmaster Flash and a more explicit politically incorrect Marx Brothers. The headline over the Village Voice's lead review said it all: "Three Jerks Make a Masterpiece."

It went on to become the first hip-hop album to top 5 million sales while bridging the chasm between rock and rap. Essential to its appeal was the perception that the trio were, in fact, jerks: arrogant, loud, snotty, foul-mouthed. Transgression has always been a linchpin of pop culture, and the trio's demand—"You gotta fight . . . for your right . . . to party!"—became an '80s MTV-generation anthem. Their rhymes were clever, hilarious and sometimes just plain idiotic—forming a lethal combination with Rubin's stockpile of rock guitar riffs. On a massive arena tour with Run-D.M.C., the Beastie Boys helped bust hip-hop out of the inner city and storm the suburbs.

The 1989 follow-up, "Paul's Boutique," was a radical left turn and confirmed that the Beastie Boys were more than just a one-hit wonder. With dense, sample-heavy production by the Dust Brothers, the Beastie Boys made an album that has often been described as hip-hop's answer to The Beatles' "Sgt. Pepper's Lonely Hearts Club Band," splicing the history of funk and soul with countless pop-culture references and audacious tag-team rhymes. The group's subsequent albums, including "Check Your Head" (1992) and "Ill Communication" (1994), affirmed the Beastie Boys' place as a key band in alternative rock's rise. They began blending live instrumentation with their expanding grasp of hip-hop's roots, exploring everything from organ-fueled jazz instrumentals to rampaging hardcore.

Along the way, Yauch began to re-evaluate his life and music, as he explained in a Tribune interview: "Shortly after we put out 'Paul's Boutique,' I really started thinking about our lyrics and how they affected people. I just began noticing more and more how lyrics that I viewed as just joking around had a longer lasting effect on people, myself included. I never smoked 'dust' (PCP), but kids would come up to me citing our songs: 'Yo, I heard you talking about smoking dust in your song and we used to smoke dust all the time and listen to your music.'

"There are a lot of lyrics on our first two albums that talk about carrying guns or being disrespectful to women. We looked at it as a fantasy, a cowboy movie, but I began to realize those things have a deeper effect, where people actually think that's who we are. And in some cases, you kind of become that, a caricature of yourself, your image."

Yauch turned to Eastern philosophy and spirituality, and in the early '90s he was trekking to Bali and Nepal to further his studies. On his second trip he encountered Tibetan refugees making their way to a refugee camp in Katmandu.

There he met Erin Potts, a social worker from San Francisco, and to-gether they established the Milarepa Fund, which since 1994 has been putting on concerts and funding projects and organizations designed to aid Tibet in its 60-year struggle to gain independence from China.

"I didn't know anything about Tibet at all," Yauch said of his first visit there. "But I was struck by how these people carried themselves. . . . I began to learn about their nonviolent approach to life, and the teach-ings of the Dalai Lama (Tibet's exiled leader)."

The more open worldview affected the Beastie Boys' art. Diamond and Horovitz acknowledged that they were skeptical about their band-mate's newfound spirituality, but the Beastie Boys began making al-bums that managed to balance their trademark wit and sarcasm with a more enlightened social consciousness. The fans embraced albums such as "Hello Nasty" (1998) and "To the 5 Boroughs" (2004), which each sold millions.

Along the way, Yauch built a recording studio, Oscilloscope Labo-ratories in New York, and began making and distributing movies, in-cluding his directorial debut, the basketball documentary "Gunnin' for That #1 Spot" (2008).

Thanks to Yauch, Oscilloscope Studios brought many quirky, chal-lenging pictures to theaters and home-screen viewing. Among the best: "Exit Through the Gift Shop," a nonfiction chronicle of a massive art prank, directed by underground graffiti artist Banksy, and "Wendy and Lucy" and "Meek's Cutoff," well-regarded projects starring Michelle Williams.

Oscilloscope has made a name for itself championing outsiders. In times of nagging recessionary timidity, Yauch's distribution "lab" carved its niche honorably, if not always profitably. His health prob-lems forced the Beastie Boys to cancel a 2009 tour, including a head-lining slot at Lollapalooza in Grant Park. "Hot Sauce Committee Part Two" was released last year *[2011]* after several delays, but the group was unable to tour afterward. When the trio was inducted into the Rock and Roll Hall of Fame last month *[April 2012]*, Yauch was un-able to attend due to his deteriorating condition.

Yauch is survived by his wife, Dechen Wengdu, and their daughter Tenzin Losel Yauch.

He also leaves behind a legacy that includes 40 million records sold and a musical career that maintained relevance for three decades. But just as notable was his personal transformation as an artist, social activist and human being. As Potts, his Milarepa partner, once told the Tribune, Yauch "showed that at any point in your life, good or bad, you can turn it around. None of us are perfect, but we all have the ability to say, 'I can start living my life right now to help other people.'"

Drake has arena-size regrets, with ego to match

JUNE 4, 2012

Drake had barely arrived on stage at the packed First Midwest Bank Amphitheatre in Tinley Park [*June 2, 2012*] and already he was wrestling with his contradictions.

"Lookin' for the right way to do the wrong things," he announced in "Lord Knows." Drake, born Aubrey Drake Graham in 1986 in Toronto, mixes swagger with regret, strip-club boasting with humble introspection. The sensitive hustler routine was massaged into a 90-minute show that affirmed his status as hip-hop's new ladies man, hit maker and power broker all rolled into one.

Drake leapfrogged from an acting career into hip-hop, and his wounded vulnerability and innocent swagger were soon championed by Lil Wayne. He capitalized on the hype with a series of song-stealing cameos on other artists' singles, a well-received 2009 EP and mixtape, a million-selling 2010 debut album, "Thank Me Later," and a 2 million-selling 2011 follow-up, "Take Care."

In concert, he was a hip-hop king dressed in a drab T-shirt and baggy jeans. He's playing venues 10 times the size of those on his first major tour two years ago, and the show has expanded accordingly. He was backed by a full band and a massive grid of 40 video screens that doubled as light portals. Despite the bigger production values and higher stakes, the show still had a loose feel, and the pacing sometimes

Drake at the Chicago Theatre Oct. 13, 2010.
MARINA MAKROPOULOS

lagged. It was marbled with cameos and a numbing 10-minute series of shout-outs to various audience members; the latter gambit was a charming detour on his first tour, but now it served only to bring a massive arena show to a grinding stand-still.

Yet Drake's charisma as a performer and prowess as a hip-hop MC who's not afraid to slip into some gray emotional areas was evident from the start. He channeled Southern gangsta rap on "Underground Kings" and then dealt with the consequences of an over-the-top lifestyle in "Over" ("I'm really too young to be feeling this old"). The sweetly yearning "Crew Love" professed devotion to family as greater than any personal accomplishment, while the gothic "Up All Night" indulged in puffed-up ego-tripping.

Drake opened up the stage to a series of proteges and friends, including 2 Chainz, Waka Flocka Flame and rising Chicago teen rapper Chief Keef, who dutifully supplied the requisite stand-on-your-chair party rap. But once you've heard a song about ogling strippers, you probably don't need to hear four.

Indeed, as Drake's audience widens, the temptation to pander will intensify. Raps rhapsodizing about cash, hookers and hustlers will never go away, and Drake's set had its share. "I guess it really is just me, myself and all my millions," he crowed as "Headlines" filled the aisles with deliriously gyrating fans, vicariously sharing in the wealth.

But what makes Drake compelling is that he realizes the characters in his songs sometimes just sound like jerks. Guilt, remorse and vulnerability—he's prone to all three. In "Amen," performed with Meek Mill, Sunday morning gospel backslides into Saturday night decadence. The protagonists in Drake's songs feel trapped between those two worlds, unable to fully commit to either.

Little wonder the most moving portions of this otherwise big, brassy concert were its most intimate. In "Take Care," Drake responded to the recorded vocals of Rihanna, as if to underline the distance between a couple who can't come clean about their true feelings for each other. The song concluded with a tumbling African rhythm, over which Drake danced, alone.

The repressed emotions spilled out in "Marvins Room," in which the narrator drunk-dials his ex-girlfriend. Drake stood, head bowed, in a spotlight, mumbling and slurring his regrets into a microphone while thousands joined in.

The singalong as pity party? Drake may not have invented that concept, but he sure owns it now.

....

Kanye West assault an uneasy listen

At times minimalist, coarse and offensive, 'Yeezus' is rarely dull

JUNE 17, 2013

Kanye West's sixth studio album, "Yeezus" (Roc-A-Fella/Def Jam), is the latest affront from an artist who keeps inventing ways to tick people off.

At first listen, it is hostile, abrasive (both sonically and lyrically) and intentionally off-putting, as if to test the loyalty of even his most ardent fans. But, as usual, that's only the beginning of West's new detour.

West is used to being written off by many as a shallow, petulant, needy, self-serving braggart, a talented artist who can't resist impaling himself on his own ego. And some of that is true, as West himself will be the first to say. But even as he barges in full-on full of himself in "Yeezus," West demonstrates that he has a lot more on his mind than just self-aggrandizement or self-immolation.

One thing on which just about everyone can agree: West is pretty good at turning sound into his personal playground. His records sound great, set standards and then move on to something new: the "dusties" soul vibe of "The College Dropout" (2004), the orchestral audacity of "Late Registration" (2005), the much-maligned-at-the-time melancholy electro-chill of "808s & Heartbreak" (2008), in many ways the most influential album of the last five years.

"Yeezus" is no exception, consolidating the worlds of '80s Chicago acid-house and 2013 Chicago drill music (the sound of Chief Keef and King Louie, both of whom have prominent cameos), '90s industrial and the avant-rap of Saul Williams, Death Grips and Odd Future. Much of it sounds harsh, brutally minimal—sometimes stripped down to little more than West's voice and a drum beat or a distorted keyboard (with production help from Daft Punk and Rick Rubin, among others). It is ruthlessly edited, with rhythms and rhymes that hit like anvils, a perfect soundtrack for dropping bombs, invading homes or bum-rushing an awards show complaining that no way did Taylor

Swift make a better video than Beyonce. But there are sudden digressions and twists within the oppression, with glimpses of old soul and gospel, a sample of Hungarian rock, even Nina Simone's version of the protest anthem "Strange Fruit." Tucked inside lurk hooks and melodies that sink in over time.

Drill even further down, and West sounds more complicated than ever, an artist willing to throw himself off the ledge not just to get a reaction, but to start a conversation about, well, just about everything that matters to him.

A wave of noise opens the album, synthesizers spazzing out in "On Sight" as West rises, "a monster about to come alive again." He rages more outrageously with each line, a terrorist who is both merciless and irresistible to all he encounters. Abruptly it breaks into a sample from a gospel record that advises, "He'll give us what we need, it may not be what we want"—a sly commentary on an album that is sure to defeat expectations about who West is and what he represents.

It is exactly those sorts of expectations that West aims to upend. A decade ago, he was creating songs about the precocious kid who hated his minimum-wage job at a retail store, a relatable, everyday figure in a hip-hop world populated by larger-than-life stars. Later he was the celebrity with a tendency to run his mouth and overstay his welcome—never as cool as his hero and mentor, Jay-Z, or as prodigiously gifted an MC as Nas. "Let's have a toast for the douche bags . . . Let's have a toast for the scumbags," he sang on the 2010 track "Runaway," before advising, "Run away as fast as you can."

West has always owned and owned up to his contradictions, and "Yeezus" is no exception, even as it tramples all in its path. It amplifies his obsession with race, class and sex (especially of the interracial variety), and how they speak to issues of control and freedom.

Over Gothic organ and ominously pingponging synths, "New Slaves" finds West protesting that many of his business partners are just new slave owners in corporate disguise. At the same time, the rapper goes out of his way to be more explicit, more tasteless than ever in rhymes that equate sex with violence and casual misogyny. At times—in particular, a racially offensive joke on "I'm in It"—he's exasperating, indulging in the kind of transgressive "humor" you'd expect from lesser artists.

But in playing into a sexual-predator stereotype, he also forces a debate about why it's perpetuated: "They see a black man with a white woman/At the top floor they gone come to kill King Kong." (West, of course, has been in a yearlong relationship with a white woman, Kim Kardashian, who gave birth to their child over the weekend.)

Thunderous jungle drums clear a path for the marauding "Black Skinhead." It's over the top by design, a worst-case scenario of King Kong run amok—a mainstream nightmare by way of Marilyn Manson's industrial screed "The Beautiful People."

On "I am a God," West flirts with all those egomaniac perceptions of his public life. He plays into the outrage, even imagining a conversation with Jesus. "I am a God," he intones, "hurry up with my damn massage . . . hurry up with my damn croissants."

Even as West threatens to turn this into the blackest comedy record he's ever made, he goes one layer deeper on the track. Here's the artist who wrote "Jesus Walks" confronting the license granted him as a celebrity. By the end, heavy-breathing screams break up the electronic pulse, before being buried beneath a dark cloud of keyboards.

"Hold My Liquor" employs a wobbly, electronically altered Chief Keef vocal to lend a weird poignancy to a tale of a damaged suitor stumbling into an old girlfriend's house seeking solace and a second (third? fourth?) chance. But "Blood on the Leaves" wastes a sample of Nina Simone's biting version of "Strange Fruit" on a tawdry tale of a man who juggles a wife and mistress, and loses them both.

On an album rife with images of oppression, it seemed like the perfect opportunity for an update of the harrowing meditation on racism, but West takes a pass.

The album winds down with the deceptively bouncy "Bound 2," as if trying to let a little light through the curtain of steel. It piles on the soul samples and a guest vocal from the Gap Band's Charlie Wilson, while West plays the rogue in pursuit of "one good girl." He talks on and on, until even he's had enough of his own babbling. "After all these long-ass verses/I'm tired, you tired, Jesus wept."

West has one final laugh at his own expense. It's an album that baits listeners into isolating and focusing on its most outrageous lines, its most brutalizing moments, independent of the whole. On the surface, he's created a polarizing album that practically demands to be loved or hated. But with West, it's never quite that easy.

PART 4

MORE

You call this country?

Chicago's crowd is maverick, direct—and true to the honky-tonk spirit

JAN. 16, 2000

A native of Wales comes to Chicago and has a hillbilly-music epiphany underneath the L tracks. The absurdity of that scenario is not lost on Jon Langford, the Englishman who helps keep a torch lit for honky-tonk and western swing in the city that has become the new anti-Nashville. As he sits on the stage of the Chicago Folk Center, Langford introduces a song about "Drink and pills and Nashville radio" with these words:

"In this song, I assume the voice of Hank Williams—or so I've been told," says the ruddy-faced singer with the soul patch on his chin and the punk pedigree in his heart. "But I can't assume the voice of Hank Williams, so I'll assume the voice of a Welsh coal miner with laryngitis."

The capacity crowd, awaiting the headlining act—Texas country great Guy Clark—laughs and is clearly taken not only with Langford's irreverent patter, but his ability to put the songs across, with clarity and passion that is just a swig or two removed from chaos. What he plays isn't Hank Williams' country, but it has something of its spirit, its fierce conviction.

In the last decade, Chicago has become home to dozens of expatriated punk rockers, brash singer-songwriters and urban cowgirls and cowboys who have given new meaning to country's long-lost traditions. Whereas Nashville now specializes in mimicking the mainstream rock of the '70s, Chicago has become home to a motley array of outsiders who have taken up honky-tonk's values—the stripped-down instrumental attack, the devastatingly direct lyricism, the punch-in-the-gut emotion—with a vengeance. Call it alternative country, insurgent country, honky-tonk punk—it's a brand of in-your-face twang made by people born long after Hank Williams curled up and died in the back seat of a white Cadillac.

Jon Langford performs during Chicago Rocks: The Honorable Story of 'The Indie City,' at the Chicago History Museum on April 5, 2012.
CHRIS SWEDA

"Punk rock is so much about youthful tear-it-all-down, make-way-for-me attitude," says Kelly Kessler, a singer-songwriter who has been booking the Honky Tonk Living Room concert series at the Hideout, a North Side club where the underground rock and country scenes merge. "Country has the same kind of populist appeal as punk, and it leaves a lot of room for maturity and wisdom while you're talking about the hard knocks of love and life."

The Chicago performers mining that populist vein include long-time hard-core country instrumentalists such as John Rice and Andon Davis; master songwriters such as Robbie Fulks and Wilco's Jeff Tweedy (whose first band, Uncle Tupelo, pioneered rock's roots-country scene in the '90s); relatively recent converts such as Langford's bandmate in the Mekons, Sally Timms and Anna Fermin; and neo-traditionalists such as Freakwater, Kessler's Texas Rubies and the Handsome Family.

Langford has become a tireless catalyst for the scene. A few nights after the Chicago Folk Center gig he is at FitzGerald's pounding out Johnny Cash and Bob Wills songs with Rice in a different aggregation, a modified country swing band known as the Pine Valley Cosmonauts. A few weeks later he's mixing punk-rock adrenaline with honky-tonk moonshine at Schubas with the Waco Brothers, a jovial party band with lyrics more blue-collar than Bruce Springsteen's that attracts both leather-jacketed rockers and cowboy-booted two-steppers. In between these gigs, Langford pays the bills with artwork that places the country tradition in a political context: Hank Williams as St. Sebastian, riddled with arrows.

Though Langford and others in the underground country community are inspired by the honky-tonk heroes of old, they rarely sound like them. "It hurt me to hear a Merle Haggard song played like that," Kessler says of the early Wacos. Indeed, what has been dubbed Chicago's "insurgent country" scene might offend longtime fans of the National Barn Dance, which from 1924 to '60 was broadcast on WLS and for a time made Chicago—and not Nashville—the national Mecca for country music.

Back then it was Southern immigrants, heading North in search of work, who brought their fiddles and mandolins and taste for Jimmy Rodgers to the big city and turned Madison Avenue into one long strip of honky-tonks. Now it's former skinhead punks, art-school students and natives of the Philippines, Wales and New York who are nurturing a scene. It includes such clubs as FitzGerald's in Berywn, the Hideout and Schubas on the North Side; shops such as Chris and Heather's Record Roundup on Montrose Avenue, run by Chris Ligon and Heather McAdams; and a handful of record labels.

Ground Zero for this surge is Bloodshot Records, which recently moved from a cramped basement office in the back of co-owner Nan Warshaw's Wrigleyville apartment into a more spacious quarters on the Northwest Side. Five years into its life, Bloodshot has released 60 records and is sturdy enough to employ a half-dozen people.

Warshaw and co-founder Rob Miller are both former punk-rock drummers who once hated the "C" word. "To me country was 'The Gambler' or '9 to 5,' appalling dreck that had a bad mainstream stigma attached to it," Miller says. But while he was attending college in Ann Arbor, Mich., in the mid-'80s, he discovered a terrific happy-hour country band whose raucous versions of Commander Cody and Tammy Wynette songs triggered a psychic connection with rootsier punk bands such as the Gun Club and the Cramps.

Warshaw went to college in Olympia, Wash.—riot grrrl central in the underground punk scene—but took a liking to then-new neo-traditionalist country acts such as Dwight Yoakam and Steve Earle. Miller and Warshaw ended up in Chicago and began deejaying country nights for jack-booted punks at the Crash Palace, later Delilahs, on Lincoln Avenue with such other unlikely honky-tonk fans as Ministry's Al Jourgenson.

"About a year later we started talking about putting together a compilation of all these cool little bands around town," Miller says. "The talent was there . . ."

"But nobody identified it," Warshaw adds. "We realized there were about 20 underground country bands primarily playing rock clubs in Chicago."

There's no consensus on how this came to be. Langford and his British punk band the Mekons were turned on to country music in the mid-'80s by a Chicago college radio deejay, Terry Nelson, and began creating their own mutant version of it on such underground albums as "Fear and Whiskey" and "The Edge of the World." When the Mekons visited Chicago, they stumbled upon a hard-core country band called the Sundowners that had been playing in the Loop since the '50s, and were staggered by the flinty, no-frills music they heard.

"Country was everything I didn't want when I was 17," Langford says. "But by the time I saw the Sundowners, I was in my late 20s, and it all started to make sense—stuff you only learn about through living: misery, loss, drunkenness, put across with these incredible harmonies, really tight arrangements and smiles on their faces."

Through the Sundowners, Langford met Rice, whose stints in bands such as Special Consensus and Jump in the Saddle made him one of the most respected of the young-guard bluegrass instrumentalists. "Langford may not have had this long track record as a country artist, but he had a purity of heart about what he was doing.

He brought a conviction and a charisma to his singing that put the music across," Rice says.

At about the same time, Janet Beveridge Bean and Catherine Irwin—two childhood friends from Louisville playing in rock and punk bands (Bean as the drummer in Chicago's Eleventh Dream Day)—whiled away afternoons by singing country songs around the kitchen table. As a lark, they decided to start Freakwater, a hard-core acoustic band built around their ghostly harmonies.

"I remember coming to one of their early recording sessions and wondering what the hell was going on," Rice recalls. "They were doing songs about babies dying in fires and leaving scratch marks on the door—it took a little while to warm up to it. But eventually I realized they were coming at this tradition of the murder ballad (that had been in country music for decades) and doing something new with it."

Kessler, an Indiana native who shucked off her notions of country's corniness after living in Kentucky for five years, found herself in Chicago cooking breakfast with her sister-in-law Jane Baxter Miller and singing country songs with her till afternoon. Soon after, Kessler and Miller—the Texas Rubies—were finding gigs around town, and even playing New York art galleries and Ernest Tubb's Midnight Jamboree; their tight harmonies belying any kitsch factor associated with their wearing cowgirl hats and boots.

"Then other things started happening that raised awareness and started planting seeds: Brigid Murphy started filling the Park West with Milly's Orchid Show (a spoof of country variety shows) and Heather McAdams started doing her country calendars," says Kessler. "Then Langford came to town (moving here permanently from Leeds, England, in the early '90s), and it became a movement. When Bloodshot got rolling, it put the movement on the map."

The debut Bloodshot release, "For a Life of Sin," came out in 1994 and documented the then-nascent scene, featuring bands such as Freakwater, the Texas Rubies, the Bottle Rockets and the Handsome Family, as well as Langford and Fulks, a brilliant songwriter who served a bluegrass apprenticeship in Special Consensus and became infatuated with old-time honky-tonk's lyrical and sonic directness.

"The lyrics were about real-life topics and there was an energy in the playing that wasn't digitally honed and edited," says Fulks, who recorded his first two raw, twangy Bloodshot albums with punk producer Steve Albini. "Suddenly after 15 years of looking around there was this label in Chicago willing to put out my stuff."

Says Miller, "Most of these bands were like us, discovering the music as they were creating it. Terms like 'alternative country' are now standard critical fare, but back then no one had any idea of what to do with it. Bands were struggling with their identities and club owners were saying, 'Country music? In a rock club? No, we don't do that.' You got blank stares or overt hostility doing this stuff."

All that changed after "A Life of Sin" took off, quickly selling out its first pressing of a thousand copies and inspiring two sequels while galvanizing scenes across the country. "We heard from people around the country, 'Hey, there are great bands like this in Dallas,' like the Old 97's, or in San Francisco, where they had Tarnation," Miller says. "It just spiderwebbed. We didn't know what we were doing, but we tapped into something."

There's nothing much commercial about this stuff—the best-selling Bloodshot releases move about 15,000 copies whereas mainstream country superstars such as Shania Twain or Garth Brooks measure their success in millions—but the movement continues to expand, attracting promising new bands such as the Blacks, the Pinetop 7 and Anna Fermin's Trigger Gospel to labels around town, and flourishing nationwide under the "No Depression" banner with bands from coast to coast. Few of these bands play country the old-fashioned way: The Blacks bring elements of Tom Waits, X and even glam rock into the equation; the Pinetops create cinematic soundscapes evocative of Ennio Morricone, and Fermin is a woman of Filipino heritage who brings a Patsy Cline-sized voice to tunes that touch on rock, rockabilly and blues.

The movement is so sprawling—from the Handsome Family's gothic narratives to Wilco's sumptuous psychedelic pop—that it no longer fits under the "alternative country" umbrella created for it only five years ago. But what it retains is a healthy respect for the song, as opposed to the marketing strategy behind it.

Fulks agrees that the alternative country scene has become "intellectually a little incoherent. The music of these artists doesn't have much in common. But it's identified in my mind this audience that is more broad-minded than your typical audience, a little more urban, an audience that likes to listen to words and think about words."

And that audience is perhaps bigger and hungrier than even these maverick country artists might suspect.

"I remember when we came out with the Bob Wills tribute album as the Pine Valley Cosmonauts and we went to Austin last March to perform it," says Rice of a South by Southwest Music Conference showcase in Texas that attracted a capacity audience. "I thought we were going to be crucified for committing this sacrilege to this icon's music. But Wills' daughter was there and gave us the thumbs up, and this big crowd just loved what we were doing. It was shocking to me."

As Bloodshot's Miller says, "This is not the music of teenage rebellion or angst—16-year-old kids in Hoffman Estates aren't going to be buying Waco Brothers T-shirts—but there is an audience for it. It's an audience that likes music where there is no veneer between the listener and the player, and that kind of music will never go away."

....

Koko Taylor
Say she's an icon, but don't presume she's the retiring type

MAY 28, 2000

They call her the Queen of the Blues, and the crown fits. Koko Taylor looks like she stepped out of a 1920s photo session, a vision of gleaming elegance: earrings and rings, a sequined blue dress fit for Bessie Smith, and a gold tooth that magnifies her smile.

It's little wonder Taylor glows: She is days away from her headlining appearance at the Chicago Blues Festival; her first album in seven years, "Royal Blue" (Alligator), will be out June 6, 2000; and since November 1999 she has had her new nightclub, Koko Taylor's Celebrity, on the southern edge of the Loop.

In the early 1970s, robust blues belter Koko Taylor brought new life to the local scene.
MICHAEL FRYER

But beneath the regal exterior, Taylor is still a tough-as-nails country girl, as anyone who witnesses one of her smoldering, sweat-soaked concerts can attest. In conversation, Taylor blends a gracious, almost soft-spoken femininity with plainspoken wisdom, often delivered with a between-the-eyes directness rare in this age of carefully calculated celebrity.

As she sips a cup of morning coffee at her nightclub's bar, the lioness roars when the word "retirement" is mentioned. Taylor's age is no longer freely divulged, but blues reference works generally concur that she was born Cora Walton on Sept. 28, 1935, outside Memphis. Given that she's a grandmother of two, with mild diabetes and hypertension, why does she insist on continuing to play at least 160 shows a year?

"A lot of people ask me the same question," Taylor says, fixing me with a stare that suggests a schoolteacher addressing a 1st grader caught with a mouthful of spitballs. "And my answer to them all is I will retire when God is ready for me to retire. He'll retire me, and no one else.

"If I retire today, what am I going to do? Watch Jerry Springer? I would just as soon go down, because that would really destroy me."

Blues guitarist Lonnie Brooks has seen plenty of veteran performers tire of the grind. "A lot of people have to be drunk or high to get motivated to go on that stage every night," he says. "But she's like a kid on the first day of spring and you tell her, 'OK, now you can go ride that bicycle.' The joy—it's no put-on. She can't wait to get to that microphone."

Bruce Iglauer, president of Chicago-based Alligator Records, which has been Taylor's home for the last 26 years, says the singer "doesn't know how to go through the motions. I saw her in South America a few years ago, and she was so ill she could barely walk. She has bouts of diverticulitis [an intestinal infection] that can leave her screaming in agony, and she spent a night in the hospital. The doctor told her she absolutely couldn't go on stage. She insisted on playing a couple of songs, and ended up doing 90 minutes. She believes she should come off the stage exhausted. She will not even take a drink of water while she's up there, because she feels that's not what professionals do."

That singular dedication to the music and her audience has made Taylor an icon, one of the half-dozen most famous living blues performers. Her records now sell in the range of 60,000 copies, extraordinary by independent-label standards, and she commands a worldwide audience on the festival circuit. She has won a Grammy and 19 W.C. Handy Awards for blues excellence, but her success has come grudgingly. Even after signing with Alligator and reviving her career in the late '70s, she still had to find work cleaning hotel rooms to supplement her income. Taylor built her career "one show at a time," Iglauer says.

"It was one great performance followed by another, and 10 people more would show up each time she'd play."

That work ethic was instilled at an early age, when Taylor grew up on a sharecropper's farm outside Memphis. She and three brothers and two sisters slept on pallets in a shotgun shack with no running water or electricity. By the time she was 11, both her parents had died. She picked cotton to survive, and while a teenager moved to Chicago in the early '50s to be with her future husband, Robert "Pop" Taylor. She found a job working as a domestic for North Shore families.

"I was on my knees scrubbing floors for $5 a day, and I was happy because I wasn't making 50 cents a day in the cotton fields," she says. "I thought I was getting rich."

On weekends, she and her husband frequented the South Side clubs, and Taylor sat in with everyone from Howlin' Wolf to Junior Wells and Buddy Guy. One night in the early '60s, she was approached by a man who was already a legend in blues circles for his songwriting, producing and arranging skills.

"I didn't know Willie Dixon from Adam's house cat," Taylor recalls. "But he says to me, 'I love the way you sound' and, 'We got plenty of men out here singing the blues, but the world needs a woman like you with your voice to sing the blues.'"

Dixon became Taylor's mentor and confidant, in addition to her musical guide. Basement jam sessions at Dixon's house at 52nd and Calumet helped her refine an already formidable voice, a heavy, accusatory alto that was the female equivalent of Howlin' Wolf's baritone growl. Dixon had to plead with her to cut a version of his ribald "Wang Dang Doodle" in 1965, but when she did, it became a huge hit for Chess Records, selling a reputed million copies. It was also one of the last major chart songs for the label, which folded in the early '70s, leaving Taylor back where she started, scrapping for a living.

"It was a devastating time for my mom," says Taylor's daughter, Joyce "Cookie" Threatt, who helps her mom run the nightclub. "It was hard to leave Chess and Willie Dixon, who was her promoter, manager and friend. When Willie moved to California, they talked every day. Then she met Bruce [Iglauer]. It was like God put him there."

But as with everything in Taylor's life, she had to work to get a break. Iglauer, who was just starting his label when the blues revival of the '60s was losing steam, at first wanted nothing to do with her.

"I kept bugging him to give me a chance," Taylor says. "He would say he would think about it, which was a nice way of getting rid of me. Every two weeks I'd call, and finally he said he'd give it a try."

Iglauer says he was uncertain of his abilities to produce a singer instead of an instrumentalist like his first signing, boogie guitarist Hound Dog Taylor. "I came from a world where guitar players ruled and stand-up vocalists didn't do very well," he says. "For me every record I made was a gamble back then, and if the gamble failed, the whole company could go."

But once Iglauer signed Taylor, he was impressed with her moxie. "Soon after I told her I'd try to get her some gigs, she called me and said, 'I've put a down payment on a van, I have four musicians in rehearsal and I'm ready to go. Get me some work.' She never expected me to hold her hand or take care of her business-wise. She was taking care of business on her own."

Taylor was already a distinctive artist when she came to Alligator, and with Iglauer's help began exploring a more vulnerable side to her persona on select ballads such as her epochal version of the Etta James hit "I'd Rather Go Blind." Even when recording other people's material, the singer put her idiosyncratic touch on it, usually singing it a cappella in the studio, with the musicians following her with chord changes and voicings.

Of all the female blues singers still active, she retains the closest connection to the raw Mississippi Delta sound that she first heard in childhood while listening to radio shows hosted by B.B. King and Rufus Thomas. "But she brings a lot of funky syncopations to her blues," Iglauer says. "Listen to the way she does 'Wang Dang Doodle' now, and it's slower, funkier and more grinding. It's her personality coming through larger than life."

With Taylor dedicated to touring, it took seven years before "Royal Blue" was completed. But the wait was worth it: Taylor sounds as tough and formidable as ever, lacing her tales of domestic strife—usually involving a two-timing lover who gets his comeuppance from the Queen—with salty humor. Taylor originals such as "The Man Next

Door," "Old Woman" and "Ernestine" work as a trilogy of stories on the subjects of lust and betrayal.

"She's writing about everyday life, though not her life necessarily," says her daughter. "She grew up singing in [the Baptist] church in Memphis, and people come into church to get washed. They don't come in there already clean."

Taylor's no-nonsense attitude doesn't just apply to her songs. She had to be tough to command respect in a male-dominated business. In addition, another foray into the club world, Koko Taylor's Chicago Blues, closed in April 1996 after being open only 14 months.

"I've seen her on nights when she was not happy with her band's performance," Iglauer says. "After the show, she'll call the band into the dressing room, and those guys come out of there shaking. She doesn't lay her hands on people, but she knows how to hurt a guy. We've been working together for 26 years, but that doesn't mean it's been a happy marriage for every moment. I've been fired more than once. I know that person laying into me. It's the person who picked cotton. She's got some calluses inside, and some rough edges. She's twice as tough as most blues performers because she is a woman, and had to fight not to be taken advantage of when she started out."

Back at the bar, the Queen is as sweet as can be. She just spent Mother's Day surrounded by friends, her daughter's family and her husband of four years, Hays Harris. After Pop died in 1989, she was devastated. But years later she met real estate developer Harris through a mutual friend and says "it feels like a honeymoon when we're together."

"The future, it isn't promised to you," she says. "But it looks good, it sounds promising and I'm looking forward to my career reaching the sky. And if we land somewhere in the clouds, I'll be happy with that."

Building her club is her way of returning a favor, providing a space for young musicians to perform the way she did 40 years ago, when she was still an unknown blues singer. "They'd say, 'Come on up and let Koko sing,'" she says with a laugh. "And I did." Little did she know that those weekend flings would soon come to define who she is.

As Lonnie Brooks says, "When she sings, it's like eating or breathing. She has to have it. She has to have this feeling to live. I do believe she'd rather die than quit."

They might be Bloodshot, but not tired at all

JAN. 30, 2004

Chicago might have seemed like an odd place for a pair of former punk rock drummers to start a roots-country label a decade ago, but Nan Warshaw and Rob Miller knew better when they mapped out a business plan for Bloodshot Records on a bar napkin. The city was teeming with disenfranchised rockers drawn to the soul of Appalachian murder ballads and honky-tonk two-steps. With their former partner, Eric Babcock (who has since left the label to run his own imprint, Catamount Records, in Nashville), Miller and Warshaw helped put the notion of "alternative country" on the map with Bloodshot's first album, "For a Life of Sin," a compilation of local twang-punk stalwarts (Jon Langford, Handsome Family, Robbie Fulks, Freakwater) released in 1994.

"For a Life of Sin" quickly sold out of its initial pressing of 1,000 copies, and now—109 albums and singles later—Bloodshot is renowned as the home of "insurgent country," ground zero for a movement that prides itself on being the antithesis of everything Nashville's Music Row stands for.

But as the label begins its 10th anniversary celebration with a concert Feb. 7, [2004] at the Old Town School of Folk Music, Miller acknowledges that the "insurgent country" imprint has become a "straitjacket."

"I know what I mean when I say country-influenced stuff, but not everybody else does," he says with a laugh. "If Creedence Clearwater Revival came out now, or [the Rolling Stones'] 'Let It Bleed,' or Neil Young, they'd all be thrown into the alt-country ghetto. Our label has some stuff in the country tradition, but there are also the Waco Brothers, Bobby Bare Jr., Neko [Case], Alejandro [Escovedo] who are country-influenced, but not really country or even alt-country in the way most people think of it. We tried to control the message at

Rob Miller and Nan Warshaw, co-owners of Bloodshot Records, posing in
their unfancy corporate headquarters.
BILL HOGAN

the start by labeling the music, but now it's sort of irrelevant. We're
not so narrowly defined anymore."

The label has had a number of successes in recent years, both artistic and commercial. Bloodshot released The Pine Valley Cosmonauts'
benefit CDs, "The Executioners' Last Songs," volumes 1–3, which
helped pour money into the successful campaign to overturn the death
penalty in Illinois; nurtured rising country-soul singer Neko Case; resurrected punk pioneer Alejandro Escovedo; and laid the groundwork
for the Old 97's.

But the label's watershed release remains Ryan Adams' first post-
Whiskeytown solo album, "Heartbreaker," which came out in 2000. Its
worldwide sales of 250,000 copies enabled the label to buy health insurance for its half-dozen employees and removed the cloud of financial doubt that had swirled around the label since its inception. Adams
wanted $30,000 to make the record and Miller and Warshaw took out
a private loan to make it happen.

"We didn't want to interfere with the daily operation of the label,"

Warshaw says, "so we went into hock to make it. But it paid off: It still sells 600 to 1,000 copies a week."

Though Adams' misadventures on and off the stage since then have been well-documented, the Bloodshot folks savor the idea that they released what remains the singer's finest album. "It's gratifying to know that record is not a flash in the pan, whatever shenanigans he's been involved in," Miller says. "That record still stands up over time."

The same could be said for the label itself, which has become part of a rich Chicago tradition. With 50-year-old Delmark at the head of the class, the city has become an incubator for successful indies: Alligator, Touch & Go, Southport, Drag City, Thrill Jockey, Minty Fresh, Carrot Top and countless others. They specialize in different brands of music, but they share a common passion for music and a commitment to their artists that resembles a family more than a business. Bloodshot, for example, has earned a reputation for being scrupulous about paying its artists; Escovedo says Bloodshot was the first label ever to pay him a royalty check in his 25-year career. It also allows its artists to record for other labels, rather than tying them down to exclusive deals.

"The longer I do this, the more I abhor the music business in general," Warshaw says. "It's like they lose sight of the fact that they exist to serve the artist, not the other way around."

"My one piece of advice about starting a label has not changed since the first day I did this," Miller adds.

"If you want to get into this to make money, you're an idiot. Do it only if you have absolutely unquenchable passion for the bands that you work with. Then you won't care if the rest of the world doesn't pick it up right away. You'll find a way, you'll build a grassroots network, you'll staple flyers to telephone poles, you'll get out there and build a website for your acts. All the business crap that you're forced to learn will change drastically, but the reason to do this never will."

House music comes home

More than two decades later, Chicago is finally listening to the sound born in its own underground

AUG. 8, 2004

Improbably, it's shaping up as the summer of house in Chicago. The gritty, homegrown brand of dance music that arose from the ashes of disco in the late '70s and became an international sound by the late '80s, has never gotten its due at home, and was almost run out of town by the city government a few years ago. But all that's starting to slowly change, thanks to a confluence of events:

Maurice Joshua took home a Grammy Award in February [2004] for best remixed recording, only the second time a Chicago-based house producer has been honored at the music industry's most prestigious ceremony.

House "godfather" Frankie Knuckles will have a street named in his honor at the site of the defunct Warehouse, the West Side dance club where he dee-jayed in the early days of house.

Knuckles is among the renowned deejays invited to spin this summer at free dance parties in Grant Park, the most high-profile city-sponsored house event in Chicago's history.

The Chicago label that put house on the international map, Trax Records, is back with wider distribution and a batch of CDs mining their revered catalog as well as new recordings.

It's enough to make even the most jaded house fan wonder what suddenly went right.

"There are a number of governmental employees, politicians and people in very important positions who've embraced this music," Knuckles says. "I'm nothing short of astounded by it all."

"I wished and hoped to see house music come to Grant Park, but I'd practically given up hope," says Joe Dale, longtime owner of Gramophone Records, epicenter for the dance-music community on the North Side. "Now it's happening and I'm happy, and the city seems to be happy. This could be a turning point."

Says Larry Sherman, the founder of Trax, back in business after an up-and-down decade, "House is an art form, a Chicago art form that Chicago didn't care about. It was created and maintained by people living in this city to entertain themselves and eventually the world. All of what is happening now indicates that Chicago is finally accepting that."

Acceptance has never come easily for house in its back yard, so it's understandable why the house community is so hungry for it. But it remains to be seen whether the overdue recognition will be good for the music.

At the 6,000-square-foot West Side offices of the newly revived Trax, one of the original house divas—Screamin' Rachael Cain—is taking a break from her usual brimming-with-optimism house cheerleader persona and slipping into a new outfit: beleaguered record-company president.

In the house

Just as disco went mainstream in the late '70s, house began cracking the pop charts about a decade after it first was heard in Chicago dance clubs. Its influence can be heard in the following songs:

• TECHNOTRONIC, "Pump Up the Jam" (1989): A collaboration between Belgian producer Joe Bogaert and Zairean rapper Ya Kid K took house to the top of the pop charts for the first time.

• HAPPY MONDAYS, "Pills `n' Thrills and Bellyaches" (1990): The Mondays were among the first British rock bands to incorporate acid-house rhythms, and broke through in the U.S. with this album.

• MADONNA, "Vogue" (1990): Always on top of the latest dance trends, Madonna explicitly celebrated the latest club fad in this No. 1 pop single.

• C+C MUSIC FACTORY, "Gonna Make You Sweat" (1991): Co-producers Robert Clivilles and David Cole brought a house groove to this massive international hit, topped by singer Martha Wash's call to arms, "Everybody dance now!"

• TONI BRAXTON, "Unbreak my Heart" (1996): The diva's No. 1 single was remixed by house "godfather" Frankie Knuckles.

• MOBY, "Play" (2000): After a decade in the clubs, Moby had his first million-seller with this mix.

"People didn't take Trax seriously for a long time. They think they can just steal from us!" She's standing in red fishnet stockings with hands on hips inside an office that befits her persona—it's outfitted in faux cheetah-skin wallpaper. Sherman looks on from the couch with a bemused grin: "Rachael is like a walking ad for her obsession, her career, her lifestyle."

Cain's obsession can be summed up in one word: house. House was built by deejays. Frankie Knuckles and Ron Hardy, and later Steve "Silk" Hurley, Farley Funk and Marshall Jefferson, strived to outdo each other with more outrageous mixes as they presided over dusk-till-dawn dance parties at South and West Side clubs. The sound combined crude digital technology, a relentless kick-drum bottom that thumped along at 125 beats per minute, and vocals that chanted, roared and pleaded for deliverance. Its ecstatic pulse was created on crude drum machines and keyboards, a kind of futuristic soul that swept dance music into the electronic age.

Pushed underground by the disco backlash that culminated with Steve Dahl's "Disco Demolition Night" at the Comiskey Park in 1979, house was largely the province of blacks, gays and Latinos until it hit the European vacation island of Ibiza in the late '80s. There house reached a new audience of teens and young adults just coming into its own, and became the soundtrack for a generation.

House had became world-renowned, but Chicago's pioneers rarely got the magazine covers, radio play or pay checks that their European disciples collected. English deejays such as Paul Oakenfold became the new ministers of dance culture, and savvier promoters and record labels in Europe usurped the Chicago sound for their own profit, eventually selling it back to North America. Meanwhile, the Chicago labels that had done the most to build the house sound faded away, victims of in-fighting and their own business and promotional ineptitude.

"The whole world adopted house, but forgot where it came from," Cain says. "Business was not our forte."

Chicago's attitude

Hometown recognition was complicated by the City of Chicago's am-bivalent, and sometimes downright poisonous, attitude toward late-night youth culture. While the city actively promoted itself as the home of the blues, it not only ignored house, it sometimes took steps that were perceived as hostile to its very existence. In 2000, the Chicago area dance scene was linked to three deaths, and the media ran wild with stories about rampant abuse of the designer drug Ecstasy at raves. That year, the city passed an ordinance that placed property owners, promoters and deejays in line for $10,000 fines if they were involved in an unlicensed dance party. The ordinance was passed without public discussion.

In 2001, another ordinance was passed holding building owners and managers criminally responsible for hosting house parties where drug use occurred. The crackdown left a stigma that made it more difficult for law-abiding fans, deejays and promoters to schedule events, and to bring out-of-town talent to Chicago. Just as rock 'n' roll had divided previous generations, dance music cleaved the city into warring extremes: the powerbrokers seeing it as a corrupt force that need to be banished before it drove their sons and daughters to drugs and an early death, the young fans and participants embracing it as the soundtrack of their lives that should be allowed to flourish anywhere, anytime.

"Some of the city people don't realize that what blues and jazz is to Chicago and an older generation, house is to the city and a younger generation," says Gramophone's Dale. "It not only has a social impact, but it can have a financial impact on the city, because there would be a huge influx of young people in this city from around the world if house were promoted properly."

In the time since the crackdown, the outlaw rave scene has faded, replaced gradually by sanctioned events where the music is the focus. This year [2004], the Chicago Department of Cultural Affairs incorporated the deejay series into its already successful Summer Dance program in Grant Park. The crowds have swelled to more than 3,000, and the atmosphere is festive, with bare-chested club kids mingling with couples pushing strollers.

The weekly events have helped overturn "the drug-culture stigma that has followed dance music around in this city," says Brian Keigher, a deejay who worked with program director Michael Orlove in the cultural affairs department to give house a foothold in city programming.

The two hope to expand the bookings in future summers, and are looking at the possibility of a house festival or conference in future years to spotlight the city's importance in international music.

"It took about the same amount of time for blues to be recognized as a significant art form," Keigher says. "There's a whole generation after the Baby Boom that has always recognized house as a legitimate style of music, and it's inundating TV commercials, so you can't say it's underground anymore. Now people on the outskirts of the music are starting to realize its potential."

Dirty immediacy

That may not be in the best interests of a music that has always been perceived as a bit of an outlaw: "primal, sexual escapism from the world outside the dance club," as Screamin' Rachael puts it. The production standards of the early house records were so low that the major labels laughed at them, but these tracks had a dirty immediacy unlike anything else.

"This was a style of music created by people who didn't have a map, who didn't know the `right' way to play an instrument, or how to play an instrument at all," says Farley Funk. "People hated me because we didn't have real drummers and real bass players on our records, yet I'd walk into a room with one machine under my arm and make a hit. We didn't have radio support, but I was selling more records out of my trunk than Prince."

The bespectacled house veteran exaggerates only slightly. He co-wrote one of the biggest house hits of all time, "Love Can't Turn Around," though getting paid royalties for it was a different matter.

"Our legend was a whole lot bigger than our wallets," says Rachael, who scored a string of major house hits, including "Fun with Bad Boys," but acknowledges that for years she and her fellow Chicago house innovators struggled to make ends meet.

Yet the music they made has achieved a longevity that even some of its early champions couldn't predict. After the first wave of deejays introduced house to the club scene, musicians fluent in the new digital gear began making records, including Vince Lawrence, Joe Smooth and Jere McAllister. "It was basically kids with new drum

machines and little synthesizers trying to capture the vibe of an orchestra," McAllister says. "It became the first multicultural dance
music, with American soul music, Afro-Cuban rhythms and other
styles mixed together." As the music filtered overseas, it became
trendy. But the bedrock of well-crafted songs—many compiled on
Trax's new "20th Anniversary Collection"—gave it a staying power
that has transcended generations.

"The Trax catalog is still selling because it had identifiable tunes,
whereas a lot of dance music now is kind of nondescript—it's basically a track without a memorable sense of melody," Gramophone's
Dale says.

What remains uncertain is whether Trax and Chicago house can
find a new audience. Dale says he still sells 100 copies a week of Trax's
vintage hits at his store, compared to 15 copies of the label's new product. "It remains to be seen whether there's a new market out there that
cares about Trax, because to them Trax is their older brother's or father's music," Dale says. "But they're working hard: They've got tenacity,
and now they've got money behind them."

A new deal with Toronto-based investors Casablanca will ensure
that Trax has a promotional and distribution reach that it lacked in
its '80s heyday. Screamin' Rachael has a new album, "Extacy," out
this month, and the Maurice Joshua-mixed "Trax Records: The Next
Generation" spotlights new songs from revered house artists such as
McAllister, Rachael, Joe Smooth and Lidell Townsell.

"Who cares about the legend?" Farley Funk says. "In dance music,
there's a turnover every two years in what's hot. You have to earn your
wings every day."

Whether house in its post-outlaw, city-sanctioned phase will still
matter to young people already hooked on hip-hop, video games and
extreme sports remains to be seen.

But for now, Chicago's house mavens are basking in the glow of
some long-overdue recognition.

"The people I meet all around the world are looking at Chicago and
the house scene with a new romanticism," Knuckles says. "Too little
too late? Personally, I'm happy to see it happen in my lifetime.

Evolution of house

• **1977:** Frankie Knuckles moves from New York to Chicago to spin records at the Warehouse on South Jefferson Street.

• **1979:** Steve Dahl orchestrates "Disco Demolition Night" at Comiskey Park, creating a fireworks show out of Donna Summer and KC and the Sunshine Band albums.

• **1979–83:** Disco doesn't die—it morphs into house and flourishes in Chicago clubs such as the Warehouse, Power Plant, Playground and Music Box.

• **1982:** Techno, a futuristic electronic cousin of house, is born in Detroit with Derrick May, Juan Atkins and Kevin Saunderson.

• **1985–86:** The golden age of house arrives in Chicago, with massive hits by Steve "Silk" Hurley ("Music is the Key"), Marshall Jefferson ("Move Your Body") and Farley Funk ("Love Can't Turn Around").

• **1987:** The British discover Chicago house, and psychedelic dance parties called raves take over the vacation island of Ibiza in the Mediterranean and clubs back on the mainland such as the Hacienda in Manchester.

• **1989–90:** A host of British bands—Happy Mondays, Stone Roses, Primal Scream—beginning melding acid-house's pulse and trippy vibe with rock instrumentation.

• **1992–95:** A second wave of house led by Cajmere, a.k.a. Green Velvet; Derrick Carter; DJ Sneak; and Bad Boy Bill puts Chicago back in the forefront of the club world.

• **1997:** Knuckles becomes the first artist associated with house music to win a Grammy Award, in the newly created category of remixer of the year.

• **2000:** The City of Chicago becomes notorious in the worldwide dance community for passing what became known as the "anti-rave" ordinance. It makes property owners, promoters and deejays subject to $10,000 fines for being involved in an unlicensed dance party.

• **2004:** House producer Maurice Joshua wins a Grammy for best remixed recording.

Pitchfork tries its hand at running its own musical extravaganza

JULY 28, 2006

Ho-hum—another summer weekend in Chicago, another festival that shouldn't be missed.

The inaugural Pitchfork Music Festival offers a madhouse of 41 bands and artists ranging across the worlds of rock, jazz, hip-hop, electronic and experimental music. It's expected that as many as 34,000 fans will attend the two-day event.

It's getting to be old hat for a city that went from virtually ignoring cutting-edge culture during its outdoor season to filling its summer calendar with events that music fans from around the world are talking about: Intonation, Move! Lollapalooza and Pitchfork.

Mike Reed, a veteran jazz drummer who had a history of booking smart but small local shows for a decade, couldn't have predicted such a windfall of music two years ago. Back then, he took aim at creating a festival in Chicago patterned after huge European musical gatherings such as Reading and Glastonbury, which showcased artists who cut across genres and generations. "I thought we needed a better display of music than we'd been getting," he says.

With his partners Jon Singer and Mike Simons, Reed enlisted Pitchfork, the potent Chicago-based Internet magazine devoted to independent music, to curate what would become known as the Intonation Music Festival last summer.

The festival drew 30,000 fans from around the world to Union Park. When Reed split with his partners afterward, Singer and Simons brought back Intonation a few weeks ago to Union Park with a new curator, the New York-based Vice record label. The two-day event again left its mark, with a comeback show by psychedelic rock pioneer Roky Erickson, a rare appearance by producer extraordinaire Jon Brion, and showcases for rising hip-hop stars Rhymefest and Lupe Fiasco.

Now it's Reed and Pitchfork's turn. Once again the e-zine has

Scott Plagenhoef (left), Chris Kaskie, Mike Reed, and Ryan Schreiber. Pitchfork, the most influential tastemakers in indie-rock, and Reed put together the Intonation Festival, one of the biggest indie rock festivals ever staged, and the first Pitchfork Music Festival.
BILL HOGAN

handpicked a who's who of its favorite artists, ranging from relative newcomers such as Art Brut and Tapes 'N Tapes to reunited '60s cult favorites Os Mutantes. Tickets are $20, up five dollars from last year's Intonation. That's still a bargain; to see Os Mutantes in New York recently, fans would've had to pay more than double that price. Weeks before the event, the festival had already sold more than 12,000 two-day passes.

"It's going to be a great event," says Chicago Park District Supt. Tim Mitchell. "It's not a big organization like [Lollapalooza promoters Capital Sports and Entertainment], so it's not about the dollars they bring in, but about helping us bring programs that we can do in other parks, like day camps. Intonation and Pitchfork are helping us attract a whole different crowd than the park district normally touches."

Reed also helped book art, film and music events throughout the city in the days preceding the festival. Afterward, he'll bring musical events to other parks in the city.

"If we're going to put on a national or international event, we have to make it about more than 41 bands in two days in a park," Reed says. Ultimately, however, the festival will be judged on the quality of its music. If anything, Reed and Pitchfork have upped the ante over last year, with more artists across a wider spectrum of music, and a genuine coup in Os Mutantes.

"We kept in mind what our audience wants to see," says Pitchfork managing editor Scott Plagenhoef. "The festival is an extension of our dialogue with the music fans on our site."

Whereas Intonation booked more heavy metal and hip-hop, Pitchfork dug a little deeper for a wider array of noteworthy underground acts. But the festivals share more aesthetic similarities than differences.

That's not a major concern for the promoters. "We're not worried whether the festivals do some of the same things," Plagenhoef says. "We're focused on doing our festival, and making sure we represent all the artists in the best light."

Ultimately, the winners are music fans, who now have two well-planned festivals to enjoy in Union Park this summer instead of just one, as in 2005, or none, as in all the years previous. Mitchell is glad to have the business. "I see them both coming back next year," he says.

....

Girl Talk easily blends appealing samples

JULY 20, 2008

In Girl Talk's world, anything is possible: The Carpenters jam with Metallica, Jay-Z collaborates with Radiohead, the Butthole Surfers pretend they're in "Flashdance."

That's just a smattering of the hundreds of seemingly absurd re-combinations conjured by former Pittsburgh biochemist Gregg Gillis on the fourth Girl Talk album, "Feed the Animals" (Illegal Art), which is available on the illegalart.net Web site at any price chosen by the buyer.

Fans dance on stage during the performance by Girl Talk's Greg Gillis at the Pitchfork Music Festival July 14, 2007.
NUCCIO DINUZZO

Two years ago, Girl Talk's "Night Ripper" album skipped from underground obscurity to party favorite through a combination of audacity, skill and relentless touring.

Just about every note heard on "Night Ripper" and now "Feed the Animals" is a provocation, a test of copyright law. Each track on both albums consists entirely of electronic snippets meticulously stitched together from hundreds of major hits, most by high-profile artists. In the process, Gillis has become a somewhat reluctant poster boy for fair-use advocates in the ongoing battle over copyright law. Girl Talk's music demands that a distinction be made between simply copying someone else's work for profit, and reconfiguring and recontextualizing it to create a new piece of art.

Modest expectations

Gillis says he never intended his music to become even remotely popular. He made "Night Ripper" and two preceding albums primarily for his friends, and as a way to play a few shows around his hometown. But as "Night Ripper" made the rounds on Internet file-sharing networks, Girl Talk became an increasingly bigger draw on the road.

Showing up with little more than his laptop and an arsenal of MP3 music files that he mashed-up on the fly, Gillis took the relatively esoteric science of sample-based composition into a new, nearly mainstream arena. He was the hit of the 2007 Pitchfork Festival in Union Park, drawing a crowd that far exceeded promoter's expectations, and this year *[2008]* has a prime slot on Lollapalooza. He's gone from playing tiny clubs for a few dozen fans two years ago to headlining sold-out clubs and theaters.

How'd he do it? DJ's had been mashing up songs in dance clubs and circulating mixes on the Internet for years. But Gillis is the first mash-up star because he took this somewhat esoteric art form live in a new and exciting way. He's a participant as much as an instigator at his own shows, often diving into the audience and leading the dancers like an electroshock pied piper.

On record, Gillis merges high and low art. Composition based on fragments of recorded material has a long and noble tradition in avant-garde circles. It was the province of academics, connoisseurs and cult figures such as John Oswald, John Cage and Luc Ferrari. Gillis brings this rigorous editing process to bear on top 40 pop, and refashions it into music that can be appreciated both for its technical acumen and its unabashed sense of fun. Add the outlaw element—none of these samples has been cleared—and you have the makings of an underground star.

Bits and pieces

On "Feed the Animals," Gillis subtly expands the template established on "Night Ripper." He packs dozens of samples into each track and more than 300 overall onto the 53-minute album. Most are recognizable, even iconic, including snippets of songs by Jay-Z, George Harrison, Radiohead, Sly Stone, Prince, Lil Wayne and Madonna.

He turns them into 14 smoothly integrated, breathlessly paced pieces of pop music, designed to be heard in sequence, like one long set at a dance club. Girl Talk does not traffic in working with obscure or obscured fragments; instead, he positively revels in the way he can put a new spin on the overexposed. Some of his source songs are so hoary that they were cliches nearly the instant they were originally released (Tag Team's "Whoomp! (There It Is)," we're looking at you). Yet by pairing "Whoomp!" with the drums from Big Country's bombastic "In a Big Country," Gillis re-energizes both tracks. Tag Team sounds suddenly more urgent, and Big Country loses some of its clenched-teeth earnestness.

The main difference between the new album and "Night Ripper" is that "Feed the Animals" isn't quite as densely packed; Gillis' edits are less frenetic, and he's more willing to ride a groove rather than send it screeching in a new direction with a precision edit. The laugh-out-loud juxtapositions, such as the Carpenters' somber "Superstar" ushering in Metallica's rivet-gun riffing in "One," are all the more enjoyable for the way Gillis makes them sound utterly natural, almost inevitable.

There's a wonderful moment near the end of the album where Lil Wayne's ubiquitous "Lollipop" slips inside John Frusciante's lyrical guitar riff from the Red Hot Chili Peppers' "Under the Bridge." They are songs separated by two decades and two cultures, but in the context created by Gillis, they couldn't be more right for each other.

....

How Lollapalooza changed Chicago's concert landscape

JULY 27, 2008

The road that Lollapalooza built in Chicago for Texas promoters C3 Presents could lead to the 2016 Olympics, if C3 co-founder Charlie Jones has his way.

"I would love nothing more," Jones says. "I don't think there is any doubt the city will get the Olympics . . . [and] when they get it, I would love nothing more than to help the city bring that event to the world. Public assembly is my passion. And I feel we're very good at it. There are people in the city who have seen our attention to detail

Lollapalooza in Grant Park in 2008.
E. JASON WAMBSGANS

and we run a pretty tight ship, and I think we are educating other event producers in town on how to elevate their game. I hope we get the opportunity, whether working any of the Olympic arenas or stuff that happens around it, or helping the city prepare for it. I'll be in the bullpen waiting."

A mix of Texas-size bravado and I'm-here-to-serve earnestness, Jones, 39, represents the heaviest new hitter on the Chicago entertainment promotion landscape. Jones' previous company, Capital Sports Entertainment, revived the Lollapalooza name in 2005 and implausibly found a new home for it at Grant Park, the city's most revered piece of public property and previously inaccessible to big rock shows. Jones and his current partners in C3, 40-year-old Charles Attal and 36-year-old Charlie Walker, also have forged contracts with the Congress Theatre to book shows at the 4,200-seat theater and with the Philadelphia-based facility management firm SMG and the Chicago Park District to bring events to Soldier Field.

Next weekend, more than 100 bands will play Lollapalooza over three days in Grant Park, and Jones says it will be the biggest festival yet, with capacity audiences of 75,000 expected all three days. Indeed, the 2008 edition of Lollapalooza has the most enticing lineup of head-liners booked by any major North American festival this year *[2008]*: Radiohead, Rage Against the Machine, Nine Inch Nails, Kanye West and Wilco.

C3 Presents is based in Austin, Texas, where it has a 75-person office and promotes events throughout the state. Attal and Jones first partnered as promoters for the Austin City Limits Festival, which began in 2002 and has grown into one of the nation's biggest and most successful festivals, drawing 225,000 people annually. Its suc-cess led to a deal with the City of Chicago to launch Lollapalooza in 2005, breaking a long-standing resistance to major rock shows in Grant Park. Later, the Texans hired Mark Vanecko, an attorney and lobbyist who is Mayor Richard J. Daley's nephew, to help them nego-tiate a five-year deal with the city to keep Lollapalooza in Grant Park through at least 2011.

The Lollapalooza, Congress Theatre and Soldier Field contracts have turned C3 into the third major force on the Chicago concert scene, along with a local institution, Jam Productions, and the nation's largest concert promoter, Live Nation. Jones says there's room for all three to thrive. But Lollapalooza is blamed by many local club owners for seriously cutting into their summer business, because of exclusivity clauses that restrict bands on the bill from playing local concerts six months before and three months after the festival.

"Bands play Lollapalooza because they get paid a lot of money," says Nick Miller, longtime club talent buyer for Jam. "It sucks up all our talent during the summer."

Ray Quinn, owner of the Lincoln Avenue club Martyrs', says, "We try to stock up the rest of the year for the long cold summer. It's like hibernation [for clubs in Chicago]."

Exclusivity clauses are common practice in the concert promotion business. Every major festival has them. They're designed to protect promoters' investment in a band against other venues. But club own-ers argue that smaller bands on the Lollapalooza schedule don't affect ticket sales that much and shouldn't be subject to the same restrictions as headliners such as Radiohead.

"If I put up trillions of dollars to put on a festival, I would want to put those [exclusivity] clauses on," says Bruce Finkelman, owner of the Empty Bottle on Western Avenue. "But I don't see how a band playing at 2 o'clock in the afternoon at Lollapalooza, opening for Radiohead, is going to make much of a difference [to Lollapalooza's bottom line]."

Attal, the primary talent buyer at C3, counters that the exclusivity clause is often just a formality. "It's in 90 percent of the contracts for all the big promoters," he says. "But if a band wants to play another show in the area, it's usually not a problem. We make exceptions all the time."

A number of artists on this year's Lollapalooza technically violated the exclusivity clause with C3's blessing, Attal says, including Yeasayer, Jamie Lidell, the National, Lupe Fiasco and West. Next year, he says, he will narrow the exclusivity clause to three months on either side of the Lollapalooza dates. "That's pretty fair, considering I'm not enforcing it anyway," he says.

The olive branch is part of C3's effort to ingratiate itself with the city and its music community. Each year, it funnels $1 million to the Chicago Parkways Foundation for park improvements. Next weekend, Lollapalooza will partner with clubs such as Metro, Schubas, the Abbey, Double Door, Empty Bottle and House of Blues to host 18 "after-parties" with 30 festival bands.

"We've got two Lollapalooza shows that are great shows," Finkelman says. "We are starting to have a relationship with [C3]."

Jones invokes buzz words such as "relationship-building," "community service" and "social responsibility" frequently. C3 Presents is in the second year of a five-year deal with the city to promote Lollapalooza, but it's already looking beyond that. It established a small office in Chicago last year, but Jones says it will expand by the end of this year to handle business for the festival as well as booking events at the Congress Theatre and Soldier Field. He's contemplating a similar move with his family, which includes his wife and two daughters, ages 3 and 3 months.

"I'm very close to moving my family here, and probably someday I will," he says. "Every time my wife comes here and brings our daughters, we get more and more comfortable. I love the city. I'm going to be around a while."

At least, it appears, until 2016.

Vinyl spins to the forefront again

OCT. 5, 2008

At a time when convenience and portability rule for consumers listening to music collections on MP3 players, the stodgy old vinyl album and turntable are making an unexpected comeback.

While CD sales continue a double-digit decline, sales of vinyl albums have doubled in the last year to 6 million and turntable sales increased 80 percent last year. The resurgence is being led not just by Baby Boomers nostalgic for gatefold album sleeves and the pops and scratches of favorite records, but by college-age consumers discovering the elaborate artwork of vinyl-album packaging for the first time, and entranced by the grittier, less-artificial sound quality.

"We're seeing the [vinyl] resurgence in all walks of life: from 50-year-old guys who want high-quality product to match their high-end stereos to 19-year-old kids who are sick of the minimalist Ikea design that has plagued dorm rooms for the last decade," says Ken Shipley, co-owner of the Numero Group, a South Side label that specializes in reissues of underground soul music. "Vinyl is the new books."

This year *[2008]*, 40 percent of the label's income is coming from vinyl sales. Sundazed Music, a New York-based reissue label, has seen vinyl sales surge 500 percent in the last three years. The percentage is far lower at major labels, but still significant enough to warrant not only reissues of classic titles such as the Beach Boys' "Pet Sounds" and Radiohead's "OK Computer," but new titles as well. Warner Brothers sold 12,000 vinyl copies of the White Stripes' 2007 release "Icky Thump" and sold out a 5,000-copy run of a $115.98 vinyl boxed set of Metallica's latest album, "Death Magnetic." Nonesuch's vinyl version of Wilco's 2007 album "Sky Blue Sky" has sold 15,000 copies.

Matador Records, home to such bands as Cat Power, Yo La Tengo and Mission of Burma, is seeing a double-digit percentage increase in vinyl sales. "We can't press it fast enough," says Matador General Manager Patrick Amory.

Record Breakers shop in Reggie's Rock Club.
BRENT LEWIS

"You have to get in line now at these pressing plants, which is amazing, because vinyl was virtually non-existent two or three years ago," adds Bill Gagnon, senior vice president of catalog marketing at EMI Music. The turnaround time at pressing plants has doubled to two months because of high demand, says Robert Griffin, who runs the Scat label out of Cleveland.

"How many commercials have you seen that involve a DJ spinning a record?" he says. "Repeat with incidences on TV shows, movies. It's being presented as a cool thing, not anachronistic, which was the late '90s attitude."

Though Gagnon says vinyl will eventually make up about 4 percent of EMI's revenue, it's a profitable business that will have long-lasting appeal, in part because a younger generation is getting hooked on it.

Eric Shah, a 23-year-old law student at Loyola University, says he didn't start buying vinyl to be cool, but because "I like the sound. It's closer to the sound you might hear in the studio when the music is being recorded. I like the idea of listening to an artist's work on vinyl. It becomes a process. You sit down, play through a side, it becomes more singular because you're more focused on it. It's not portable. You have to pay attention, turn the record over when it's done. It encourages active listening."

Allie Samata, a 20-year-old studying architecture at the University of Illinois at Chicago, rhapsodizes about "the emotional connection of placing the record on the turntable, putting the needle down and sitting there with your friends to listen. It's definitely a community experience, which I don't get from downloading an MP3 file. It's as close to going to a concert as you can get."

The disadvantages of vinyl are numerous: tough to transport, bulky to store, easy to damage. MP3 files have enabled consumers to essentially pack their entire music collection in a device the size of a cigarette box and listen to it any time, anywhere. Clearly, digital is the future of music, and the re-emergence of vinyl won't change that. But hard-core music lovers are a demanding bunch, and they still want a tangible connection to the music that a digital file can't provide.

"There's an art to making a vinyl album, and it invites serious listening," says Matador's Amory.

"For me, vinyl is more of a personal listening experience," says Ben Meyerson, 22, who is studying journalism at the University of Maryland. "I have my turntable in my room, and it's hands-on—a compensation for the lack of physicality you get from a hard drive and iTunes. It's fills a void in my musical experience."

There are also legions of album junkies who insist that no digital format, whether compact disc or MP3, can compare to the sonic richness of a stylus penetrating the grooves of a vinyl record.

"There's a huge difference," says singer Sam Phillips. "It has a little grit and texture compared to digital. It's heartbreaking not to have all that sound on an MP3 file. I love my vinyl, and I play it all the time. Nothing sounds like it. Who would've thought? In the early '80s, we were trying to take all the noise out by making these really precise recordings. And now, we want it all back because it sounds more real, more like the work of a human being instead of a machine."

The new market for albums is in part directed at these audiophiles, with heavier 180-gram discs made out of so-called "virgin" vinyl (which contains no recycled plastic) more resistant to the degradation and warping that accompany cheaper materials. With fewer pressing plants and more expensive material, the packaging can get pricey: Some vinyl albums sell for double the price of a CD. The situation was reversed 25 years ago, when compact discs first came on the market and were double the price of most vinyl albums. In addition, the nuances of an audiophile vinyl album won't be apparent unless the listener has a turntable of sufficient quality to pick them up. A hand-me-down turntable from an uncle or a flea-market bargain special won't necessarily yield sonic results that satisfy any more than a low-grade MP3 download.

But the romantic pull of turntables and vinyl is strong, both for an older generation that grew up with them, and younger listeners looking for a deeper connection with the music they love.

"Everything old is new again," says Tom Biery, general manager of Warner Brothers. "Now that iPods and MP3s have become your parents' music, too, kids want something different. The kids in the dorm with the turntable are the cool kids now."

Classics on vinyl

• THE 13TH FLOOR ELEVATORS, "The Psychedelic Sounds of . . . " (Sundazed): The Holy Grail of psychedelia by Roky Erickson's acid-drenched garage band, available in the original (and vastly preferred) mono for the first time in 40 years.

• BEACH BOYS, "Pet Sounds" (Capitol Records): The limited-edition double album released in 2006 contains both mono and stereo mixes of the 1966 masterpiece.

• JOHNNY CASH, "At Folsom Prison" (Columbia Legacy): The master in his element, in a recording that captures the palpable excitement of his 1968 performance at one of the country's most notorious penitentiaries.

• METALLICA, "Master of Puppets" (Elektra): Available in both 33-r.p.m. and pricier 45-r.p.m. pressings, a revelatory reissue of a metal landmark.

• VARIOUS ARTISTS, "Don't Stop: Recording Tap" (Numero Group): Proof that packaging counts, nobody does it better than this Chicago label. Detailed liner notes augment lovingly restored music from the last golden era of disco, with an entire bonus album of tracks unavailable on the CD version.

....

How much is music worth?

In a business previously dominated by personalities and movements, this decade belonged to the fans

DEC. 22, 2009

" t's up to you"—so said Radiohead when fans clicked to download the band's "In Rainbows" album from its website in 2007.

Radiohead had become the equivalent of the busker on the street corner, playing for tips. But as one of the biggest bands in the world, Radiohead also was posing a question: "What's music worth?"

That was the decade's signature moment in pop music, a sign that fans—once a faceless marketing demographic—were now de facto distributors, marketers, publicists and co-conspirators.

Previous decades were dominated by personalities and movements, larger-than-life figures such as Elvis Presley and The Beatles, and cultural shifts such as hip-hop, rave music and punk. But the 2000s belonged to music technology and delivery systems. Most of all, the decade belonged to fans.

The combination of broadband Internet access and file-trading software such as Napster seized power and control over music from a handful of corporations and transferred it to the laptops and cell phones of consumers. Since 2000, the industry has seen its business cut by one-third to less than $10 billion annually, while compact disc sales have been chopped in half, to fewer than 500 million annually.

Though sales of digital music have increased, those gains are far outweighed by rogue peer-to-peer file-trading networks. Web-tracking services estimate that for every digital file that is sold, 40 are traded in violation of U.S. copyright law. Even as massive judgments were awarded to the music industry in highly publicized copyright infringement trials against Jammie Thomas-Rasset and Joel Tenenbaum, jurists noted the inadequacy of 20th century copyright law in addressing the new digital reality. Though a jury ultimately awarded the record industry $1.92 million in damages because Thomas-Rasset was found to have made 24 copyrighted music files available on her home computer, she "acted like countless other Internet users," U.S. District Judge Michael Davis said.

"Her alleged acts were illegal, but common."

Copyright holders have reason to gripe. Intellectual property that consumers covet is certainly worth something—as Radiohead's "In Rainbows" marketing strategy implied. Yet the industry is hardly blameless in the shift to illegal file-sharing. As consumers made their desires clear by shifting from physical product to digital music, important catalogs such as The Beatles and AC/DC still can't be purchased from legitimate music stores like Apple's iTunes. But fans can download the songs of any band through countless black-market sites; indeed, just about any song you can possibly think of is a mouse click away, for free.

---

10 key rock events of the decade

In chronological order:

1. 'N Sync rides the wave. The boy band caps an unrivaled run of prosperity for the music industry by selling 2.4 million copies of its 2000 album "No Strings Attached" in a single week.

2. Radiohead's "Kid A" leaks. Despite hitting the Internet months before release, the album debuts at No. 1 on the Billboard chart anyway, with computer-savvy fans leading the charge.

3. Metallica sues Napster. The band files suit in April 2000 and brings the wrath of the music industry down on peer-to-peer file sharing. The move didn't exactly endear the band to music consumers, and online backlash came swiftly. Napster filed for bankruptcy in 2002 and now exists as a paid, subscription-based service.

4. Kelly Clarkson tops Justin Guarini. In winning the first "American Idol," she helps ignite the most popular mainstream music industry franchise of the decade.

5. Festivals jump-start touring. After a false start in 1999 followed by years of inactivity, the Coachella Valley Music and Arts Festival relaunches in 2002 in California. In Tennessee, the Bonnaroo Music and Arts Festival debuts. The two events kick off a decade of major destination festivals, including Lollapalooza and Pitchfork in Chicago, and help rejuvenate the touring business.

As recently as a decade ago, it could take the dedicated fan months to track down obscure releases. Now they can be found in a matter of seconds, turning music into the cultural equivalent of tap water or oxygen. More music is more accessible to more people than ever, and yet that very ubiquity makes it feel somehow less essential.

Music fans hang on to their portable music players, the iPod in particular, rather than the music they hold. They collect music and then dispose of it, certain they can replace it with a few mouse clicks.

Just about everything (except for maybe the latest "American Idol" star) feels smaller, more niche. The age of The Beatles, U2 and Madonna—the all-encompassing global superstar—is in decline. Within this fragmented culture, in which every movement no matter how obscure has its own website and cult following, great music still is

---

10 key rock events of the decade, cont.

6. Apple opens its digital media store iTunes. It is the music industry's most successful response to the file-sharing crisis.

7. Recording industry cracks down. In 2003, the Recording Industry Association of America opens a lengthy campaign to sue consumers accused of sharing copyrighted digital songs. Most consumers avoid trial by paying a $3,000 fine.

8. The Arcade Fire catches fire. An obscure Canadian band, the Arcade Fire, hits big with its 2004 debut, "Funeral," fueled by massive Internet buzz fed primarily by Chicago-based e-zine Pitchfork. The next year, the website begins curating its own festival, and a host of indie-rock bands would enjoy unprecedented mainstream attention.

9. File-sharers pay. Culminating four years of lawsuits against file-sharing consumers, a jury awards the music industry $222,000 in the infringement trial of Jammie Thomas-Rasset, who is accused of making 24 copyrighted songs available on her home computer. The award is increased to $1.92 million in a retrial the next year.

10. Live Nation and Ticketmaster join forces. The industry giants in 2009 announce plans to merge the nation's largest concert promoter and ticketing company. Despite major concerns about a monopoly that could send ticket prices spiraling even higher, the merger is still in play as the decade ends.

Alligator Records producer Bruce Iglauer (left) with blues artist
Lil' Ed Williams at Joyride Studios on Feb. 9, 2011.
BRIAN CASSELLA

Koko Taylor, have died; the record business has been in a decade-long
economic decline; and the blues is a mere sliver of the U.S. music market, representing less than 1 percent of its sales.

Yet Iglauer remains an enthusiast, a vigorous advocate for the blues
who runs his label with an energy that can verge on manic. He puts in
long days, doing everything from producing records and listening to
demos to assisting artists who need help paying bills and drumming
up overseas business. He is currently exploring a licensing deal with a

Shanghai media conglomerate to bring Alligator recordings to China. With a staff of 15, Alligator Records remains a blues cornerstone, a $2 million-a-year business that dispenses $500,000 in royalty checks to artists annually.

"I run this business with the knowledge that the grandchildren of Hound Dog Taylor are counting on me to make smart decisions," he says, sitting next to a coffee table brimming with stuffed alligators (the label was named after Iglauer's habit of clicking his teeth together in time to music) and a pyramid-shaped Blues Foundation trophy awarded to the imprint for "Keeping the Blues Alive."

In an interview, Iglauer reflected on his favorite subject: the blues, and how to ensure that future generations will hear it.

Q: How's business?

A: We took a really bad hit in 2009, but the last year *[2010]* turned out to be profitable. Our international business has actually grown. We have so many artists who are successfully touring in Europe and we've been aggressive about building those marketplaces. Our download market is growing. For our more straight-up blues artists the digital market is fairly small, but newer artists like JJ Grey and Mofro and Anders Osborne can sell as much as 45 percent digital.

Q: In 1991 on your 20th anniversary you estimated gross revenue of $4 million for Alligator. What's your revenue like now?

A: Our cash flow is about half of what it was 20 years ago. The sales of all recordings in the world are about half of what they were in 1999. We've all taken a hit.

Q: Many in the industry blame file-sharing for the decline. I know you feel it's hurt the business.

A: It didn't hurt us as much directly because of our adult consumer base, which likes to buy physical product. But there are many fewer stores today carrying our records. The implosion of commercial recordings started in 1999, and Napster started in 1999. I don't think that's coincidental. There is some legal action against file-sharing in the U.S. It's a good sign. But burning a CD and sending it to your friend is unstoppable. That's here to stay. We can't as publishers keep up with all our songs that are showing up on YouTube. We've given up. It's an impossible fight.

Q: But is there any benefit to people exposing their friends to your music this way?

A: Certainly people hear about music from friends. I used to have friends come over and I'd play my new records for them, and some of them went out and bought them. But when you give away all the music, burn the entire album and give it to a friend, then no, your friend is not going to go out and purchase it later. . . . The effect of downloading is much more negative than positive.

Q: How have recording costs been affected?

A: The cost of making a record has actually gone down in the last 40 years. I was making deals for $100 to $120 an hour for studio time to record albums, now I pay half that. I used to spend $2,000 on tape alone. No more. I will cut songs on tape, then dump them into Pro Tools, then re-record over the tape. I'm not afraid of digital. I think those records sound as warm and live sounding as analog records. If the music is great, most of the public doesn't care what it sounds like. The important thing is the song and the performance.

Q: You used to produce most of the albums you put out, but you seem to have cut back. Why?

A: Because I'm not the right producer for a lot of the artists I sign—JJ Grey, Marcia Ball, Anders Osborne. I'm a good blues producer. If you want to make a good-sounding blues record, I'm your man. If you want to make something more complex than that, I'm not your man. I'm not a musician. I don't read music. I'm no Arif Mardin, I'm no Glen Ballard. But I think I can make a better Lil' Ed record than anyone in the world. I have other artists, they come with a vision of their own, their music is more complex, and they want to make their own personal statement.

Q: Blues is shrinking as a percentage of the national music market, right?

A: Yes, straight-up blues is less than 1 percent of the U.S. market. Blues hasn't had a champion, a new artist in quite some time, since Stevie Ray Vaughan's death (in 1990). There are a lot of younger listeners who don't have a way into the music.

Q: Eric Clapton says the blues has become like classical music—but is that a good thing for its future?

A: I think blues has a future as long as it doesn't spend too much time repeating what already has been done. It's in a double bind. A lot of established blues fans really want their blues to sound like what they grew up with. But it was never a static thing. When Muddy Waters

---

Some classic Alligator recordings

• HOUND DOG TAYLOR, "Hound Dog Taylor and the Houserockers" (1971): The album that started it all, a blast of unrivaled, grit-coated South Side boogie.

• KOKO TAYLOR, "The Earthshaker" (1978): A voice robust enough to knock down walls at any gin joint in town.

• ALBERT COLLINS, "Ice Pickin'" (1978): A master class in guitar tone brimming with shiver-inducing accents.

• LONNIE BROOKS, "Bayou Lightning" (1979): Expressive blues guitar streaked with Louisiana soul.

• LUTHER ALLISON, "Soul Fixin' Man" (1994): The first domestic release by the guitar great in 20 years ignited his late-career rise.

• COREY HARRIS, "Greens from the Garden" (1999): Among the most adventurous albums Alligator ever released, with convincing forays into funk, Cajun, reggae and folk.

• HOLMES BROTHERS, "Speaking in Tongues" (2001): Sublime harmonies steeped in the church, underlined by soul grooves.

• MAVIS STAPLES, "Have a Little Faith" (2004): The legendary gospel vocalist launched her comeback with this profoundly spiritual plea.

• CHARLIE MUSSELWHITE, "The Well" (2010): Starkly personal songs from the gentlemanly harp virtuoso.

• VARIOUS ARTISTS, "Alligator Records: 40th Anniversary Collection" (2011): Fine two-disc overview of the label's history with liner notes by founder Bruce Iglauer.

started playing electric guitar at Chess he didn't sound like Robert Johnson, and Robert Johnson inserting jazz chords into his songs didn't sound like Son House. To survive, the blues has got to speak to a contemporary audience lyrically, it's got to be something people can dance to, it's got to feel like blues but not regurgitate what's already been done so well.

Q: Do you ever see yourself walking away from this?

A: Very few people have been able to create a label with a vision that has opened doors for musicians and created an audience for them. There were a half-dozen labels that started in Chicago around the time I did, and they're not around anymore. As good as my people are here, I don't know if any of them has the overall vision to find the artists, produce the artists and lead the music company forward for the next 15–20 years. As much as I'd like to work for the ACLU or political campaigns, I think the chances are I'll be here the rest of my life.

....

Wax Trax celebrates its misfit founders

APRIL 10, 2011

Throwing a party in honor of Jim Nash and Dannie Flesher, the founders of Wax Trax! Records, is a daunting task. There were parties, and then there were Wax Trax bacchanals. But Jim Nash's daughter is giving it a try.

"They were great guys—crazy, but great," says Julia Nash, who is spearheading a series of tribute concerts dubbed the "Wax Trax! Records Retrospectacle" next weekend at Metro for the two gone-but-not-forgotten life partners (Jim Nash died in 1995, Flesher in 2010).

"After Dannie passed, we thought, 'This is it, the end of an era,'" Julia Nash says. "It was time to celebrate what they had done. But I've gotten overwhelmed with how huge it has become. It started out kind

Artists play Revolting Cocks songs at the Wax Trax! Retrospectacle at the Metro on April 16, 2011.
CHRIS SALATA

of intimate and small, and it's become this huge thing that I am trying to reel in before I lose it completely."

Among the former Wax Trax bands and artists scheduled to play at the three-night Metro blowout are Front 242, My Life With the Thrill Kill Kult, Rights of the Accused, Luc Van Acker, Ministry's Paul Barker, Chris Connelly and members of the Revolting Cocks and KMFDM.

Somewhere Nash and Flesher are probably laughing at such excess being committed in their honor. They wouldn't have it any other way.

When the two fled Topeka, Kan., in the early '70s their goals were relatively modest: "We worked lousy jobs in construction and got tired of it," Jim Nash once told the Tribune. "So we thought, 'OK, now how can we retire at the tender age of 23?' "

They did much better than that. Their desire to live a less-structured life led to Denver, where they opened a record store, then relocated it to Lincoln Avenue on Chicago's North Side in 1978. The store, Wax Trax, a couple of doors down from the old Biograph Theater, instantly became just about the coolest place in Chicago to hang out for the city's most colorful outcasts. It was stuffed with punk, glam and subterranean-dance records, and was the Midwest headquarters for fanzines and news about all the latest underground shows. It instantly attracted a clientele that liked their music harsh and their clothes provocative. Combat boots, bombardier jackets, dyed hair, tattoos, piercings and ripped fishnets mingled with the blare of the latest singles by Throbbing Gristle and Joy Division.

Within a couple of years the store expanded into a record label, first as an outlet for Nash and Flesher to put out records by their friends that wouldn't stand a prayer of being released by anyone else. The releases included a punk EP by locals Strike Under, a single by John Waters' film star Divine, and fey synth-pop sung in a fake British accent by a record-store employee, Al Jourgensen, in the band Ministry.

But soon Jourgensen was pumping up the volume and the aggression, and a particularly brutal brand of electronic music was born. Some called it "industrial" (though Jourgensen and most of his labelmates hated the term) and Wax Trax became its epicenter. Other bands and artists from around the world—most notably Nine Inch Nails—made millions a decade later capitalizing on the aggressive, technology-abusing blueprint established by Ministry and other Wax Trax artists.

A gleeful irreverence underlined much of it—how could anything associated with Nash and Flesher not have a certain frivolity attached to it? But the music also flashed a pointed political edge, sometimes overt (as in the case of Ministry), most often implied by a wicked, against-the-grain attitude. Wax Trax was a rude gesture, a style defined by its refusal to conform. Its primary messages? Think for yourself. Take nothing at face value. It's OK to march to your own drum machine. In the era of AIDS and Reaganomics, the Wax Trax culture struck a chord with kids allergic to the Cold War and boilerplate pop music.

"The plan was there wasn't any plan," Jim Nash once said. "We weren't going after the Bananaramas of the day. The music we liked, it's not exactly pleasing."

The label owners blew past the nuances of running a business, but they were passionate about music and culture and the people who made it. Wax Trax broke bands such as Germany's KMFDM and Belgium's Front 242 before those groups were well-known in their home countries.

"I came from Scotland with Fini Tribe, a band that worked very hard but couldn't find anyone to (care) because we didn't sound like the Pastels or the Jesus and Mary Chain or the Soup Dragons, who were big at the time," says Chris Connelly. "Chicago was the one place in the world where there was more than one human being who heard our record and liked it. Jim could get a record played at (underground dance club) Smart Bar or at a college radio station like WZRD, and we felt our band was taken seriously for the first time."

Connelly and the early incarnation of the Revolting Cocks crashed at Julia Nash's apartment in 1987, and Connelly recalls a steady stream of meals and cash from Jim Nash and Flesher that helped tide over Wax Trax artists as they got their careers off the ground.

The owners' openhearted attitude and handshake deals with many of their artists eventually doomed the label. Wax Trax plunged into bankruptcy and was bought out by another label, then quietly disappeared after Nash died of AIDS at age 47 in 1995.

Julia Nash, who ran her father's record store in its waning years and was friends with many of the artists, eventually went into private business (she now owns a gift shop in Oak Park). For her, the label's legacy is less about music than it is the extended family it created, which is why proceeds from the Metro concerts will benefit the Center on Halsted, a community hub for the Midwest's gay, bisexual and transgender population.

"It's a community place for misfits, the disenfranchised, much like Wax Trax was," Julia Nash says. She adds that there are no plans to revive the label, which remains tied up in litigation, but Connelly is hopeful that the reunion of some of electronic music's most vivid personalities will light some sparks.

"It's a nostalgia show, but we've pulled back from the 'has-beens getting together for the money' aspect by doing it for charity," Connelly says. "If Jim and Dannie were here, they'd love the party and the cause, but they'd also be bullying us to do something new, which would be fantastic. They would always encourage us to make records, no matter how esoteric or strange, and they would be happy to foot the bill."

Wax Trax's greatest hits

Here are a few of Wax Trax's greatest hits, arranged chronologically:

• MINISTRY, "Everyday is Halloween" (1984): Before transforming himself into a rabid, technology-fired pit bull, Al Jourgensen dominates the Chicago clubs with Euro-influenced synth-pop singles like "Everyday is Halloween" and "Cold Life."

• FRONT 242, "Official Version" (1987): Brutal beats, stentorian vocals and sample-heavy sound collages turn this Belgian outfit into one of electronic music's defining groups.

• LAIBACH, "Opus Dei" (1987): Goose-stepping stomps merge harsh Germanic vocals and even harsher rhythms as part provocation, part fascist satire.

• THE YOUNG GODS, "The Young Gods" (1987): Swiss bombast-mongers add rock crunch and classical grandeur to their electro attack.

• THE KLF, "Chill Out" (1990): A landmark of so-called ambient house music, a perfect companion for the 5 a.m. comedown after a night of frantic dancing.

• REVOLTING COCKS, "Beers, Steers + Queers" (1990): Life as an out-of-control toga party for this Jourgensen side project, the hedonistic flip side of Ministry's dark grind.

• MY LIFE WITH THE THRILL KILL KULT, "Sexplosion!" (1991): A campy romp that would be the perfect soundtrack to any number of grindhouse exploitation movies.

• CHRIS CONNELLY, "Shipwreck" (1994): The early-'70s glam-rock influences make this an anomaly in the Wax Trax catalog, but its songcraft is undeniable.

• VARIOUS ARTISTS, "Black Box—Wax Trax! The First 13 Years" (1994): Superb three-disc overview of the label's embrace of twisted exotica, from Divine's "The Name Game" to 1000 Homo DJs' cover of Black Sabbath's "Supernaut," with Trent Reznor on lead vocals.

• KMFDM, "Nihil" (1995): The German band's seventh album is one of Wax Trax's commercial high points, putting a polished pop spin on industrial's characteristic harshness, with club hit "Juke Joint Jezebel."

Don Cornelius
Powerful engine of 'Soul Train'

FEB. 2, 2012

Don Cornelius, who died at 75, was a civil rights pioneer disguised as a dance-music show host. He used to sign off the "Soul Train" show he founded in Chicago by wishing his viewers "love, peace and soul," and devoted every programming minute to proving he meant it.

The baritone-voiced host slipped into many roles on "Soul Train" and made it look easy, as if he were trying on just another tailored double-breasted suit. He was a music tastemaker, fashion leader, smooth talker and business innovator, a national icon who could broker a deal or bust a move on the dance floor without seeming to break a sweat.

But his role as a civil rights leader is perhaps his most significant contribution, even though he isn't often portrayed that way. Cornelius worked uplifting community messages into his programming, and he created a social context for "Soul Train" that was as radical and empowering as any civil rights speech or rally.

As Roots drummer Ahmir "Questlove" Thompson wrote after Cornelius was found dead of an apparently self-inflicted gunshot wound at his Mulholland Drive home in Encino, Calif., "Next to (Motown founder) Berry Gordy, Don Cornelius was hands down the most crucial nonpolitical figure to emerge from the Civil Rights era post-'68."

Thompson went on to amplify that assertion on his blog at Okayplayer.com: "To say with a straight, dignified face that 'black is beautiful' was the riskiest, (most) radical life-changing move that America has seen. And amazingly enough for one hour, for one Saturday out (of) the week, if you were watching 'Soul Train,' it became contagious. Next thing you know you are actually believing you have some sort of worth. The whole idea of Afro-centrism in my opinion manifested and spread with 'Soul Train' in its first six years."

To do it, Cornelius had to break through the walls that had barred African-Americans from power in television and music.

Cornelius was born in Chicago on Sept. 27, 1936, and grew up on

Don Cornelius is presented with a street sign during the Soul Train Labor
Day concert at the Pritzker Pavilion on Sept. 5, 2011.
NUCCIO DINUZZO

the South Side. After graduating from DuSable High School in 1954,
he served a stint in the Marines. He sold tires, cars and insurance before taking a course in broadcasting in 1966. In 1970 Cornelius began
hosting a local, low-budget African-American answer to Dick Clark's
"American Bandstand."

By the next year he was going national, and soon every major black
performer was clamoring to be on his syndicated show. James Brown,
Aretha Franklin, Al Green and Sly Stone were among his guests. Barry
White showed up in a black velvet tux with a 40-piece orchestra in the
midst of his larger-than-life heyday.

At a time when commercial radio was segregating across lines of
style and race, Cornelius presented the richness of black music in all its
variety to a national audience. He effectively became the most powerful DJ in America.

He also showed the ability to adapt, keeping the show relevant
through the disco and hip-hop eras, even though he was not particularly a fan of either style of music. He hosted the most important hip-

hop artists of the time, including L.L. Cool J, (then) Snoop Doggy Dogg and Public Enemy. For many of these acts, "Soul Train" would be their first national television exposure.

"We didn't get nationally known until we did 'Rebel Without a Pause' on 'Soul Train' in 1987," Public Enemy's Chuck D said on Twitter. "We thanked Don forever."

"Soul Train" did more than just passively present the music. At its core, Cornelius' show was about a community responding—creatively, spontaneously, ecstatically—to the music made for it. The palpable excitement of that interaction opened up African-American culture to the rest of the world and made it not only more accessible but also desirable, hip, fun.

Cornelius' primary ambassadors were the dancers he hired. Initially they were teenagers and young adults he met at the parties he used to DJ in Chicago. A number went on to become famous in their own right: Jody Watley, M.C. Hammer and future Bears running back Walter Payton. They brought a street flair to the show and their dance moves—the pop and lock, robot, moonwalk—were studied and often emulated by viewers, including a young Michael Jackson.

The show's cultural cachet—spreading the gospel of not just music but African-American dance, slang, hairstyles and fashion— was tied to Cornelius' acumen as a businessman. As Berry Gordy was to music, Cornelius was to the intersection of music and television. He cut a path for future African-American music moguls such as Russell Simmons, L.A. Reid, Sean "Puffy" Combs and Jay-Z, as well as Bob Johnson, who founded the Black Entertainment Television cable network in 1980. Cornelius partnered with George Johnson and Johnson Products, another black-owned Chicago institution, as an early sponsor.

"At the time, there weren't many black advertisements or black figures appearing in ads, so there really was no place else to put them," said Todd Boyd, a professor of critical studies at the University of Southern California. "If you want to go back in the late 1950s, Nat King Cole's show was canceled because they couldn't find a sponsor. By the '70s, Don Cornelius was pushing the (black) culture into the mainstream and also introducing concepts around sponsorship and advertising that previously had no other places to exist except the pages of John Johnson's publications (Jet and Ebony)."

Cornelius quit as host in 1993, but he continued to oversee everything from behind the scenes until the show's demise more than 15 years later. (Tribune Entertainment syndicated "Soul Train" from 1985 to 2007.)

In September 2011, Cornelius was coaxed back to Chicago from his California home for a week of festivities honoring the show's 40th anniversary. About 15,000 people attended a concert at the Pritzker Pavilion in Millennium Park headlined by his friends Jerry Butler, the Impressions, the Emotions and the Chi-Lites. Cornelius, dressed in black leather, got the biggest ovation, the decades of memories compressed into a sustained moment of appreciation.

"It was pretty emotional," said Richard Steele, the old friend who co-hosted the concert with DJ Herb Kent. "To look out and see all those people who came because it was 'Soul Train,' he was really moved by that."

"At the end they also presented him with a street sign," said Steele, now a host and producer at WBEZ-FM 91.5. "He was pretty shook up. . . . When he did the customary sign-off he used to do, 'Love, peace and soul,' well, they went crazy."

Donna Summer
Disco diva was a true revolutionary

MAY 18, 2012

Donna Summer was typecast as the disco-era "bad girl," the diva who was too salty and sexual for some radio stations to play in the '70s. But she was also a musical revolutionary, a versatile singer who created a radical new template for dance and pop music with such songs as "Love to Love You Baby" and "I Feel Love."

The singer died in Florida at age 63 of cancer. She is survived by her husband, Bruce Sudano, and three daughters, Brooklyn, Mimi and Amanda.

Donna Summer at the Ravinia Pavilion, Aug. 15, 1999.
NUCCIO DINUZZO

Summer, born LaDonna Adrian Gaines on Dec. 31, 1948, out-side Boston, came from a devoutly Christian background, singing in church before branching out into pop. In the late '60s, she joined a psychedelic rock band influenced by Janis Joplin and then ventured to Europe, where she sang in musicals. In the early '70s, she met producers Giorgio Moroder and Pete Bellotte while working as a backup singer in Germany, and they began forging one of the era's great musical partnerships.

Their first success, "Love to Love You Baby," ushered in the disco era in 1975; it was a 17-minute track with a pulsing, trancelike rhythm over which Summer cooed, cried and moaned. The track's overtly erotic tone scared away some radio programmers, but an edited version became a pop hit anyway, and the extended version (among the first 12-inch singles) became a staple of dance floors worldwide.

In a Tribune Newspapers interview more than a decade later, Summer reflected on the image created by the song. "People didn't think I could sing, because I was whispering," she said. "And it was a persona. . . . It was never something that I felt comfortable with. I struggled with it from the beginning . . . but it's nothing I'm ashamed of."

She escaped the one-hit wonder typecasting so prevalent in the disco era. Moroder, Bellotte and Neil Bogart, president of her record label, Casablanca, put her in settings that showcased her as an artist with a stunning vocal range. A succession of double albums, side-long suites and extended tracks created a new type of progressive music, largely with keyboards, that expanded on some of the innovations of electro-pop and avant-garde artists such as Kraftwerk.

In 1977, the producers and Summer collaborated on a concept album that surveyed several decades of music, "I Remember Yesterday." Its "future" segment included the track "I Feel Love," which lived up to the hype: hypnotic waves of synthesizer rhythm suggesting some kind of science-fiction metropolis, with Summer's voice rising and falling as if riding the celestial highway's curves.

It was not only a No. 2 pop single; it would prove to have a lasting impact on music. Brian Eno, while in recording sessions in Berlin with David Bowie at the time, proclaimed the song "the sound of the future." Which, Bowie added, "was more or less right."

"We had the music, and we wrote so many lyrics that didn't work— they were too dense," Summer said of "I Feel Love" in a recent interview. "And I said, 'This is a chant—this is euphoric' and started to sing simpler things . . . and it was so natural. It still sounds great—when you're on the cutting edge of something and you hear it back, sometimes it sounds so dated, but this still sounds fresh to me."

Summer, Moroder and Bellotte kept up a feverish pace, producing four double albums between '77 and '79, including the disco Cinderella story "Once Upon a Time . . ." The run included the sprawling "Bad Girls" album, which featured not just a "disco queen," but a woman whose past in rock, soul and ballad-singing was equally apparent. During this period, Summer released an audacious remake of Jimmy Webb's baroque-pop epic "MacArthur Park" and the valedictory "Last Dance," in many ways the capstone of the disco era.

Summer transcended that period even as she was going through a number of personal upheavals at the onset of the '80s. She changed labels, divorced, remarried, had children and proclaimed herself a born-again Christian. Yet the hits kept coming, with the "She Works Hard for the Money" album and title track (1983) and "Another Place and Time" (1989), produced by the then-hot London production team of Stock Aitken Waterman. The latter collaboration netted her final Top 40 hit, "This Time I Know It's For Real."

The singer battled depression and took up painting as a release. "Performing is what I do for other people," she once told Tribune Newspapers. "Painting is what I do for me. Being on stage is a lot of stress. You have to be perfect. Look perfect, your weight has to be perfect. Painting is a lot easier. I don't have to be beautiful or skinny."

She never quit music, though, continuing to tour and record while raising two daughters, Brooklyn and Amanda, with husband Bruce

---

Donna Summer essentials

• "Love to Love You Baby" (1975): Worth it if only for the 17-minute title song, a disco landmark.

• "I Remember Yesterday" (1977): A concept album about music, with the "future" defined by the groundbreaking "I Feel Love." Dance and pop music would never be the same.

• "Bad Girls" (1979): The Summer collaboration with producers Giorgio Moroder and Pete Bellotte was never better, branching out into rock, soul and ballads, and yielding hit singles in the title track, "Hot Stuff" and "Dim the Lights."

• "She Works Hard for the Money" (1983): Summer is a more confident singer than ever on her 11th studio album as she reinvents herself for the post-disco age with a blue-collar anthem.

• "The Donna Summer Anthology" (1993): Solid overview of her first two decades, with the mostly excellent '70s on Disc 1 and the more hit-and-miss '80s on Disc 2.

Sudano (she had another daughter, Mimi, from a previous marriage). Her 2008 album, "Crayons," hit No. 17 on the U.S. album chart, her highest entry since 1983. It included a track called "The Queen," in which she pokes fun at her lasting image as the "Queen of Disco."

That she was able to play with icon-hood and embrace it was a triumph of sorts for Summer, among the more introspective talents produced by an era noted for its glitter and glam.

After she turned 40, she told Tribune Newspapers that entering her fifth decade "was traumatic. But we, the black people, have a saying; it's, 'Black don't crack.' It made me think of a lot of things I want to do, and I don't want to die without doing them. It was like putting a fire underneath me. At first, it scared me, and then I thought, 'Let me make the best of the next 40 years, and let me leave an anchor for my kids and their kids.' That's my goal."

The Flatlanders' latest

Forgotten recording surfaces, reminding Joe Ely of band's true inspiration and sound

APRIL 5, 2013

The Flatlanders—the West Texas trinity of Joe Ely, Jimmie Dale Gilmore and Butch Hancock—were about 50 years behind the times and 15 years ahead of it, Ely once surmised. The band recorded a batch of songs in 1972 and then disappeared, leaving a legacy that inspired countless bands and movements over the decades. As the Velvet Underground were to punk and post-punk, the Flatlanders were to outlaw and outsider country.

For decades it was assumed that the Flatlanders' only recordings during their one year as a band were the 13 songs that surfaced on their "More a Legend than a Band" album, widely released domestically 20 years after it was tracked in Nashville, Tenn. But last year *[2012]*, "The Odessa Tapes" (New West) turned up, essentially a demo recorded two months before the Nashville sessions that shows Ely, Gilmore and Hancock in a more relaxed, natural light.

The Flatlanders, Joe Ely, Jimmie Dale Gilmore, and Butch Hancock at Navy Pier Aug. 8, 2002.
JOHN BARTLEY

"It was a demo to show the Flatlanders might be a country band, even though we didn't even really think of ourselves as a band," Ely recalls. "We drove 140 miles from Lubbock (where the Flatlanders were based) south to Odessa and recorded 14 songs in a studio there from sundown to sunup.

"That was the demo tape sent to (producer) Shelby Singleton, and it got us an opportunity to record our album in Nashville two months later. For a long time, people thought that was our first record. I thought it was our first record (laughs). I had completely forgotten about the Odessa tape."

The recording turned up in the closet of the bass player on the sessions, Tony Pearson, in an outdated three-track format. It took Ely about a year to find a tape machine that would even play the original demo so that it could be converted into a modern format.

"When I finally heard the session, I was completely stunned," Ely says. "It's not a perfect record. We were still learning the songs. I was just learning to play dobro; I had been playing it for about a month. We were working out the harmonies. That whole band was not together for more than eight months at that time.

"But it gave me some insights into what we recorded in Nashville two months later. In Nashville, I realized they overdubbed some studio players, a slew of guitars to cover up some of our 'flaws.' It was still 90 percent us, but the Nashville guys tweaked it. There is something about the Odessa tapes that is truer to what we were. There is this pure simplicity. No frills, no weird things added. There is an innocence about it.

"We were not used to the recording studio. Me and Jimmie had recorded three songs with Buddy Holly's daddy in 1969 in Lubbock, but those tapes never surfaced. We were complete novices, but it was more true to how we lived and played at the time."

The Flatlanders set up shop in a three-bedroom house near the Texas Tech campus in Lubbock in 1971. Hancock, Ely and Gilmore had all grown up in the city and melded divergent interests in music, books and movies. Their home became a misfit hangout that bridged generations: '40s and '50s beatniks, college students, drifters, philosopher poets and just about anybody who had a guitar or a song. The group's "gigs" largely consisted of casual performances in living rooms, basements, cafes, even the roof of their house during evenings when the oppressive Lubbock summer weather became tolerable.

"There was a tremendous amount of material," Ely says. "The Odessa tapes took the songs that were more in a country vein, because the idea was to target something that Nashville might want. We had no idea, because we did all kinds of stuff. I was more out of a rock 'n' roll world in Lubbock; my stuff was a little more rocking and didn't quite fit the record, so we left it off. Butch's stuff was more in folk vein. Jimmie sang most of the vocals because he sounded more 'country' than the rest of us. It was just a small slice of the kinds of music we were interested in."

But the hyperliterate lyrics by Hancock, Gilmore and their friends were still more metaphysical and mystical than standard country drinking-cheating-lusting fare.

"We were totally uninterested in the music business, so the offer to make a demo for a Nashville recording session came as a complete surprise," Ely says. "We were on a quest to discover great music, whether it was The Beatles or Leadbelly or Butch's collection of bluegrass records.

All our friends came to our house, and we'd stay up all night playing songs and learning songs. It became almost a Lubbock nightclub. People would bring over a casserole or tacos, and we'd play until dawn. Playing wasn't just a hobby but our lives 24 hours a day."

When the Nashville recording was deemed too strange for mainstream commercial radio, the Flatlanders went off in different directions. Gilmore, Ely and Hancock each made their mark in music separately, only to reunite a little more than a decade ago to pick up where the Flatlanders left off: more cosmic Americana from the "flatlands" of West Texas.

"We were gypsies," Ely says. "Coming out of the '60s, everybody was open for anything. There were no rules. That's how our music evolved too. A lot of those songs don't follow any rules. I think that's still the reason we're together today. There was no big audience for our stuff until later, so we didn't have to fight about money. Nobody made a penny. But it was a rich period of time for all of us."

....

Music in the cause of justice
How the civil rights movement got its soundtrack

AUG. 25, 2013

I t was 50 years ago when gospel, folk music and the civil rights movement cemented their bond on the biggest stage in America.

The March on Washington that punctuated the civil rights movement and brought hundreds of thousands to the Lincoln Memorial to hear Martin Luther King Jr. deliver his "I Have a Dream" speech began not with pronouncements and demonstrations, but with music.

At 10 a.m. Aug. 28, 1963, Joan Baez began serenading the early arrivals at the starting line, the Washington Monument, with "Oh, Freedom," and she was followed by Odetta; Peter, Paul & Mary; Bob Dylan; the Freedom Singers; and other performers. Marian Anderson performed the spiritual "He's Got the Whole World in His Hands," and Mahalia Jackson delivered the gospel anthems "I've Been 'Buked and I've Been Scorned" and "How I Got Over." Later, Jackson exhorted King from the audience to go off script and rhapsodize: "Tell them about the dream, Martin."

It capped a day of eloquence magnified and intensified by music. An estimated 250,000 people attended the gathering, designed to advocate for minority jobs and voting rights, and massive media coverage brought it to millions more nationwide. It was a symbolic turning point in the struggle, presaging passage of the Civil Rights Act in 1964 and the Voting Rights Act in 1965.

It was a revolution with a soundtrack, a protest movement in which music and message were inextricably mixed. At rallies, meetings and marches, songs inspired the unarmed soldiers of the movement as they waded into streets lined with baton-wielding police, snarling dogs and water cannons.

For more than a century, the church had been the center of African-American life, the sanctuary where blacks could be themselves and speak their minds. The words of ministers were amplified by choirs and underlined by songs that sought redemption, if not in this world, then possibly in the next. The civil rights movement brought the voice of the oppressed into music that reached far beyond the black community. King called the music "vital" to the peaceful revolution he led, as did Newsweek: "History has never known a protest movement so rich in song as the Civil Rights Movement."

Here are 10 musical signposts, arranged chronologically, from this tumultuous era.

1. Max Roach
"WE INSIST! FREEDOM NOW SUITE" ALBUM (1960)

Within the musical rebellion that was bebop and later free jazz, a political consciousness arose. In 1960, Charles Mingus' "Fables of Faubus" railed against Arkansas Gov. Orval Faubus, who had called out the Arkansas National Guard to prevent black students from integrating a Little Rock high school. John Coltrane's 1963 tone poem "Alabama" mourned four black girls killed in the bombing of an Alabama church. And the great drummer Max Roach collaborated with lyricist Oscar Brown Jr. on

"We Insist! Freedom Now Suite," a masterpiece that combined activism and improvisation. The concept album takes black history from the slave and sharecropping days through the onset of the civil rights movement and joins it with the struggle in apartheid-racked South Africa. Singer Abbey Lincoln, who was then Roach's wife, animates the poetic imagery with a performance that veers between tender and volcanic.

2. Mahalia Jackson
"HOW I GOT OVER" (1963)

The greatest voice in gospel music had recorded a version of the hymn "How I Got Over" in 1961. By then it was already deeply entrenched in the African-American consciousness, a standard in churches around the country. It was written in 1951 by Clara Ward, in response to a racially charged incident while she and her family were traveling through the South. Jackson returned to the song during the March on Washington, accompanied by Hammond organ and rhythmic hand claps from the audience, her voice rising to a fever pitch as if anticipating King's famed "I Have a Dream" speech. "I'm gonna join the heavenly choir/ And I'm a-sing and never get tired," Jackson testifies.

3. Freedom Singers
"IN THE MISSISSIPPI RIVER" (1964)

The Student Nonviolent Coordinating Committee played a huge role in the civil rights movement, particularly in the South. In 1962, it set up the Freedom Singers to spread the message of nonviolence nationwide. The group, which included Bernice Johnson, Rutha Harris, Charles Neblitt and Cordell Hull Reagon, among others, traveled 100,000 miles in 1962 and '63, including performances at the Newport Folk Festival and the March on Washington. The group often adapted traditional spirituals and hymns such as "This Little Light," "Down by the Riverside" and "Will the Circle Be Unbroken," inserting topical lyrics into familiar songs that had been part of the black church vernacular for a century or more. But it also introduced original songs, never more powerfully than with "In the Mississippi River," written by Marshall Jones. It documents the search for three civil rights workers in Mississippi in summer 1964. During the search for their bodies, dozens more slain African-Americans were pulled from the river. The toll becomes a chilling incantation: "You can count them one by one, two by two . . . five by five."

4. Nina Simone
"MISSISSIPPI GODDAM" (1964)

The fiery singer was incensed by the murder of civil rights leader Medgar Evers in Mississippi and the Alabama church bombing that left four children dead. At a series of Carnegie Hall concerts, she described "Mississippi Goddam" as "a show tune, but the show hasn't been written yet." The jaunty melody contrasts with the rising indignation and frustration in the lyrics. "Me and my people," she sings, "just about through."

5. The Impressions
"KEEP ON PUSHING" (1964)

Curtis Mayfield, who grew up in the Cabrini-Green housing complex in Chicago, made his early reputation as an evocative lyricist in the vocal group the Impressions with pop-soul numbers such as "Gypsy Woman" and "It's All Right," but "Keep on Pushing" took him into a new area: a song of resilience and empowerment for the embattled African-American community. Other classics in the same vein followed—"People Get Ready," "We're a Winner," "Choice of Colors"—but "Keep on Pushing" was the first to crack the Top-10 pop singles chart.

6. Sam Cooke
"A CHANGE IS GONNA COME" (1964)

The star vocalist, who grew up on Chicago's South Side, had a reputation for singing it suave and smooth after transitioning to pop from gospel in the late '50s. But he was deeply moved by Bob Dylan's "Blowin' in the Wind" when he first heard the protest anthem in 1963. In response, Cooke wrote his greatest song, an emotionally transparent depiction of the frustration that many blacks felt as they were denied entry into the so-called "brotherhood" of man. Even though it was eventually released as a B-side in the weeks after Cooke's death in 1964, it became a Top-40 hit.

7. Staple Singers
"FREEDOM HIGHWAY" (1965)

In the wake of the bloody Selma to Montgomery, Ala., march in 1965 protesting a civil rights worker's murder in Alabama, Roebuck "Pops" Staples wrote this classic. The song debuted with his family—daughters Mavis and Cleotha and son Pervis—in a scintillating live performance at New Nazareth Church on Chicago's South Side. "I made up my mind, and I won't turn around," roars Mavis, her voice bristling with angry resolve.

8. James Brown
"SAY IT LOUD—I'M BLACK AND I'M PROUD" (1968)

After the assassination of King in April 1968, the black power movement gained traction, and the music got tougher and funkier. Brown wanted to uplift with "Say It Loud" and enlisted a group of children to shout the refrain, an explicit message of African-American pride. He later said the song cost him the crossover audience he had always nurtured, but that it was a necessary tonic for a community that was in shock and despair after the loss of its spiritual leader.

9. Temptations
"BALL OF CONFUSION (THAT'S WHAT THE WORLD IS TODAY)" (1970)

Motown came late to the protest era. Label founder Berry Gordy had always sought to make music that would appeal across lines of race, generation and gender and not stir up any political dust. But producer Norman Whitfield, along with his songwriting partner Barrett Strong, brought a harder psychedelic edge to the tracks they cut with artists such as the Temptations, a reflection of how civil-rights-era protests had turned violent. "Cities in flame in the summertime," the Temptations sing, "and the beat goes on."

10. Kim Weston
"LIFT EVERY VOICE AND SING" (1972)

The Wattstax concert at the Los Angeles Coliseum, a benefit for the Watts community ravaged by rioting in the '60s, drew more than 100,000 people. It was described by many as the largest public gathering of African-Americans since the March on Washington. The concert featured the artists on the Memphis-based Stax label, including Isaac Hayes, Johnnie Taylor, Rufus Thomas and the Staple Singers. And it kicked off with a resounding version of what had become known as "the black national anthem," a turn-of-the-century poem by James Weldon Johnson that was set to music and became a testament to African-American struggle and perseverance. Kim Weston's powerhouse interpretation of "Lift Every Voice and Sing" launched a day of peaceful protest in the guise of a soul-music concert.

ABOUT THE
AUTHOR

Greg Kot has been the Chicago Tribune's music critic covering pop, rock and hip-hop since 1990. He is the cohost of the nationally syndicated public radio show *Sound Opinions* and the author of several books. He lives in Chicago with his wife and two daughters.

CPSIA information can be obtained
at www.ICGtesting.com
Printed in the USA
LVHW041420150523
747042LV00004B/219